Advertising and Public Relations Research

Advertising and Public Relations Research

Donald W. Jugenheimer • Samuel D. Bradley

Larry D. Kelley • Jerry C. Hudson

M.E.Sharpe
Armonk, New York
London, England

Library of Congress Cataloging-in-Publication Data

Advertising and public relations research / by Donald W. Jugenheimer ... [et al.].
    p. cm.
  Includes bibliographical references and index.
  ISBN 978-0-7656-2418-5 (pbk. : alk. paper)
  1. Advertising—Research. 2. Public relations—Research. I. Jugenheimer,
Donald W.

  HF5814.A32 2010
  659.072—dc22   2009020564

Printed in the United States of America

The paper used in this publication meets the minimum requirements of
American National Standard for Information Sciences
Permanence of Paper for Printed Library Materials,
ANSI Z 39.48-1984.

CW (p)   10   9   8   7   6   5   4   3   2   1

Contents

Preface

Research is a crucial component for any advertising or public relations campaign. Yet there is a lack of college textbooks that discuss advertising and public relations research. Most mass communications research textbooks used in undergraduate classes are typically published to educate graduate students. Furthermore, most textbooks focus on general mass communications topics that include advertising and public relations but also include journalism and broadcasting. Plus, the content covers mostly quantitative methods with limited coverage given to qualitative methods, which is a large aspect of research in the advertising and public relations profession.

That is why we have designed this research book specifically for undergraduate students enrolled in advertising and public relations curricula. The book is intended to be used in junior- and senior-level research courses or as a supplement to explain research techniques in upper- or exit-level advertising and public relations courses. The book might also be used in master's-level research courses; however, that is not the primary intent.

To serve the intended audience of undergraduate advertising and public relations students, the book concentrates on the uses and applications of research in advertising and public relations situations. Although the design and conduct of research are included and discussed in detail, the primary goal is not to make researchers of students. Instead, the goal is to provide information needed by future practitioners to commission and apply research to their work problems in advertising and public relations. Students must be critical consumers of research design and be prepared to evaluate data. Practitioners must be able to recognize valid and reliable research in making intelligent decisions for their organizations or clients.

It is quite possible that the textbook could be used as a resource and training tool by advertising and public relations practitioners, particularly by advertising agencies. Many public relations and advertising hires are persons who do not have research skills or adequate knowledge to identify valid and reliable research methods, so on-the-job training is common in many small- to medium-sized shops.

This book follows a logical sequence of topics, starting with the very simplest concepts and progressing into more complex topics. In Part I (chapters 1–4), we have included the needs for research in the business of advertising and public relations along with some basic research terms and concepts. Part I also includes some research planning and designing instructions. We discuss secondary research in Part II (chapters 5–8), including commonly used secondary sources from the practice of advertising and public relations; syndicated research sources and measurements are also examined. Part III (chapters 9–11) covers primary research, specifically qualitative research. Part IV (chapters 12–23) covers more primary research, specifically quantitative research, and includes detailed discussions of survey research, including sampling, questionnaire development and question formulation, interviewer training, response problems, and research applications to advertising and public relations situations. This section also provides simple instructions for the novice researcher to learn about the construction of questionnaires, scales, and questions. The final chapters in this section include information about experimental research, experimental approaches, quasi-experimental research, and eye-tracking and psychophysiology techniques. Part V (chapter 24) is a brief treatment of other research methods, including historical and legal research methods and critical analysis. The next section (Part VI, chapters 25–29) includes information about handling research findings and data, various tabulation options, scaling and mapping techniques, along with statistical knowledge, application, and analysis. Because this book is intended to be used at the undergraduate level, the explanation of statistics is simple and straightforward, rather than in deep mathematical terms. Finally in Part VII (chapters 30–33), there is a discussion of research ethics and appropriate uses of research in advertising and public relations; this section also includes consideration of who should actually conduct the research and how to prepare a research report.

Each chapter begins with a bullet-point list of the learning objectives followed by the text. At the end of each text, we have included a brief summary of what was covered in the respective chapter, along with discussion questions to help expand and test students' comprehension of the material. There are also suggested research exercises that might be used in classroom situations. Finally, there are suggested sources for additional information.

We would like to express our utmost appreciation to our colleagues, students, and family members. Thanks to Melissa Wofford for creating the figures in Chapters 12–16. Thanks for FKM for providing important industry information. Thanks also go to the great staff at the publisher, M.E. Sharpe, Inc., and especially to editor Harry Briggs.

PART I

INTRODUCTION TO ADVERTISING AND PUBLIC RELATIONS RESEARCH

1 Needs for Research in Advertising and Public Relations

LEARNING OBJECTIVES

This chapter is intended to help you:

- See why research is so necessary in public relations and advertising;
- Understand some of the advantages of conducting research;
- Learn why you will need to be able to work with basic research techniques;
- Comprehend how research findings can help you with your job in advertising or public relations.

WHAT RESEARCH DOES

As the public relations manager for a local humane shelter, Sheila is responsible for the upcoming fund-raising campaign. She needs to know why people give to the shelter and especially what motivates the biggest givers to donate as much as they do. She designs a research survey to find the answers to her questions.

Jason is the copy chief at a large advertising agency. He likes the campaign that has been running for his biggest client, but he also wants to be certain that there is no stronger message that he might be using instead. After asking all his copywriters to come up with one new idea each, he has almost a dozen advertising appeals on hand as possible replacements for the existing campaign. To determine which might work best, he plans a copy testing study.

As the advertising manager for a large consumer packaged-goods company, Roberto receives lots of suggestions from consumers about possible improvements to existing products, as well as concepts for new products. He needs to know which of these ideas are sound and which are not likely to be cost-effective. Predictive market and advertising research will help him.

Barney is the vice president of public relations for a national airline. As fuel prices fluctuate, so do airline ticket prices. Various additional costs imposed on flyers have increased the revenue stream but at the expense of customer goodwill. Barney needs research to help him find the best ways to explain these price increases to customers and to try to maintain their patronage.

Advertising is increasing for the Internet but at the expense of traditional media.

Brittany works in advertising media sales for a cable television company. She needs research to help her uncover advantages for her advertising medium that will offset the current trends toward new media and will bring the maximum return for her advertiser clients.

As store manager of one unit of a regional retail chain, Hal must handle both advertising and public relations, as well as merchandising, promotions, and personal selling. He must have many kinds of research to help guide his decisions.

THE NEED FOR RESEARCH

Each of the situations described above can be aided by research. Research does not automatically provide answers to questions, but it can aid in suggesting directions, providing insights, and eliminating unproductive approaches.

Much of advertising and public relations communications is one-way, from the company or organization out to the customers or publics. Research, by contrast, is inward-directed communication, bringing in information that can be used to make sound and productive decisions. Much of the contact between companies and their publics is mediated—conducted through the mass media, the Internet, or even less-direct means of contact. Research helps shorten this lengthy communications channel. Research helps overcome the major separations between firms and their publics: geographic distance, value differentials, time and timing factors. Research helps promote the features of products, services, and ideas that the firm wants to disseminate.

Research is a critical competitive tool in modern business. Research learns what the public wants. Research uncovers pathways that may not have been previously considered. Research helps prevent mistakes and unnecessary expenditures. Research improves efficiency.

THE BENEFITS OF RESEARCH

If you work in public relations or in advertising, research brings many benefits.

First, research can save money, by avoiding incorrect decisions, by helping to find the correct strategies, by shortening the time required to introduce new initiatives, and by indicating opportunities for new products or services. Of course, it is necessary to weigh research costs against the potential benefits, because very expensive research may not be offset by the future gains.

Research also lets you gain on your competitors. Either by tracking what the competition is doing or discovering new opportunities before the competition does, research can be invaluable.

Research lets you adapt to change, whether in society, in the economy, in your generic business, or in your specific firm or organization. At the same time, research may help you maintain your business, grow your business, and reap profitable rewards from your business.

Research can also help with your internal operations. It may lead to synergy between departments or people, or at least to greater cooperation.

Exhibit 1.1

Some Commonly Used Demographic Categories

- Age
- Income
- Educational level
- Occupation
- Marital Status
- Gender
- Number of children in household
- Ages of children in household
- Race or ethnic group

APPLIED RESEARCH

Applied research is research that utilizes existing knowledge and research approaches for a specific purpose, often for a commercial or client-driven reason. In contrast, basic research is driven by a scientist's own curiosity or interest in some scientific question; it is also sometimes known as fundamental research or pure research. The rationale for basic or pure research is to expand human knowledge, rather than to create or invent something.

So basic research is conducted to increase our understanding of fundamental principles. Over the long term, basic research may lead to applied research.

Most advertising and public relations research is applied research, intended for a specific purpose or application, often in a particular, proprietary situation. You may still avail yourself of all the research methods and approaches that are available, just applied to a specific situation or problem.

PREDICTIVE RESEARCH

There is an increasing need for research that attempts to establish predictability. We try to use what we know today to predict what may occur tomorrow. A marketer relies on that fact when he assesses our buying patterns to predict our likely preferences. Consumer attitudes are somewhat predictive; if we know people's attitudes about themselves, we may have a fairly accurate idea of which brands they will prefer.

Demographics provide only a little predictability, but still, advertising agencies often plan their campaign target based primarily on demographic data.

Predictive research can help us in many ways. Customers change, and research can help us predict what they will want in the future; however, designing a new automobile may take as long as seven years, and consumers are unlikely to know what they will want or buy that far into the future. Markets also change; with the proper research, effective stimuli can be found to help shift the changes in directions that will generate more interest and sales. Environments change, leading to new fads and the passing of older interests, and research can help predict these changes—or perhaps even bring them about. The economy changes, sometimes rapidly, and foresight can help take advantage of these global alterations.

Exhibit 1.2

Some Commonly Used Segmentation Categories

- Geographic
- Demographic
- Psychographic
- Socio-graphic
- Geo-demographic
- Benefits
- Lifestyle
- Product or service usage

SPECIFIC USES OF RESEARCH

In uses of the mass media, including in advertising and public relations, there are some primary areas that are focal points for research. First, we are concerned about the credibility of the source of information, the sender of the message—especially if it is we ourselves. Much research involves source credibility, and the characteristics of the sender that affect the receipt, use, and application of the mass communications message.

Second, we study the audiences who receive our messages. What will make them pay attention to what we have to say, what will make them absorb this information, what will make them trust us, and what will make them act upon our suggestions? How can we segment the audiences into similar groupings?

Third, we study the messages themselves. Are there better ways to present our message? Can we precede our message with some things that will make it more palatable, even more attractive? How can we be sure to communicate what we want to in our message? How can we offer meaningful benefits?

Fourth, we study the media, the channels that carry our message. Which channels are most trustworthy? Which are most attractive? To which media do audiences pay the closest attention? Which media choices are most efficacious as well as economical?

Finally, we study the outcomes of our communications efforts. Did people actually listen to us, did they understand us, did they do what we hoped they would do, and are they pleased as a result?

NEGATIVE RATIONALE FOR RESEARCH

As we saw above, we must balance the costs of research against the potential gains from the findings. So research that is too expensive to provide a return on its investment is one negative rationale for research, but there are others.

Sometimes research can be done for the wrong reasons. In advertising and public relations, it is common for a team of workers to have a creative idea that they want to test with research. They are not using research to determine a course of action, only to confirm their initial beliefs and ideas. If the research comes back in support of their views, they can discount the research as telling them only what they already knew; if the research comes back opposed to their idea, they ask whether the research is reliable.

And many times, that particular research is not reliable because they simply asked for a small study, something "quick and dirty that will tell us we're on the right track." So conducting the research was an exercise in futility, not a worthwhile venture.

A related situation will be when research is commissioned to prove a particular point of view. Be very cautious when research is intended to prove or support a certain perspective or opinion. Research should be used to determine whether that viewpoint is correct, not to prove that it is correct. By designing a study with a particular aim or by manipulating research findings in a certain direction, it may be possible to support almost any views with research. But that is not a good use of research and certainly not the intended use of research.

In a later chapter, there is a more thorough discussion of the appropriate uses of research in public relations and advertising, as well as a look at misguided applications of research.

SUMMARY

Research can be very helpful in advertising and public relations. Most of the research used in these industries is applied research and much of it is predictive research. Although there are many benefits in the use of research, there are also possible problems and negative repercussions for research that is not intended for the proper purposes.

DISCUSSION QUESTIONS

1. What can research do to help those who work in public relations?
2. What can research do to help those who work in advertising?
3. What are the most likely research problems encountered in advertising? In public relations?
4. When should research be used? When should it not be used?
5. When is research unproductive or even harmful?

EXERCISES

1. Collect advertisements from a single sponsor. (Print advertisements are easier to save than broadcast commercials.) Analyze the entire set of advertisements to determine how you think research may have contributed.
2. Gather annual reports for several businesses. Analyze how research may have contributed to those reports.

ADDITIONAL READING

Davis, J. 1997. *Advertising research: Theory and practice.* Upper Saddle River, NJ: Prentice-Hall.
Aaker, D., G. Day, and V. Kumar. 2007. *Marketing research,* 9th ed. Hoboken, NJ: Wiley.
Hair, J., R. Bush, and D. Ortinau. 2009. *Marketing research.* Columbus, OH: McGraw-Hill.

2 Research Plans

LEARNING OBJECTIVES

This chapter is intended to help you:

- Understand what constitutes a research plan;
- Understand the trade-offs in doing research;
- Learn when research is appropriate and when it is better to use intuition.

WHAT IS A RESEARCH PLAN?

You have a burning desire to learn more about a topic that you feel can benefit a client or a campaign. It could be to better understand your target audience or it could be to determine what the best message is to motivate your audience.

Regardless of what you want to know, you will need to develop a plan to fill in that knowledge. On the surface, research plans are like any other business plan. You have an objective or goal. You are seeking a strategy to best meet that objective. You need an action plan on how to implant that strategy. You have resource constraints to deal with, such as budget and timing.

However, unlike business planning, research planning has one other key variable. That is the amount of ambiguity you can accept in the answer that the research may give you.

RESEARCH TRADE-OFFS

In a perfect world, you would have the proper amount of time and the money necessary to determine the proper course of action. But, business is far from being a perfect world. There are always time and budget constraints. These two elements greatly influence the research plan that you will develop. The final aspect of the research trade-off is the level of ambiguity that you can tolerate in making the decision.

In subsequent chapters we will discuss the confidence level of research. In simple terms, the level of confidence is the likelihood of the answer being the same time and time again. Academic research papers work within a 95 percent level of confidence. That means that a result at this level is very factual. There is little ambiguity that the

Exhibit 2.1   **Research Trade-Off**

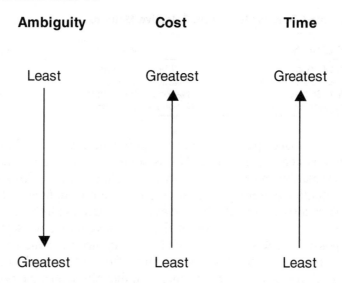

Ambiguity	**Cost**	**Time**
Least	Greatest	Greatest
Greatest	Least	Least

result will deviate from the reported result. Business decisions, on the other hand are typically made at less than a 60 percent level of confidence. In fact, many business decisions are made on very sketchy information. Why is this?

You pay for reducing the level of ambiguity in decisions through time and money. For example, would you be satisfied that consumers liked your commercial if 9 out of 10 people in your office you talked to liked it? Or would you feel better if you fielded a national survey where 900 out of 1,000 surveyed liked it?

Obviously, you would feel better if you could say that 900 out of 1,000 liked it. However, to get to this level of certainty requires significantly more money and more time than talking to a few colleagues in the hallway. So, as a general rule of thumb, the more confident you are in a research result, the more people you need to talk to, which costs more money and takes more time.

Time and money become the key ingredients in developing your research plan. Those are the first two questions you should ask once you decide if research is necessary to answer your question.

- When do we need an answer to this question?
- What is the budget for this project?

The amount of time weighs heavily on the outcome of any research plan. If you need to answer a question today, then it is unlikely that you can conduct a primary research study with a large sample size to answer the question. Time can dictate if the number of people you talk to is "good enough" or is enough to feel reasonably confident about the result.

Time may dictate if research can be considered in the first place. Suppose you are an account manager of a public relations firm and your client calls with a crisis. The

Exhibit 2.2

Estimated Time for Research: Selective Methods

Type of Study	Scope	Estimated Time Range
Focus Group	1 Market–2 groups	2–3 weeks
Online Focus Group	National–2 groups	3–4 weeks
Online Survey	National–300 Sample	4–6 weeks
Telephone Survey	National–2,000 Sample	6–8 weeks

client is a large poultry producer and is telling you that they have just learned that their chickens have bird flu. This is not the time to suggest that you conduct research to test various messages on how to handle the crisis. Obviously, you must react to the situation and use your best judgment on how to handle it.

Time also can dictate the size and scope of a research plan. If you want to conduct focus groups in three different cities but have only a week to do so, then it may not be possible. The same would be true if you need to conduct a large national survey. Most primary research takes anywhere from a few weeks to a few months to complete. If you don't have the time, then that eliminates the possibilities of doing that method of research.

Just like time, the other major constraint of developing a research plan is money or resources. Primary research costs money. You can pay a research company to recruit respondents, pay the respondents an incentive, and then pay for the actual research and analysis. Depending upon the size and scope of your research project, you can spend as little as a few thousand dollars to well over $100,000.

Time is also money. Even if you engage in secondary research or some other form of in-house or ad hoc research, it all takes time. Advertising and public relations agencies bill clients for their time. So, if the agency takes on a research assignment, it will likely cost the client some billable hours.

Time, money, and the tolerance of ambiguity all play a central role in shaping the research plan. Each of these elements forms some type of trade-off. It is best to understand any limitations you may have to developing a research plan prior to finalizing it. Or you will have wasted even more time and money.

Research Plan Development

A research plan consists of a series of interconnected events. The first step in the process is to define the problem. The second step is to determine the methods for solving or understanding the problem. Once a method has been determined, the third step is to execute the research. This begins with fielding the research or data collection. Once the data is collected, the fourth step is to analyze it and draw conclusions. The final step in the process is to determine what action you will take or recommend as a result of the research study. Also, at this stage of the process, you may elect or recommend conducting further research to delve deeper into the problem or to track the action you are taking as a result of the research. If this is the case, you start all over again.

Exhibit 2.3 **Research Plan Development**

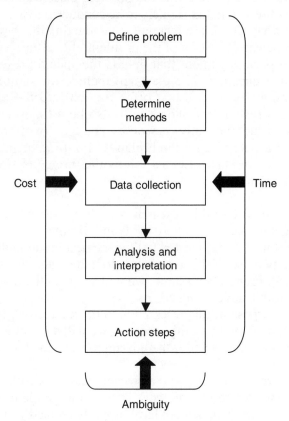

As you read further in this textbook, there will be details on various research methodologies, data collection methods, and analysis techniques. Before you do research, it is important to properly define the problem. This is particularly true in the case of advertising and public relations where many problems involve consumer behavior or attitudes towards a brand or company.

You want to make sure that your problem is specific and actionable. For example, suppose your client asks you if advertising works. Is this a question or problem that you would want to research? It is like asking how many galaxies there are in the universe. It all depends. Now if your client asked whether it is better to advertise in magazines rather than on television, that is a question that could be framed as a problem for research.

Defining the problem or objective of the research is crucial, since it sets into motion the rest of the research plan. The following are examples of research questions for advertising and public relations:

- What message will best motivate my target audience to purchase my brand?
- What do consumers think of my brand?
- Is my advertising or public relations program helping to change the perception of my target market?

All of these questions define the problem clearly and concisely. You can visualize the type of research that is likely to be conducted to answer these questions. You can also see what actions are inherent in conducting this type of research.

With a clear definition of the problem, the research plan then typically consists of a two-page document that details the specific research method to be used to answer the question. The plan will include the sample methodology and some-times sample questions that offer context into the types of things that will be asked of a respondent. There will also be a timeline showing how long it will take to conduct the study, as well as a budget for either internal or external costs. The final aspect of a research plan will outline the action steps to be taken as a result of the research. Let's see how the three questions above lead to examples of action plans.

- The purpose of this research is to determine what message best motivates our target market to purchase the brand. From this research, we will learn which of the four messages tested will be the best in motivating our target.
- The purpose of this research is to understand the consumer perceptions of the brand. From this research, we will segment the market, which will be the basis for future advertising efforts.
- The purpose of this research is to track the advertising/public relations impact on our target. From this research, we will determine if the message is resonating with consumers and if there is appropriate media weight behind the message.

A research plan starts with a problem and ends with a result. It is a good exercise to start from the result and work back to the problem. If your result doesn't sound actionable, then you may not have properly defined your problem. Try it a few times on your own as you craft a research plan.

RESEARCH VERSUS INTUITION

There is an old saying that "research is used in business like a drunk uses a lamp post, more for support than illumination." Because businesspeople want to make informed decisions, many rely on research to support decisions that may be obvious or need no support.

For example, you likely don't need an in-depth research study to tell you that the majority of students do not like tests. Just as you don't need research to tell you that parents want their children to succeed. These are "human truths." They are cultural or societal norms. They don't need to be researched unless you want to dig deeper into motivations or changing attitudes toward these topics.

A question you need to ask yourself prior to any research is: Is this research really necessary? Or can I solve the problem based on my own knowledge and intuition?

Given the pace of business and the time and cost of conducting primary or formal research, the better your "gut" or intuition, the quicker you can be to enact an adver-tising or public relations program.

Beyond things that are just common sense or are just known, you should be able

Exhibit 2.4

Research vs. Intuition Decision Matrix

Situation	Research	Intuition
Decision is significant	✓	
Decision is complex	✓	
Decision requires new knowledge	✓	
Decision is of low risk		✓
Decision is simple		✓
Decision requires no new information		✓

to use your intuition to help you with many potential research issues. For example, if you develop a television commercial that shows a child playing with a puppy, do you really need to research it to see if consumers will feel warm and fuzzy? The answer is probably not. Your intuition should tell you that this is a warm moment in anyone's eyes.

As you work in the field of advertising and public relations, you will be faced with numerous situations where you are dealing with public perception. Research is an important tool to help understand public perception but it is good to remind yourself that you can also help shape public perception.

It is important not to rely on research to tell you each and every facet of what consumers may think. Your own observation of consumers and your intuition can many times be more powerful in generating insights than the fanciest research study.

We have indicated that it is important to use your intuition when a problem is readily known and is of small importance. On the other hand, research is crucial for determining areas where you need more knowledge or insight and when the decisions are of a major magnitude.

For example, if you were about to invest $30 million in a national advertising campaign, you would want to take the time to test the message and creative to ensure that it will be successful. A $30 million campaign is not one that you would like to leave to chance.

Similarly, if you were faced with a decision on how best to target your message that could result in a $20 million sales swing for the brand, you would probably want to invest in some form of research to help guide you.

To conduct research or not becomes a cost–benefit trade-off. Is it worth the time and money to conduct the research? Is it worth the risk if there is no research conducted? All of these questions feed into the development of the research plan.

SUMMARY

You need to formulate a research plan before you can tackle any research project. However, prior to developing a research plan, you first should determine if research is needed at all. It is also important to make sure that research is worth the investment. If the decision is that research is required, you should understand the time and cost constraints that could impact any research effort. Based on a clear understanding of any constraints, you can then proceed to develop a comprehensive research plan. Finally, it is always good to keep in mind that you want to use research to gain insights that you currently don't have rather than as a crutch for making a decision.

DISCUSSION QUESTIONS

1. What is a good use of research? What is a good time to use intuition?
2. What is the difference between public relations and advertising needs for research?
3. What are other trade-offs in determining whether to conduct research?
4. Can you think of situations when you would rely on your intuition rather than conduct research?
5. Can you think of situations where you must conduct research?

EXERCISES

1. Read the current trade press, such as *Advertising Age* or *PR Week*. Highlight the problems faced by a company or other organization. Then decide how you might use research to solve this dilemma.
2. Repeat Exercise 1 above, but this time decide how you might solve the dilemma without utilizing research.

ADDITIONAL READING

Allen, K., R. Sharp, and B. Budlender (eds.). 2000. *How to do a gender-sensitive budget analysis: Contemporary research and practice.* London: Commonwealth Secretariat.

Boardman, A. (ed.). 2005. *Cost-benefit analysis: Concepts and practice.* Upper Saddle River, NJ: Prentice-Hall.

3 Some Research Definitions

LEARNING OBJECTIVES

This chapter is intended to help you:

- Learn some of the basic terms used in advertising and public relations research;
- Understand how those terms relate to one another;
- Learn that some important research terms have more than one use and meaning;
- Try to practice comprehending these basic research terminologies.

There are many terms used in the practice of research. The use of some of these terms is similar to, or the same as, their usage in other spheres or practices. Yet there are some terms that have a different meaning in research than in other uses, and then there are terms that are unique to research. To understand and use research in public relations and advertising, it is essential to have a working knowledge of research terminology and its meanings.

These terms will be used throughout this book, and you will use them when you are involved in formal research projects and in evaluating research that others have done. So it is important to know and comprehend these basic research terms.

SUBJECT

A research subject is any person, object, practice, or process that is observed for research purposes. In survey research and opinion polling, the subject is often referred to as a respondent. In research that uses human subjects, two important concerns are informed consent and protection of the human subjects. There are many guidelines, all to ensure that the subjects are clearly informed of what the study will be, what their participation will involve, any possible consequences, that they can quit any time without consequences, whom to contact with questions, and so forth. Any research involving human subjects should include human-subject protection.

OPERATIONAL DEFINITIONS

To serve its customers better and to target its public relations plans more accurately, a real estate firm wanted to learn more about how people felt about the process of buying a home. A simple survey was designed. The subjects were supposed to be people who had bought a home, so the first question was a qualifying question, to make sure that people had undergone the home-buying process. The question that was asked was, "Do you own your home?" and the answer choices were "Yes" and "No." But after the trial test of the survey, it seemed that very few of the respondents said they owned their homes, even though they had bought homes through this same real-estate firm.

A series of telephone calls to the test respondents found that, even though they had gone through the process of buying a home, many homeowners had checked the "No" answer on the qualifying question. The homeowners realized that they had a mortgage loan to help them buy their homes and the lending institutions owned more of the home than they did, so the respondents marked the "No" response even though they had bought a home.

The problem was that the definition of homebuyers was people who had bought a home, but that was not working in this survey. So the initial qualifying question was changed to "Do you own your home or do you rent?" and the answer choices provided were "Own" and "Rent." The operational definition of a homeowner was anyone who checked the "Own" box in response to the first question.

The actual definition may not be useful in research, or may actually hamper the study. So we develop operational definitions that fit our particular circumstance. An operational definition involves defining a word in terms of the specific process or application at hand, using a set of validation tests to determine its meaning.

Think about trying to survey students at a large university. Coming up with a definition may be complicated; some students may be on leave, or studying overseas, or conducting thesis research at some other location. Defining the term "Mega State University student" may be more complicated than it is worth. Instead, think of an operational definition. Conduct a survey with a question that says, "Are you a student at Mega State University?" and those who answer "yes" are students for the purpose of your study. You let the respondents put themselves into the category where they feel they belong, and your defining process is much simpler.

VARIABLES

As the word implies, a variable is anything that varies. That is, it is anything that can change during the process of conducting research. Variables can usually be measured; variables can also be controlled not to vary, as will be explained below.

INDEPENDENT VARIABLES

An independent variable changes on its own, not as a result of some other factor. If one variable causes another to change, the first is the independent variable. In research, we often manipulate the independent variable to observe the outcome or effect on other variables.

DEPENDENT VARIABLES

Dependent variables change as the result of some other factor. In research, dependent variables change as the result of the independent variable or variables. For example, if you run a retail advertisement for a new cell phone and customers come into the store seeking to buy that cell phone, the advertising is the independent variable and the sales response is the dependent variable.

INTERVENING VARIABLES

Intervening variables operate between the independent and dependent variables. Much of the time, the intervening variable is a dependent variable to the original independent variable; in turn, the intervening variable becomes a new independent variable to the eventual dependent variable. Let's imagine a large company that reduces its public relations budget; a year or so later, the company finds that its customers do not have as strong a positive view of the firm as they did before the budget cut. The budget cut may be the independent variable and the lowered public opinion may be the dependent variable, but in the intervening time, there have also been many intervening variables: reduced public relations efforts, some public relations tasks left undone, customers becoming increasingly frustrated with the company, and so on.

CONTROL

Certainly we all know what it is to control something. In research, control takes on a special meaning: to hold certain variables steady and unchanging while the research takes place on a different independent variable. If you want to test a new advertising campaign, the new campaign is the independent variable and the sales results are the dependent variable. But you want to make sure that the sales-level changes would not have occurred anyway, even without the new campaign, so you keep using the old campaign in some markets and test the new campaign in other selected markets. Using the old campaign in some markets is controlling that campaign, keeping it unchanged, while testing the new campaign elsewhere. The markets where the old campaign ran are called control markets.

HYPOTHESES

A hypothesis is what you expect to happen. In research, your research hypothesis is your prediction of the outcome of the research. In most research in public relations and advertising, you cannot actually "prove" anything; all you usually do is to examine the hypothesis and to determine whether you will accept or reject your hypothesis—that is, whether you conclude that your prediction of the research outcome was correct.

Later in this book, you will see that we often establish certain statistical measures to determine whether to accept the hypothesis. We also sometimes make mistakes in research, and we use statistical methods to determine how often it is likely that we will make a mistake, such as rejecting a hypothesis that should have been accepted (because it was true) or such as accepting a hypothesis that should have been rejected (because it was not true).

Exhibit 3.1

Examples of Research Hypotheses, Null Hypotheses (H_0), and Research Questions

Hypothesis 1

> H_1: Participants will report more favorable attitudes toward billboards they recall seeing than those they do not recall seeing.
> H_0: There will be no difference in attitudes as a function of recall.

Hypothesis 2

> H_2: Experienced gamers will recall more billboards than non-experienced gamers.
> H_0: Gaming experience will not be related to recall.

Research Questions

> RQ_1: Is there an increase in skin conductance following an exposure to a billboard in a video game?
> RQ_2: Will participants show greater skin conductance in response to billboards?

NULL HYPOTHESES

The null hypothesis is any outcome other than the one that you projected or predicted as your hypothesis. So if you hypothesize that your sales will increase because your advertising campaign was altered, there are two possible null hypotheses: that sales went down or that sales remained the same.

In research, we often examine the null hypothesis rather than the hypothesis. Remember that the hypothesis is what you expected, so the null hypothesis is what you did not expect to occur. Because the null hypothesis is the unexpected result, it is often easier to examine—simply because it is not expected and thus it is not the norm, it is unusual, and it is easier to find and examine something that is unusual or not normal than it is for something that occurs all the time.

RESEARCH QUESTIONS

After developing the research hypotheses and null hypotheses, the research question is usually the next step in the course of the research—or the research questions could be developed before the hypotheses. The research questions indicate what the researcher wants to know most in this particular study and what is the highest priority of the research.

In many studies, there will be several research questions. These questions are designed so that their answers will help to determine whether to accept or reject the research hypotheses.

UNIVERSE

In research, the universe is not the same as the astronomical term for the vast expanse of space. We use universe to define all the research subjects that fit the study topic.

POPULATION

Much of the time in research, we cannot study the entire universe. It is too vast, with too many research subjects. So we narrow the scope to those research subjects that we can study, which we call the population.

Maybe you want to know what students majoring in public relations in college think about their discipline. So your universe is all public relations majors in all colleges and universities throughout the world. But you cannot easily study all of them, or even find all of them. So you decide just to study public relations majors in U.S. universities, and you further narrow the scope of the population to those studying at accredited public relations institutions of higher learning. Your population is this smaller group, those who might be included in your study, while your universe was all the PR students in the entire world.

The population need not be only people. If you want to study the ways that magazine advertising has evolved over the years, all the advertisements that have appeared in magazines might be the population, and advertisements appearing in U.S. publications between, say, 1970 and the present time might be the population. So the population may be comprised of things as well as of humans.

SAMPLE

Although the research population is likely to be much smaller than the original universe, it may still be too large—too numerous to enable us to study all the research subjects in the population. To solve this dilemma, we often study a part of the population, and those who are included in the study make up our research sample. All members of the research population can be possible members of the sample, but only a small section of the population is used for the actual sample.

PARAMETER

The word parameter has two separate and different definitions in research.

Originally, parameter was a mathematical term, and because numbers are important in much research, the term parameter became widely used in the field of research. In this original sense, a parameter is a constant, a value in an equation such as a constant in the equation of a curve or line that can be varied to represent a larger collection of curves or lines. So in research, a parameter can be a variable that does not vary or that remains the same throughout the study, whether it is controlled or not.

Yet there is another meaning for parameter in research, one that is used more commonly than the original mathematical definition. A parameter is the boundary of the research, the outside limits of what is being studied. If your research parameters are adult females who purchase bread for their families, then any other group or person would be outside the parameters of your study.

This second meaning for parameter probably derived from a similar word, perimeter, meaning boundary, and over time the word parameter took on this new meaning.

Because parameter has two usages in research, it helps to make things clear by including an explanatory phrase when you use the word: for example, you might say something such as "the mathematical parameter or unchanged variable" for the first meaning and "the research parameter limits" for the second meaning.

SUMMARY

There are many terms used in much if not most formal research, so it is important to know what they mean. It will be helpful to group like terms together. The terms variable, independent variable, intervening variable, and dependent variable all are related to one another. Similarly, universe, population, sample, and research subject all relate closely to one another. The terms hypothesis, null hypotheses, and research question are also related to one another.

DISCUSSION QUESTIONS

1. How are operational definitions different from regular "dictionary" definitions?
2. How do operational definitions aid in research?
3. What is the difference between hypotheses and null hypotheses? Which are usually easier to examine with a research study?
4. In research, what is the difference between a universe, a population, and a sample group?

EXERCISES

1. Use an operational definition to define the persons enrolled in your research course.
2. You want to study whether audiences read a public relations news release. State a hypothesis for your study. Now state the null hypothesis (or null hypotheses).
3. For the same study, state your research question(s).

ADDITIONAL READING

Leedy, P., and J. Ormrod. 2005. *Practical research: Planning and design.* Upper Saddle River, NJ: Pearson Prentice Hall.
Bordens, K., and B. Abbot. 2008. *Research design and methods: A process approach.* Hightstown, NJ: McGraw-Hill.

4 Planning and Designing Research

LEARNING OBJECTIVES

This chapter is intended to help you:

- Learn some basics about research methods;
- Understand the differences between certain common research terms;
- Observe certain concerns that arise in the conduct of research;
- See how these concerns may relate to public relations and advertising research;
- Understand that research often involves reasoning, and that two kinds of reasoning are involved.

METHODS VERSUS METHODOLOGY

The terms "method" and "methodology" are often misused in research, especially by those who do not conduct research on a regular basis and by those who wish to make their work seem more important, as well as by those who simply do not understand the differences between these two words. A research method is simply how one goes about conducting the research at hand—the manner or mode of the research procedure, usually in a logical, orderly, or systematic way of conducting the research. There are many research methods available, including empirical research, experimental research, quantitative research, qualitative research, and historical research. Each of these research methods is discussed in detail later in this book.

"Methodology," on the other hand, really means the study of methods, so a methodology is not a research method but rather the study and analysis of various methods. Too many researchers refer to their research methodology when they really should use the simpler and more apt term, research method.

Because the error of misusing the word "methodology" is so common, the word is beginning to be understood as a synonym for "method." Careful writers and researchers, however, will want to differentiate between these two common research terms.

RESEARCH CONCERNS

In the previous chapter, we examined many of the common basic terms used in research. Here we will expand the list of terms to include those that apply to specific research concerns or potential research problems.

RELIABILITY

In research, reliability occurs when a study is repeated and arrives at the same results as the original study. If repeating the research results in different findings, then there is a problem of lack of reliability.

Let's say you want to find out how much airline companies spend on their public relations operations. In winter, you send out a survey to the public relations departments at several major airlines. Just to verify the results, you send out the same survey in summer, and to a different list of airlines, and you find that the results are widely varied from the original survey's findings. The discrepancy may be caused by a number of problems: different times of year will affect the airlines' passenger traffic; different airlines likely have differing opinions on how important public relations may be, which could affect their budgets; different airlines may define certain functions differently, so not all functions are counted as public relations by all the airlines. In any case, you have a problem of reliability, because replicating the original study came up with different results.

VALIDITY

In simple terms, validity questions whether the research really studied what it proposed to study. Did it really find out what it was trying to find out, about the subjects that it intended to study?

Internal Validity

Internal validity applies to the study itself. Did this particular research project or study really find out what it said it was going to find out? If it did not, there is a problem of internal validity: within the study itself.

There are many possible common problems of internal research validity. Suppose, for example, that part of your study involves getting information about respondents' ages and incomes. These are questions to which people often provide misleading answers—in fact, outright lies. Many respondents will lie about their ages, indicating a younger age than their true age. Similarly, respondents often lie about their incomes, indicating larger incomes than their real incomes.

These are also topics on which respondents often refuse to respond. Respondents who withhold their age or income do not provide the necessary information, so those non-response problems also create difficulties with internal validity.

External Validity

Another type of validity concern is external validity. Even if the study has internal validity, there may be external validity difficulties.

External validity is the validity of generalized statements based on limited research studies, or implying that one variable caused another to vary when such conclusions are unwarranted. These problems often arise when studies in a controlled research laboratory situation cannot be replicated outside the lab.

The most common problems with external validity come from the fact that experiments using human participants often employ small samples obtained from a single geographic location or with idiosyncratic features, such as using volunteers rather than a representative sample, or forcing unwilling respondents to provide information. If you study the response to an advertisement in a small group, you cannot be certain that these responses would be the same in a mass audience. If you study the effectiveness of public relations fund-raising campaigns in New York, there may be completely different problems in, say, California. We cannot be sure that the conclusions drawn from a certain research study actually apply in other geographic locations or with different features.

Projectability

If the results of the internal study cannot be projected to a larger external population, then there are problems of projectability.

Many survey-research studies are conducted using college students as subjects. Yet college students are hardly representative of the entire population; they are younger than average, have lower personal incomes, are more highly educated than the mean of the general population, and in many cases are still forming their opinions about world problems and events. Using research from college students and trying to project those results onto the general populace is a common problem of projectability.

REASONING

Most good research involves logic and reasoning. There are two kinds of reasoning, and both can apply to communications research.

DEDUCTIVE REASONING

Deductions involve logic, which moves from something known to be true (or strongly believed to be true), called a major premise, then onward through a supporting idea or rule (a minor premise) to the conclusion. For example, if we assume that all advertising is paid for, and we see or hear some advertising, we can safely conclude that the advertising we see or hear is paid for.

However, it is easy to go too far with deductive reasoning. If we assume that all good advertising speaks directly to the audience, and our advertising speaks directly to the audience, we cannot assume that our advertising is good—because there is much more involved in good advertising than simply speaking directly to the audience.

INDUCTIVE REASONING

Induction is another form of reasoning, which makes general conclusions based on individual observations. If you observe that good public relations programs and good advertising campaigns support one another, you may logically conclude that good advertising and good public relations should work hand-in-hand.

However, it is essential to recognize that inductive reasoning may be false simply because the observations you made may not be universal, that is, they may not always be true even though they were true in your case. If you work on many public relations efforts and those that were successful took a long time to accomplish their goals, you might conclude that effective public relations efforts require a long time to be successful. Yet there may be some public relations programs that were successful in a shorter time, but you did not experience or see those campaigns. In this instance, your inductive reasoning is faulty.

There are several kinds of inductive reasoning. The differences between the various types are subtle but it may be helpful just to know the kinds of mistakes that people make with inductive thought.

Simple Induction

The simplest kind of induction starts with a premise based on a sample group and leads to a conclusion involving another individual. If you survey your customers and find that those in the sample react better to fund-raising campaigns based on emotional appeals, you may conclude that the next individual from whom you solicit a donation will respond to an emotional appeal. That may or may not be true.

Generalization

Similarly, an inductive generalization goes from a premise based on a sample group and leads to a conclusion about the entire population. If you are running an advertising campaign in Louisiana, and you think that most Louisianans understand some French, then you may reasonably conclude that using some French in your advertising may make it more direct and acceptable to your audience. Again, that may or may not be true.

Causal Inference

Causal inference is drawing a conclusion about a cause-and-effect relationship, based on your observations of some occurrence and the conditions that existed at that time, which you assume to be the cause. If you find that harsh winter weather brings greater sales of automobiles with anti-skid brakes (ABS), you may decide to prepare an advertising campaign about your cars with ABS to run the next time there is bad winter weather. Of course, that may work or it may not.

Prediction

Prediction involves a future conclusion from some sample in the past. If you surveyed industrial buyers during the last economic downturn and found that they were cutting back on their expenditures, you may predict that some future customer will cut back in a future downturn. That may not actually occur, however.

Statistical Syllogism

Going from a generalization to a conclusion is statistical syllogism. If you find that 90 percent of persons over age fifty-five are concerned about saving for retirement, then you might assume that the next person you meet who is over age fifty-five is also concerned about saving for retirement, whether that is the case or not.

Analogies

Inductive analogies go from similarities between two things to a conclusion about some additional attributes of both things. Let's say your company's stockholders tend to own only small bundles of your stock. You might assume that your closest competitor's stockholders would be much the same as your own stockholders and may similarly own only small bundles of the competitor's stock. This may or may not be true.

SUMMARY

There is a difference between research methods and research methodology. Reliability is getting the same results from replicating a research study. Validity asks whether the research really studied what it proposed to study, and there can be problems of both internal and external validity. Projectability concerns the ability to project the research results from a sample onto the larger population. Reasoning is involved in most good research, there are both deductive and inductive reasoning, and there are many kinds of inductive reasoning.

DISCUSSION QUESTIONS

1. How would you use inductive reasoning to study a mass media audience?
2. How would you use deductive reasoning to study a mass media audience?
3. Do all research studies depend on reliability? On validity? On projectability?
4. Why is it necessary to differentiate between methods and methodology?

EXERCISES

1. Design a simple research plan that involves projectability.
2. Design a simple research plan that does not involve projectability.
3. Conduct a quick Internet search to find all the types of research methods that you can.

ADDITIONAL READING

Creswell, J., and V. Plano Clark. 2007. *Designing and conducting mixed methods research.* Thousand Oaks, CA: Sage.

Keppel, G., and T. Wickens. 2004. *Design and analysis: A researcher's handbook.* Upper Saddle River, NJ: Pearson Prentice Hall.

PART II

SECONDARY RESEARCH IN ADVERTISING AND PUBLIC RELATIONS

5 | Introduction to Secondary Research

This chapter is intended to help you:

- Understand the difference between primary and secondary research;
- Understand the advantages and disadvantages of secondary research;
- Understand the different types of secondary research used by advertising and public relations professionals;
- Understand in what situations you should use secondary research.

SECONDARY VERSUS PRIMARY RESEARCH

When a client asks you to solve a problem with research, he likely doesn't care if you use secondary or primary research to find the answer. He just wants to know the facts. Or he may want to know the answer in the quickest and most inexpensive manner possible.

However, as the one providing the answer, you will need to know not only the difference between primary and secondary research but when to use each approach.

When most clients use the term "research," they usually refer to primary research. Primary research is defined as the collection of data that does not already exist. So, primary research is used to find out something that cannot be found out without collecting new information.

Secondary research, on the other hand, is defined as the summary, collation and/or synthesis of existing data. Secondary research then uses existing information to answer the question. The easiest way to think about the differences between the two methods is that primary research involves conducting new research while secondary research involves analyzing existing research.

This doesn't mean that conducting secondary research is as simple as Googling the topic you are interested in and writing down the result. Conducting secondary research is as rigorous as primary research. In the case of secondary research, you must review a variety of existing information sources rather than conducting a single piece of research. You must then summarize what you have found and provide a point of view regarding the information that answers the question posed by your client.

It takes the same diligence and thoughtfulness to conduct a secondary research study as it does to develop and conduct a primary research study. Both methods result in a point of view that helps a client solve a problem. However, they differ markedly in what problems they are effective at solving.

ADVANTAGES AND DISADVANTAGES OF SECONDARY RESEARCH

Your client asks you how many 18–24 year olds attend college. How do you find this out? You could conduct a survey of 18–24 year olds and ask if they attend college or you could look it up in the U.S. Census data. The first approach would take time, cost quite a bit of money and yield an answer that may not be precise. On the other hand, in less than ten minutes you could give your client the specific answer by looking it up in the Census. Case closed.

Therein lies the beauty of secondary research. Since you are reporting or interpreting existing research, the major cost associated with secondary research is the time you spend researching, analyzing, and reporting the information. Unless you must purchase a syndicated study, the cost is minimal. That is one of the key advantages of secondary research.

In the example above, another key advantage to secondary research is that the U.S. Census is a huge and trusted source. It is unlikely that your client would come close to spending the money necessary to complete such an extensive study of the population as the Census. Since the U.S. Census Bureau is a trusted source, it is highly credible.

Another way to approach secondary research is to consider multiple sources. This is a journalistic viewpoint in research. You may see how the Census Bureau compares to a syndicated survey such as MRI or the Pew Research Center on this topic. If the Census Bureau states that 50 percent of 18–24 year olds go to college, compared to 52 percent by MRI and 49 percent by Pew Research Center, you can be relatively certain the answer lies around 50 percent.

You couldn't afford the time or the cost of conducting three national studies on this topic, each by a credible research source. You get the benefit of multiple studies that collaborate on a conclusion.

The final advantage to secondary research can be the resulting time you have to analyze a study. Many times when conducting primary research, there are so many steps to complete the study that analyzing the results can sometimes get short changed. However, with secondary research, you are not concerned with developing the study, only with analyzing and interpreting the results. Thus you have the luxury of time, which may not be possible with a primary study.

However, as strong as secondary research is in solving problems, it does have its drawbacks. Suppose your client now wants you to tell him what college students think of his brand of toothpaste compared to other brands in the market. Is that something you can readily find in secondary research? It is possible but highly unlikely that a specific study was done just for your client without your client actually funding it.

One of the key disadvantages of secondary research is that it is difficult to get specific data on your topic. This specificity can be both in the form of deeper attitudes or issues that may not be studied, as well as timeliness of the information.

Exhibit 5.1

Secondary Research: Advantages and Disadvantages

Advantages	Disadvantages
• Inexpensive	• Not specific to topic
• Multiple studies	• Limited knowledge of research methodology and collection
• Large studies	• Conflicting viewpoints
• Time to analyze	• Lack of depth
• Trusted source(s)	

For example, when the price of gas went from $2.00 a gallon to $4.00 a gallon, it changed behavior and attitudes towards gasoline and driving. However, unless you were studying this market at the time of the gas price spike, you may still be using consumer attitude information from when the price of gas was just $2.00 a gallon. Since secondary information is historical in nature, it is not likely to reflect what is going on at the present moment in time.

Another drawback of secondary research is that you may have limited knowledge of the research methodology and collection of data. Imagine you just told your client that, based on a secondary research study, the best radio station to reach his market is KRAB/FM, a rock station. However, you may not have known that this research study did not properly sample Hispanics and African Americans, who represent 60 percent of the market. Obviously, this would have a big bearing on the outcome of this radio listenership study. The information you have given to the client may lead to an ill-informed decision.

Not knowing how a study asks specific questions is also very problematic. Imagine if you were asked to rate a television commercial on how well you liked it. One study asks you to rate it on a five-point scale from like it very much to not like it at all. The other study asks if you either like it or don't like it. In the first study, only 20 percent say that they like it somewhat or a lot but in the second study 50 percent say that they like it. What do you do? Without knowing the details of questions and the specific results, it is difficult to draw any true conclusions.

This brings us to research that offers conflicting viewpoints. If two research studies measure the same thing but come at it from different methods or times, you can get conflicting viewpoints. This can cause doubts as to what you should report to your client. Do you tell your client that there is a mixed viewpoint on the issue or do you continue to see if you can find other studies to break the tie?

Finally, one of the key drawbacks to any secondary research is the lack of depth on a topic. Because you do not have access to all the data collected for the study, it is impossible for you to go beyond what is reported. If your client wants to know if men are more likely to respond to sale ads than women yet the only study you can find on the topic surveys "adults," then you can't answer the question with authority.

TYPES OF SECONDARY RESEARCH

Secondary research falls into some broad categories. There is syndicated research, published research, articles, associations, government, and user-generated media.

Exhibit 5.2

Types of Advertising and Public Relations Secondary Research

Types	Examples
Syndicated Audience Rating Measurement	Nielsen
	Arbitron
Syndicated Multi-Media Audience Measurement	MRI
	SMRB
	Scarborough
	Media Audit
Academic Journals	*Journal of Advertising*
	Journal of Advertising Research
Track Publications	*Advertising Age*
	Adweek
	AdMap
Associations	American Association of Advertising Agencies
	Public Relations Society of America (PRSA)
	Television Advertising Bureau
	Interactive Advertising Bureau
Syndicated Trend and Consumer Behavior	Yankelovich
	Iconoculture
Government	U.S. Census
	U.S. Department of Labor
	Statistical Abstract
Blog/Social Media Analysis	Nielsen Buzz Metrics

Each area has a variety of research that will be covered in greater detail in subsequent chapters of this textbook.

Syndicated research in advertising and public relations is typically comprehensive studies that provide information on media audiences, consumer buying, and cultural trends. Syndication is where a research company licenses the use of the information to multiple parties. In essence, it is syndicating the information. For example, Nielsen broadcast measurement service conducts research regarding television and cable consumer media habits. Advertising agencies pay a subscription to Nielsen for information on how best to purchase broadcast advertising while media companies purchase it to help them sell or market their programming on their stations. Syndicated research is one area of secondary research that is not free.

Published research papers and articles in trade publications or consumer publications, however, are free to be repurposed for other analysis. Trade publications such as *Advertising Age* or *Adweek* provide a wealth of information on the advertising industry. Published research in academic journals such as the *Journal of Advertising* or the *Public Relations Journal* also offer an opportunity for gaining a great amount of knowledge.

Trade associations provide ongoing research and collect research for their respective industries. The American Association of Advertising Agencies maintains a huge database of information for the advertising industry. Specific media also have their own trade associations that offer free research studies.

The government is an excellent source of information on a variety of topics. The U.S. Census is a key source for demographics in the country. The Bureau of Labor

Statistics offers ongoing measures on the economy of the United States. States and sometimes local municipalities also collect and publish information on their respective constituents and economic factors.

There is a wealth of secondary information a mouse click away. If you Google any topic, you are likely to find a number of studies on it. Plus, if you go to blogs and social forums, you can also find viewpoints on a variety of topics. While there are companies that aggregate and analyze this information, you can weave your way through social media on your own. There is not a lack of opinion on any topic on the Internet.

BEST USES OF SECONDARY RESEARCH

Secondary research is certainly a valuable way to get the answers to many questions. It can be readily accessible, credible, and inexpensive. However, we know that secondary research doesn't fit all needs. The following are three broad areas where secondary research is most effective.

- When the secondary source is the industry standard
- When you need general background information on a topic
- When you need a known fact

There are instances where secondary research is the industry standard. This is quite true in the case of media audience research where broadcast sources such as Nielsen and Arbitron are the industry standard. This can also be true of various market research studies that are industry specific. For example, another division of Nielsen measures grocery purchases.

When you are developing background or context for a topic or issue, secondary research can be the tool to provide that information. By analyzing and collating various studies, you can provide background or add context to a situation analysis.

Secondary research is at its best when you need to get at a known fact. For example, when you need to find the population of Des Moines or the number of Boy Scouts, secondary research is clearly the path.

SUMMARY

Primary research is often necessary in advertising and public relations work, but it usually makes sense first to determine whether secondary research will suffice. Secondary research provides information faster and more economically than primary research can. Even if primary research is necessary, conducting secondary research first will guide the primary research and make it more productive and useful.

DISCUSSION QUESTIONS

1. How would you summarize the differences between primary and secondary research?

2. Can you think of an example of when secondary research would be preferable to primary research?
3. Can you think of an example of when secondary research is not appropriate?
4. When might secondary research be harmful?
5. How has the Internet changed secondary research? What makes a credible source?

EXERCISES

1. Go to your local or college library. Determine which secondary research resources are available for public relations.
2. Now do the same for advertising.

ADDITIONAL READING

Schmidt, R., M. Smyth, and V. Kowalski. 2008. *Lessons for a scientific literature review: Guiding the inquiry.* Santa Barbara, CA: Libraries Unlimited.

Williams, F., E. Rogers, and R. Rice. 1988. *Research methods and the new media.* New York: Free Press, Simon and Schuster.

6 Syndicated Research

This chapter is intended to help you:

- Understand the different types of syndicated research;
- Understand the uses of syndicated research;
- Develop a fundamental understanding of the basic concepts of major syndicated research in advertising and public relations.

TYPES OF SYNDICATED RESEARCH

Syndicated research is frequently used in advertising and public relations. Syndicated research offers some big benefits to the industry. Syndicated research differs from other primary research in that it is not single-sponsored. The idea of syndicated research is to have a number of parties fund the research so that each individual company gets a lot of information for a relatively small amount of money. Frankly, without syndicated research, there would be no advertising industry as we know it today.

This is particularly true in the area of media measurement. Syndicated research is the backbone of the media marketplace. Syndicated research actually is the currency in the industry. Each medium has either one or more syndicated studies that provide audience measurement in terms of ratings (how many people see or hear a medium) and composition (who is watching or listening to a given media vehicle).

The following are the key media measurement syndicated research studies.

- Television and Cable: Nielsen
- Radio: Arbitron
- Magazines: MRI (Mediamark Research and Intelligence)
- Newspaper: Scarborough, Media Audit
- Interactive: Nielsen, Comscore
- Out-of-home: TAB (Traffic Audit Bureau), Nielsen

All of the above syndicated research tools are staples in the industry. The allocation of billions of dollars of advertising is based on the audience research that these tools provide.

A number of the above syndicated research tools offer multi-media audience research. The key national sources for multi-media audience research are MRI and SMRB (Simmons Market Research Bureau). On a local level, the key sources are Scarborough and Media Audit.

MRI is the primary resource for aiding advertising agencies and specifically media planners in helping define target audiences and media habits for their clients. MRI is a national study conducted twice a year with a sample of over 26,000 adults 18+. MRI provides information on over 500 product categories and over 6,000 individual brands plus over 1,000 different media vehicles.

SMRB is also a large nationally syndicated tool that offers similar research to MRI's. In the past few years, SMRB has moved away from competing directly with MRI to providing a number of psychographic studies that can be cross-referenced to media and product categories.

Scarborough is a primary resource for measuring local markets and media. Scarborough surveys the top 75 markets in the United States with a total sample over 200,000 adults 18+. While MRI and SMRB focus on national brands, retailers, and media, Scarborough focuses on local retailers, attractions, and media.

The Media Audit is similar to Scarborough in that it measures local markets and media. The Media Audit differs from Scarborough in terms of the depth of markets that it surveys, over 100 local markets compared to 75, and offers some unique brands and media types.

Multi-media research is just what it sounds like. All of these syndicated research studies measure consumer media habits for television and radio, magazines and newspapers, outdoor, and online. Where they differ from the other research tools is that they provide information on an annual or semi-annual basis. Nielsen, Arbitron, and Comscore provide much more frequent views of their respective media, ranging from quarterly to daily collection of data.

The other area of syndicated research that is used in the industry is consumer trend data. Yankelovich is an icon in this field. The Yankelovich firm has been studying consumers since 1971. Their most well-known syndicated study is the Yankelovich Monitor. To measure consumer attitudes, values, and lifestyles each year, the firm conducts in-person, door-to-door interviews with over 2,500 adults over the age of 16. This interview coupled with a self-administered questionnaire forms the basis for the firm's ongoing tracking study of American culture.

Another firm that many advertising and public relations firms subscribe to in this area is Iconoculture. Iconoculture offers a unique method of evaluating trends within the context of consumer values. Rather than fielding an ongoing study such as Yankelovich, Iconoculture relies on a strategic team of research analysts who constantly feed observations and trends to a central database. These trends are then analyzed and plotted against the 136 consumer values that Iconoculture has identified. Once this is complete, these trends are rolled up into a set of 43 larger macrotrends.

USES OF SYNDICATED RESEARCH

There probably isn't a day that goes by that syndicated research is not used by advertising and public relations professionals. Imagine that you have developed a public rela-

Exhibit 6.1

Top Ten Broadcast TV Programs, Week of November 17, 2008

Rank	Program	HH Network	Rating	Viewers (000)
1	Dancing with the Stars	ABC	12.5	19,631.0
2	Dancing with the Stars Results	ABC	11.4	17,590.0
3	CSI	CBS	11.3	18.446.0
4	NCIS	CBS	10.9	17,990.0
5	Criminal Minds	CBS	10.2	16.334.0
6	CSI Miami	CBS	10.1	15.464.0
7	Grey's Anatomy—Thu 9 PM	ABC	10.1	15,913.0
8	The Mentalist	CBS	9.8	15,844.0
9	NBC Sunday Night Football	NBC	9.5	15,168.0
10	Two and a Half Men	CBS	9.3	15,184.0

Source: Nielsen.

tions campaign that resulted in a mention of your client's product on "Good Morning America." You would want to know how many people were exposed to that message. The same is true for scheduling an advertising campaign in a variety of media.

MEDIA EXPOSURE

One key use of syndicated research is to tell us how many people were exposed to our message. We may want to know not only how many total people were exposed to a given message but also specific demographic groups within that overall audience.

Exhibit 6.1 shows the top ten prime-time programs for the week of November 17, 2008. Nielsen is the company that provides this rating analysis. In this case, the top ten programs are based on the number of households tuned to that program. Based on this sample, Nielsen then projects how many viewers there are to that program. For example, the top program for that week was "Dancing with the Stars," with 12.5 percent of all homes with a television (99.9 percent of all homes) watching this program for that week. That translates to 19,631,000 viewers. The 12.5 percent is called a rating. That is the percentage of homes or a specific target audience that is watching a program. The 19,631,000 is called gross impressions. This is the actual number of people who watched the program.

One key use of syndicated research in the advertising and public relations field is to understand the magnitude of the media that you are working with.

MEDIA PROFILE

Your client wants to know the difference in the make up or composition of MySpace and Facebook. This involves looking beyond the total number of people who visit these social networking sites. In this case, you would want to develop a media profile. A media profile will tell you who is reading, watching, or listening to a specific media vehicle.

The purpose of profiling a media vehicle is to understand if it is an appropriate audience for whatever communications strategy you are employing.

Exhibit 6.2

Houston Chronicle Readership Profile

Characteristic	% Read Yesterday	Index
All Adults	28.0	100
Men	29.6	106
Women	26.4	94
18–24	7.2	26
25–34	18.0	64
35–44	21.0	75
45–54	33.1	118
55–64	38.8	139
65–74	56.5	202
75+	70.4	251

Source: The Media Audit.

For example, your client is a local Houston, Texas, retailer. Because many retailers use the local newspaper as an advertising vehicle, they want to know more about who is reading the paper.

Exhibit 6.2 shows a partial profile of the *Houston Chronicle.* In this profile, you can see what age groups are more or less likely to read the newspaper. If your retail client was targeting adults 18–24, the newspaper wouldn't be as strong an alternative as it would be if the retailer was targeting adults over the age of 45.

Depending upon the medium, you would use different syndicated research to better understand or profile that media vehicle.

TARGET AUDIENCE MEDIA PROFILE

You know how large an audience is and you know the dimensions of it but you really don't know how a given medium fits into the grander scheme of someone's life. One popular way to look at a target audience's media habits is to develop a target audience media profile.

Just because your target watches "American Idol" doesn't mean that they watch a lot of television. If this is one of only a handful of programs that they watch, it might not make sense for you to produce a television advertising campaign. Conversely, if your target reads a large number of magazines every month, that may be the place to put your advertising emphasis.

Through the use of multi-media syndicated research, you can better understand how a specific target audience uses all different types of media. Are they avid readers or are they television couch potatoes? Do they spend all day online or do they spend their day in the car listening to the radio? All of these questions can be answered using multi-media syndicated research.

For example, Exhibit 6.3 shows the daily media consumption for the average drinker of Budweiser Beer. Nearly two-thirds of their media consumption is with television and radio. Print media such as magazines and newspapers represent a small fraction of the time they spend with media in a given day.

Exhibit 6.3 **Daily Media Consumption of Budweiser Users, 8 hours**

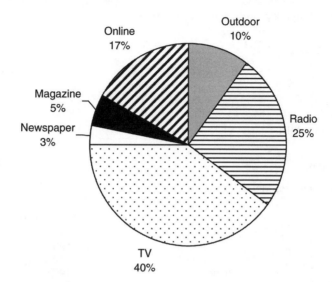

Another way that syndicated research is used to provide a target audience media profile is by determining how that audience uses each medium. Media usage is broken into quintiles or five equal groups. For example, the average consumer watches 4 hours of television a day or about 24 hours a week. That would represent Quintile 3 or the average viewer. Quintile 1 on the other hand is defined by consumers who watch over 40 hours of television a week. Conversely, Quintile 5 is represented by those who watch less than 10 hours of television per week.

Each medium has its own usage pattern. By reviewing this quintile analysis or distribution of media consumption, you can gain a significant amount of insight into a target market's media habits.

Exhibit 6.4 shows the media quintile analysis for the frequent drinker of Budweiser. If you scan across Quintile 1, you will see that this frequent Budweiser drinker is a relatively strong user of radio and magazines; an average user of television, newspapers, and outdoor and a below average user of the Internet. The way to determine this is to review the index number. One hundred is the average. Numbers above 100 such as the 125 for Quintile 1 radio usage suggest a strong or above average number. On the other hand, a 65 for Quintile 1 online usage suggests a less than average usage of this medium.

Syndicated research can help you pinpoint a target market's media habits, which are one of the key factors in developing an advertising or public relations program.

TARGET AUDIENCE PROFILE

There is nothing more important in advertising or marketing than to understand your target audience. Knowing who your target is, what they do, and what they feel forms the basis for any marketing program.

Syndicated research, such as that provided by MRI and SMRB, is designed to an-

Exhibit 6.4

Media Usage by Budweiser Heavy User

	Quintile	TV	NSPR	Radio	Magazine	Online	Outdoor
Heavy	1	109	95	125	113	65	94
	2	108	91	111	103	84	104
	3	91	116	92	108	77	98
	4	105	98	92	87	95	95
Light	5	87	101	92	90	120	105

Source: MRI.

Exhibit 6.5

Budweiser vs. Miller Lite Users

	Characteristic	Budweiser TTL Users	Miller Lite TTL Users
ALL	(000)	24,847	10,492
	% of Brand	100	100
	% of Population	12.1	5.11
	Index	100	100
College Brand+	(000)	5,655	3,797
	% of Brand	22.8	36.2
	% of Population	11.6	7.8
	Index	96	152
No College	(000)	12,264	3,661
	% of Brand	49.4	34.9
	% of Population	12.2	3.6
	Index	101	71

Source: MRI.

swer those questions. Through the use of this research, you can determine who uses a specific brand, what their demographic traits are, what their media habits are, and to some extent what their psychographic make up is. You can also compare your brand's audience to the competition or to people who do not use the category at all.

Suppose you were trying to determine whether you should target college-educated consumers for a beer advertising campaign. You could review syndicated research to see if college-educated consumers drink beer and which brands they might drink.

Exhibit 6.5 shows a comparison between Budweiser and Miller Lite users on the dimension of college education. If you had to pick the brand that had the greatest composition of college-educated drinkers, which would it be? The answer is Miller Lite: 36.2 percent of their drinkers are college educated compared to 22.8 percent for Budweiser. In fact, nearly half of Budweiser's audience (49.4 percent) has not gone to college compared to only 34.9 percent for Miller Lite. So, Miller Lite drinkers appear to have more education than Budweiser drinkers.

However, since Budweiser has many more drinkers than Miller Lite, there are actually more college-educated Budweiser drinkers than that of Miller Lite. Statistics show that 12.1 percent of all drinking-age adults drink Budweiser compared to only 5.11 percent that drink Miller Lite.

Through this type of analysis, you can get a comprehensive profile of your target audience. This leads to developing a strategy of messaging and media that should be much more relevant and focused.

CONSUMER TRENDS

The syndicated research that we have cited offers a wealth of data about media and target markets. However, since it is all based on surveys, it is capturing a moment in time. In developing communications strategy, you want to understand not only what people are thinking today but what they might think in the future.

That is where syndicated research such as Yankelovich and Iconoculture come into play. There is no need to craft a message of luxury indulgence when consumer sentiment says that it is time to be thrifty. Nor is it a good strategy to tout superior service when all the consumer wants is convenience.

Consumer trends then become the context from which you can develop the appropriate messaging strategy. You use consumer trends to get "inside the head" of the consumer. You use consumer trends to help you understand what the consumer might be thinking in the future. Since you are managing to the future, consumer trends play a vital role in any marketing communication program.

SUMMARY

Syndicated research is the mainstay of the communications industry. It forms the basis for understanding how media work. It also is the basis for the economics of the business. There is no single syndicated research tool that serves as both currency for the medium as well as the industry standard of measure. Therefore, you will need to become fluent in a variety of research methods and companies when you work with the major syndicated research studies. The role of syndicated research is expansive. It provides vital information on the target audience. It provides information on underlying consumer trends in the marketplace. It provides details on the size and composition of all different media types.

DISCUSSION QUESTIONS

1. What are the different types of syndicated research?
2. Why do you think there is no single company that provides media audience research?
3. What role does syndicated research play in terms of advertising and public relations?
4. What is the difference between total audience and composition of audience?
5. How do you best determine what your target audience media habits are?
6. What is a consumer trend? How is it used in communications?

EXERCISES

1. Look back at the exercises for the preceding chapter. Search out the library sources that you think will be most useful to you.

2. After examining these research sources, determine what kinds of research data would be most useful to a practitioner in your discipline: public relations or advertising.

ADDITIONAL READING

Schmidt, R., M. Smyth, and V. Kowalski. 2008. *Lessons for a scientific literature review: Guiding the inquiry.* Santa Barbara, CA: Libraries Unlimited.

Williams, F., E. Rogers, and R. Rice. 1988. *Research methods and the new media.* New York: Free Press, Simon and Schuster.

7 Online Resources

LEARNING OBJECTIVES

This chapter is intended to help you:

- Understand the online universe;
- Understand the online media research tools;
- Learn about emerging media research and tools;
- Understand primary research online methods.

When most people say the word online, they are usually referring to the Internet. The view of the Internet is usually limited to searching for information on one of the ISPs, or Internet service providers. This viewpoint is like looking at Mars through a telescope without taking into account the universe around it.

Today, the online—or more aptly put, the digital—world is ever expanding and extremely complex. Access to information and entertainment is moving rapidly from the computer to mobile devices. Television is converging with the digital world in both form and function.

Most businesses and organizations today have a Web site. For some businesses the Web site is their method of conducting business. For others it tells their story. Regardless, it is one of the most important marketing assets a company possesses in today's digital world.

From an advertising and public relations perspective, there are a myriad of digital methods to be aware of and to consider in a communications plan. Internet advertising is dominated by search. There are two aspects to search. One is search engine marketing, or SEM, where an advertiser is bidding on keywords so that its ad appears in a relevant context. The other is search engine optimization, or SEO, which is the method to have your brand appear organically when a person types in a relevant search term. Each of these areas offers tremendous amounts of research and learning opportunities.

Until recently, advertising on the Internet has usually consisted of using SEM and serving ads on various publisher networks or sites. Now there are opportunities to either advertise or join a conversation with consumers on social media sites, online games, blogs and forums, and even virtual reality worlds.

All of these aspects of digital media require research to understand who one's audience is, how engaged they are with the medium, and what impact advertising or public relations can have on them.

Online versus Offline Measurement

The universe of advertising and audience measurement for such media as television, radio, print, and out-of-home media appears to be rather simple and tidy compared to that of the online world.

As we have previously discussed, there is typically a singular form of ratings currency used in each of these industries to help set pricing. Each industry has a dominant research company that is the industry standard such as Nielsen in the television and cable markets and Arbitron in the radio market. The Audit Bureau of Circulation, or ABC, forms the major third-party auditing service for both the newspaper and magazine industry. Although there is always something new in research methodology in these industries, the information is more evolutionary than revolutionary.

This is not the case in the online or digital world. The media is still emerging, as are the research companies and methods used to provide information. Unlike the offline media world, there is a deeper and richer set of information available in the online space. This can be positive as well as negative. The opportunity to gain insight is very great but the opportunity to be lost in the minutiae is equally as great.

There are three types of online measurement in the advertising space: media measurement, campaign measurement, and Web site optimization.

Media Measurement

You have a client who wants to understand the audience of a specific commercial Web site. The question may become what Web site do you place advertising on or send a press release to. There are two methods currently in place to provide the answer to this question. The first is the use of metered tracking through means of an online panel and the second is telephone surveys.

It may seem a bit strange to discuss telephone surveying within the realm of measuring online behavior. Metered tracking technology records Web sites that users visit via software that panel members voluntarily install on their computers. While certainly more accurate than other methods, the software is often banned from work computers so there is an underrepresentation in this area. That is one reason why audience research companies also use telephone surveys to understand online behavior.

The two leading measurement companies in this area use a combination of both, depending upon the service. ComScore Networks and Nielsen//Netratings are the two leading providers of online measurement. Two other syndicated tools previously mentioned, The Media Audit and Scarborough, also provide general online media habits in their syndicated studies.

ComScore tracks over two million continuously measured Internet users on a worldwide basis. This huge metered panel provides reports on both surfing and buying activity of consumers as well as demographic analysis of who is visiting specific sites and of their online purchase dynamics.

Nielsen//Netratings offers a suite of products that competes with ComScore. There are two primary products that Nielsen//Netratings offers in this area: @plan is a tool for media planners to assess online audiences and NetView is the online audience measurement service.

NetView provides measurement of both home and work users with its 28,000 metered panel. NetView reports on unique visitors to a site, page views, and time spent on a specific site. Just like ComScore, it provides reports on demographics, site trends, and other web usage metrics.

Both services then use telephone surveys to add more depth to their panel information. Each service calls a random group within their panel to gain more depth in terms of the user's lifestyles, purchase behavior, and other online information.

Unlike offline research that is done once or twice a year, both ComScore and Nielsen track their panelists on a 24-hour, 365-day-a-year basis. So, the trends and information data are extremely robust and up-to-date.

CAMPAIGN MEASUREMENT

The beauty of doing an online campaign is that you can get instant feedback on what is working and what isn't working. The companies that provide this information are called third-party ad servers.

A third-party ad server technology is fairly simple. When a page loads on a Web site and an ad request is made to a publisher's server, there is a redirect to a third-party server. The third-party server then counts an impression for that publisher.

Third-party ad servers provide tools to measure impressions, clicks, and conversions. For large-scale advertising campaigns, there is the opportunity to determine what creative unit is performing the best and what Web sites are also performing the best. Based on this information, adjustments can be made to the schedule to optimize performance.

There are two dominant third-party ad servers in the market today, Atlas Solutions and Doubleclick. Both Atlas and Doubleclick use similar technology to track the various actions of a campaign. Both can provide reports that allow the advertiser to understand the cost per action of a campaign.

These two services along with others in the category provide the action or direct results of a campaign. However, the limitation to these services is that not all online campaigns should be measured like a direct response campaign. Just like other media, there can be a brand enhancement benefit.

There are companies that specialize in providing the brand impact of online advertising. These companies provide information on the awareness, advertising recall, message association, and future purchase intention of online campaigns.

One of the leading companies in this area is Dynamic Logic, which is owned by a large research company, Millward Brown. Dynamic Logic uses an online panel that can be then divided into a control and test group to measure the brand impact of online advertising campaigns.

Online advertising campaigns are highly quantifiable. The third-party ad serving companies provide the specific behavior of the advertising; who sees it, who responds to it, and how deeply engaged with the content they are. On the other side, there are companies who can provide a longer term brand view of online campaigns. Combining the two methods provides a tremendous amount of information for an advertiser to fine tune any campaign.

Web Site Optimization

Probably one of the most important business tools today is your company's Web site. If you are a dry cleaner, you want your Web site to pop up when someone types in "dry cleaning" in their favorite search engine. Likewise, you want to understand who is coming to your Web site and how long they are staying there.

This is all a part of the online measurement world called site-side analytics. Just about any advertising or public relations program has a component that drives the consumer to a company's Web site. Site-side analytics then become a crucial component to measuring success.

There are a number of companies that provide research tools in this sector. The largest company is Google. Google Analytics tools are very robust. Many of them are free with the hopes that you will use them to increase your search engine marketing budget. However, there are other companies such as Coremetrics, Webtrends, and WebSideStory that also provide a wide range of analytics.

These companies produce reports that companies can use to redesign their Web sites to sell more effectively or to elicit a specific response. All of these companies have tools that can tell the company which search words generate the most visits or the highest conversion rate. Anything—from site registration to completing an application, finding a local store to playing a game, writing on a blog to participating in a forum—can be tracked.

As a researcher, there is no better way to understand consumers who want to interact with your brand than to track their behavior. Site-side analytics offers you a deep dive into this realm of consumer behavior.

Social Media

While social media such as Facebook, MySpace, and LinkedIn can all be tracked with some of the aforementioned research tools they also offer a wealth of research possibilities in their own right.

All social media sites include extensive user profiles that can be accessed for marketing use. For example, if you wanted to find out how many consumers put "rap music" in their Facebook profile, you can quickly determine it. Or if you want to find out how many accountants are on LinkedIn, you can find that as well.

Social networking sites also offer research features. You can ask those on a social site to participate in a research study. Some sites such as Facebook offer a polling feature where you can post a question for the group to answer.

As these media forms emerge and seek to monetize their audience, there will be more and more research potential available in this space.

EMERGING MEDIA

It seems that every day a new forum of consumer-generated media appears on the Internet landscape. People are talking and today there are plenty of blogs, forums, online video sites, and social networking sites to satisfy anyone's sense of personal expression.

From a brand perspective, these new forms of consumer-generated media are both an opportunity as well as a threat. People are talking all right, and you may or may not like what they might be saying about your company.

One of the problems with consumer-generated media is trying to get a handle on what the conversation is all about and how you fit in. To help aggregate this consumer discussion, various research companies have begun to develop tools for marketers to make sense of it.

One of the pioneers in this area is Nielsen. Nielsen BuzzMetrics is a service that monitors these new media to provide marketers with diagnostics that measure the amount of discussion they are involved in, as well as a positive versus negative ranking of that discussion. Nielsen BuzzMetrics is used extensively by television networks to monitor the "buzz" that a program's storyline is generating. In fact, many networks use this information to help guide script development of episodic shows.

There are other competitors to Nielsen in this space including Umbria and Radian6. Both of these companies provide measurement of consumer-generated media and also offer methods for public relations professionals to interact with this new type of journalism.

This area of consumer-generated media offers a tremendous opportunity for marketers to better understand what consumers truly think about their brand. This is consumer feedback in its rawest form so the clinical bias is taken out of the equation.

PRIMARY RESEARCH APPLICATIONS

Primary research has been greatly impacted by online technology. Both quantitative and qualitative research now has viable alternatives to former methods. The criticism regarding online research has been that those who are online are different from the general population. Therefore, it is difficult to draw a random sample from an online universe.

With broadband penetration now past 60 percent, and the widespread availability of online access either at home, work, school, and even in libraries, the myth that only the wealthy have online access is rapidly fading. The acceptability of online research methods is certainly now mainstream.

Quantitative research is largely done by telephone. Before telephone, the most popular method was by mail. Telephone polling is still the dominant method for determining consumer perception. However, the rise of online panels has provided a popular alternative in fielding quantitative studies.

Panel studies have been around for a long time. Panels are made up of like individuals who may share a demographic or behavioral trait. This had been done largely by collecting product questionnaires or warranty information. Now online panels play a big role in research. The benefit of a panel is that the group you want to research is already

Exhibit 7.1   **Online Universe**

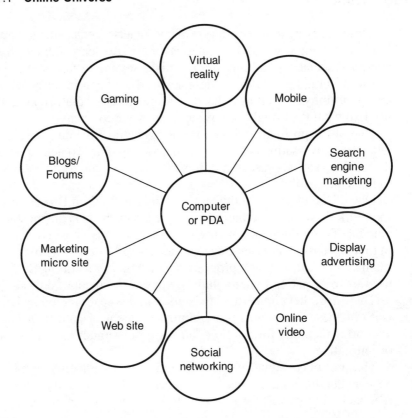

pre-recruited. The downside of a panel is that this group may participate in a variety of research studies. However, typically the pros outweigh the cons when using a panel.

Online panels can offer efficiencies. Costs are usually relatively low compared with fielding a primary study and the speed in which you can gain information is relatively fast. With online panels, you can also provide visual stimuli such as advertising for consumers to react to.

Online panels are very popular methods to research typically difficult to reach audiences. There are medical panels that contain physicians and other hard to reach medical professionals. There are high-level business panels that contain senior executives of Fortune 500 companies. And there are ethnic panels where you can research different cultures.

Online research is also making its way into qualitative research. Qualitative research usually involves meeting with consumers face-to-face either in a focus group setting or in more natural settings. The goal of qualitative research is to gain a more emotional insight to a consumer's psyche than quantitative research can provide.

You may feel that online is not suited for qualitative research. However, with technological advances in both video and voice over Internet, there is the opportunity to have a discussion with a respondent face to face. One of the popular aspects of online qualitative research is that respondents can talk to you in a comfortable setting such as their living room or home office.

Online research methods are becoming popular alternatives to traditional research methods. Online is not the panacea for research. There are many methods that are relatively new and have yet to be proven. Traditional methods have been proven to be effective. But, the online application of traditional research methods gives the researcher more alternatives to consider.

It is good to keep in mind that while online research methods can be very innovative, the goal of research is to find consumer insights. Sometimes that can be as low tech as hanging out with the consumer. That being said, online methods do offer many exciting new ways to get at those insights that marketers need to help them push their brands forward.

SUMMARY

The online universe continues to grow, driven by both new forms of media and consumer-generated media. Each medium has its own research idiosyncrasies. There are tremendous research opportunities within the online universe. Since the online universe captures so much information, there is an opportunity to gain insight into consumer behavior on a continual basis. As with any rapidly emerging area, there are many research companies vying to be the standard for their respective niche in the digital marketplace. All aspects of the research business have been and will be impacted by the growth in this area.

DISCUSSION QUESTIONS

1. What are the strengths and weaknesses of online primary research?
2. How would you measure an online advertising campaign?
3. How would you use information from consumer-generated media in a public relations program?
4. How do you feel about privacy issues regarding online research?

EXERCISES

1. Go to the Internet, search Google or Yahoo and type in "advertising research data." How many sources do you find listed?
2. Now do the same for "public relations research data." How many sources do you find listed?
3. How valuable do you judge these online resources to be?

ADDITIONAL READING

Plummer, J., S. Rappaport, R. Barroci, and T. Hall. 2007. *The online advertising playbook: Proven strategies and tested tactics from the Advertising Research Foundation.* Hoboken, NJ: Wiley.

Zinkhan, G. 2000. *Advertising research: The Internet, consumer behavior, and strategy.* Chicago: American Marketing Association.

Kelley, L., and D. Jugenheimer. 2008. *Advertising media workbook and sourcebook.* Armonk, NY: M.E. Sharpe, especially ch. 2, "Working with media web sites."

8 Other Useful Resources

LEARNING OBJECTIVES

This chapter is intended to help you:

- Understand the types of research sources available for the advertising and public relations professional;
- Learn about the different industry associations that represent the advertising and public relations business;
- Learn about key industry and academic media sources.

RESOURCE OVERVIEW

As you have gathered by reading the prior chapters of this text, there is a wealth of information in the advertising and public relations field. The syndicated research makes up the backbone of the industry. The new digital world offers a tremendous opportunity for learning about consumer behavior and what works and doesn't work in the communications field.

Beyond these areas, there are other helpful resources that can be tapped into. These resources fall into three broad categories.

- Industry trade organizations
- Industry and academic publications
- Government organizations

These organizations, industry journalists, and academic researchers all approach the advertising and public relations business from their own unique direction, and all provide differing viewpoints. Industry trade organizations exist to help their members profit in their respective areas. For example, the American Association of Advertising Agencies provides support for the advertising agency sector of the industry. The Television Advertising Bureau or TVB does the same for television stations. Each organization has a vested interest in the well being of their respective portion of the advertising industry.

On the other hand, news periodicals that follow the industry such as *Advertising Age* and *Adweek* provide a journalistic viewpoint of the industry. They report on strengths and weaknesses of the business and of specific companies within the industry. Academic journals such as the *Journal of Advertising Research* provide research that is typically not sponsored by an industry member or corporation. Therefore, the research found in most academic journals is usually without an industry bias.

There are a number of government agencies that impact the advertising and public relations industry. Some such as the Federal Trade Commission (FTC) help regulate the industry while others such as the Census Bureau provide a myriad of information that is valuable to the industry.

INDUSTRY ORGANIZATIONS

Industry organizations offer an excellent resource for anyone wanting to know more about advertising or public relations. There are two sets of industry organizations that are valuable in the research process. The first set is organizations that directly serve the industry:

- ANA—Association of National Advertisers
- 4As—American Association of Advertising Agencies
- AAF—American Advertising Federation
- AAA—American Academy of Advertising
- PRSA—Public Relations Society of America
- DMA—Direct Marketing Association
- IPR—Institute for Public Relations

These organizations serve various constituencies within the advertising and public relations field. The ANA is the client or advertiser side of the business. The 4As serves advertising agency and advertising holding companies. The AAF serves to unify advertising professionals through clubs organized on an individual market basis; students interested in advertising may become involved via college chapters. The PRSA represents the public relations profession. The DMA is a clearinghouse for agencies and/or advertisers who work in the direct marketing arena. All of these organizations house numerous research studies. Many of these organizations fund research specifically to help their members learn more about the impact of advertising and public relations.

Two other organizations that help to bridge the gap between academia and the industry are the AAA or American Academy of Advertising and the Institute for Public Relations (IPR). The AAA is an organization of scholars and industry researchers with interests in advertising research and advertising education, while the IPR is a nonprofit organization that maintains a repository of research for the public relations industry.

The second set of organizations that is important to the advertising industry centers on the media. Each medium has its own trade organization that is dedicated to furthering its cause. The following highlights some of the key media organizations:

- TVB—Television Advertising Bureau
- RAB—Radio Advertising Bureau
- NAB—Newspaper Advertising Bureau
- IAB—Internet Advertising Bureau
- MPA—Magazine Publishers Association
- OAAA—Outdoor Advertising Association of America

Each of these organizations conducts research to help position their respective medium to be able to gain more advertising revenue. Their research studies are quite in depth and are typically presented to the advertising agency and advertiser community. Each of these organizations offers research on all facets of using their medium including who uses it, how they use it, and which advertisers are using it most effectively.

For example, if you had a question about the relative impact of a banner ad compared to a rich media ad online, the IAB has a study on it. In a similar fashion, the TVB has research on the impact of 30-second commercials compared to 15-second commercials in terms of effectiveness. The MPA has extensive research on the impact of adding magazines to the media mix to provide balance to a television-only media plan. So, specific media information is readily available at these organizations and their corresponding Web sites.

INDUSTRY PERIODICALS

The two advertising industry weekly news publications are *Advertising Age* and *AdWeek. Advertising Age* takes a balanced view of advertiser and advertising agency while *AdWeek* is geared towards the advertising agency world.

Advertising Age publishes numerous guides that can be very useful to anyone wanting to dig into the advertising business. For example, the Guide to Digital Media and Guide to the Hispanic Marketplace are both very good secondary sources into each topic. *Advertising Age* also offers a resource center that has other guides, historical views of advertising, and other topical articles.

AdWeek also offers a resource center that includes some industry studies plus a regular review of current advertising. Like *Advertising Age,* it provides key industry statistics and topical articles on the advertising business.

Admap is a monthly publication that is a bridge between industry and academia. *Admap* is the publication of the WARC or World Advertising Research Center. The WARC is a tremendous international research resource. All of the articles in the monthly *Admap* are published by professionals using an approach that might be termed "academic journal light." Research is provided for most articles but not in a formal academic manner. The WARC is perhaps the gold standard for industry research.

Other publications of interest include the *Polling Report,* a twice-a-month newsletter that summarizes recent public opinion polls, and *Quirk's Marketing Research* review, a monthly magazine that details best practices in research and publishes comprehensive guides to the marketing, advertising, and public relations research community.

ACADEMIC JOURNALS

Academic journals provide an important perspective on the advertising and public relations industry. The following are the leading academic journals in this field:

- *Journal of Advertising*
- *Journal of Advertising Research*
- *Journal of Public Relations Research*
- *Public Relations Review*

In addition, there is considerable research into advertising and public relations in the *Harvard Business Review* as well as the *Journal of Marketing* and *Journal of Marketing Research.*

If you are interested in certain topics—such as developing a model to measure advertising effectiveness or to understand the relationship between advertising recall and persuasion—these academic journals will be a valuable resource.

Although publishing a paper in an academic journal requires much intellectual skill and determination, you—as the reader—don't need your own Ph.D. to get a lot out of the resulting work. The nature of an academic paper is to provide a complete review of the topic at hand and then to discuss how the paper's own research furthers this particular area of interest. So, if you are interested in a subject such as measuring advertising or public relations effectiveness, the most recent journal papers in this area will contain an extensive bibliography of prior published research. Studying this, you can quickly get up to speed on all the research that has been published on a topic.

Academic research is typically more rigorous than research conducted in the practice of advertising and public relations. As a result, the conclusions drawn from the research are normally statistically significant. This means that you can assume that if a primary research study was conducted and is published in an academic journal, it is of the highest quality. The conclusions are not subject to serve anyone's agenda other than to provide the results of the study.

Since the great body of research in the field of advertising and public relations is either proprietary (not published) or is designed to promote a specific agenda, academic research is the one area you can turn to for an unbiased viewpoint of the industry.

GOVERNMENT SOURCES

There are two types of government resources that are important for the advertising and public relations industry. The first are government agencies that provide federal regulation of advertising and the second are government agencies that provide information that is beneficial for marketing.

Your client wants to make a specific claim in their advertising. How do you know if it meets the legal requirements? You would turn to the Federal Trade Commission (FTC). The FTC is the major regulator of advertising for products sold in interstate commerce. The FTC's mission is to ensure that our markets are competitive and that consumers are offered complete and not deceptive information about their brands.

Any product claim including comparative advertising is reviewed by the FTC. The FTC is a key source for ensuring that your advertising message is fair and can be substantiated.

You are working on the promotion of a new pharmaceutical product. One organization that you will need to research is the Food and Drug Administration (FDA). The FDA ensures that the food we eat, the medicines we use, and the cosmetics we wear are safe and effective. The FDA works with manufacturers on proper labeling and disclosure of information. The FDA also oversees the promotion of these products, which means that you are likely to need to know FDA policies if you work in these sectors of the economy.

You are consulting with a media client regarding the purchase of a television station in the market to add to the other affiliate that they own. You would need to understand the rules and regulations of the Federal Communications Commission (FCC). The FCC is the federal agency with jurisdiction over radio, television, telephone, satellite, Internet, and cable television industries.

You are asked by your client to provide a viewpoint on trademarks and copyright protection for his brand and your advertising. The place to turn to would be the Patent and Trademark Office and the Library of Congress. These are great resources that offer counsel on intellectual property—which advertising is.

You are given the task of researching demographic trends in the United States plus economic trends in the food industry. Rather than pore through numerous publications or Google incessantly, you can turn to two government agencies to help you out. The Bureau of Labor Statistics is the repository for all economic trends and business facts in the United States. The Census Bureau is the official collector and publisher of demographic information for the United States. Both of these sources provide tremendous background information on the demography and economy of the United States.

Although not government sponsored, nonprofit organizations that provide research such as the National Opinion Research Center at the University of Chicago and the Pew Research Center also offer a tremendous volume of research that can be valuable in this area.

Summary

There is a tremendous amount of information available to the advertising or public relations researcher. The trick is to determine what information is relevant to your needs. From there, you need to determine how much trust you will put in that information. For any research topic, a good place to start your search is with the industry trade publications. They are becoming more of a repository for research in this digital age. There are a myriad of industry trade organizations that also have valuable information and conduct research on behalf of their members. Depending upon the nature of the study, these organizations can offer valuable insights. The academic world offers a rich amount of research that can give you a historical perspective on the research topic. The government has a deep body of facts that can help any researcher build a foundation for a plan.

DISCUSSION QUESTIONS

1. What are the strengths or weaknesses of these alternative research sources?
2. When would you be comfortable using trade organization information? How about trade publications?
3. Is academic research in this area relevant?
4. In what situations would you use government information?
5. How would you resolve conflicts in information from competing sources?

EXERCISES

1. On the Internet, go to Google or Yahoo and type in "advertising trade organizations." Do the same with "public relations trade organizations." How many do you find? Do you think all of them will be useful to you in your career?
2. Now do the same by typing in "public relations publications." Then do the same with "advertising publications." Again, how many do you find, and do you think all of them will be useful to you? Which will be most useful?

ADDITIONAL READING

Jones, J. 2000. *Advertising organizations and publications: A resource guide.* Thousand Oaks, CA: Sage.

Scott, D. 2007. *The new rules of marketing and PR: How to use news releases, blogs, podcasting, viral marketing, and online media to reach your buyers directly.* Hoboken, NJ: Wiley.

PART III

PRIMARY RESEARCH IN ADVERTISING AND PUBLIC RELATIONS: QUALITATIVE RESEARCH

9 Uses of Qualitative Research

LEARNING OBJECTIVES

This chapter is intended to help you:

- Understand what qualitative research is;
- Determine why qualitative research is necessary;
- See how qualitative research is conducted;
- Learn how qualitative research may apply to public relations and advertising;
- Observe some qualitative research techniques.

QUALITATIVE RESEARCH

Qualitative research in the mass media observes what people say and do. While the other major type of research—quantitative research—tends to measure and count the number of responses, qualitative research attempts to delve into concepts, ideas, definitions, characteristics, meanings, and symbols.

Because the mass media serve human beings, the study of people is an essential part of advertising and public relations research. The humans who comprise the public relations and advertising audiences are influenced by a number of factors, including the setting in which the communication occurs, the meanings that people attribute to certain terms and derive from certain messages and media, and the behavior of the audience members after they receive and process the messages' information. Qualitative research encompasses all these factors.

Qualitative research tries to describe things, such as meaning, comprehension, and processes. Qualitative research necessarily must go to the people or the setting where the communication occurs. The outcome is not as important to qualitative research as is the process of communication.

To define a problem and generate research questions and hypotheses, qualitative research is often used in public relations and advertising. The number of respondents is often low, so the results cannot be projected onto a larger population. Knowing what behaviors people might exhibit and their motivations is important in the media business and qualitative research can do this well.

In a qualitative study, the people in the study are often asked to respond to general questions, and the researcher then formulates additional questions to probe deeper into the respondents' feelings, interpretations, and responses. Because of this methodological approach, qualitative research depends heavily on the researcher, who must be intimately and actively involved in the research itself.

In qualitative research, we assume that the issues involved are complicated and, thus, difficult to measure and interpret. We are concerned with the perspectives, interpretations, and settings in which the communication occurs. The researcher is not only involved but is often partial, as opposed to the impartiality so often expected of research. Inductive reasoning is involved as the researcher looks for patterns and connections. Instead of starting with theories and hypotheses, qualitative research starts with a blank sheet and tries to help develop hypotheses that may eventually lead to theories.

There are numerous qualitative approaches used in advertising and public relations research, and we shall examine some of the most common. There are other uses of qualitative research, of course, for other disciplines, but those are beyond the scope of this book. Entire books are written on the conduct and use of qualitative research, so these chapters will provide only an introduction to qualitative research as used in public relations and advertising.

SOURCE CREDIBILITY

How credible is the person or institution that sent out the message? Source credibility does not solely refer to the credibility of the media; in addition, it refers to the credibility of the sender, whether that be the U.S. president's press secretary, the public relations officer of a corporation, or the advertising from a retail store.

Studies of source credibility often deal with the way credible sources may influence selection of a message by an audience member, the believability of the message, attitude change, and perhaps even resulting actions.

Why do some advertisements work and others do not? Why are some political candidates more successful in persuading others? Why do some audiences consider a source as credible while the same source is seen as not credible by others? Credibility is controlled, in main part, by the receiver, the audience member. Sometimes demographic factors may come into play; a young audience may not believe things said by an older speaker. So age, economic level, political or religious affiliations, and gender may affect how a recipient views the credibility of a source.

Because source credibility can be so subjective, it is difficult to quantify and thus most often is the subject of qualitative research. The basic step of determining what constitutes credibility is a major focus of this research, as is finding the various factors that contribute to source credibility.

Determining how much the receiver appraises a source as credible constitutes a *factor* model of source credibility. A *functional* model tries to determine how well the sender satisfies the recipient's needs for information, persuasion, justification, and similar factors. Finally, analyzing how the receiver handles and reacts to the source is a *constructivist* model.

Perhaps surprisingly, source credibility studies have found results on two extremes and at almost every measure in between: that a credible source affects the attitudes of the receivers, or that it does not affect the receivers' attitudes, or that it may sometimes and not at others. Yet because message selection, believability, attitude change, and resulting action or inaction are so important in advertising and in public relations, this topic remains an important one for media researchers.

To conduct research into media credibility, it is common to ask respondents to compare some choices, such as "From which source is sales information more truthful, advertisements or salespersons?" and then to repeat with similar questions comparing other matches of information sources. Such research might be preceded with other questions, like "Where do you receive most of your news? Where do you receive most of your product purchase information?" For any such questions, a good researcher will follow up with probing in-depth questions. This kind of research can also be conducted with lists of media and possible scores, say from 1 to 5, for media trust, but such an approach would be quantitative rather than qualitative.

CONCEPT TESTING

Both approaches to research, quantitative and qualitative, can also be used for concept-testing studies. This research is most often conducted prior to the introduction of the advertising or promotional campaign, and perhaps even before the introduction of the product, service, or idea to be marketed. Respondents are asked to evaluate various benefits of the item to be marketed, such as a car that helps park itself or a liquid laundry detergent that weighs less but cleans just as well as another even though less of the product is used. If this research involves checking off scores or rating scales, it would be quantitative. On the other hand, qualitative research into concept tests would likely utilize personal interviews, focus groups, and perhaps field studies; these specific approaches will be discussed later in this chapter. Modern concept testing often makes use of the Internet, which may not be as personal as face-to-face research but may allow the respondents to view sample campaigns in a realistic format. The Internet makes it feasible to conduct online in-depth interviews with respondents who are geographically diverse, which can permit repeated interaction with larger numbers of respondents.

Concept testing can be used to evaluate proposed marketing, advertising, and public relations ideas and themes, as well as basic product or service concepts, prices, brand names, product and service features, and market positions.

COPY TESTING

Testing copy is similar to testing concepts, although it may come a bit later in the marketing program. Copy testing can be used in public relations although it was formulated specifically for advertising purposes to test potential advertising themes and appeals, as well as message recall, comprehension, and relevance. This particular type of research is sometimes known as pretesting, although it is important not to confuse pretesting of messages with other types of pretests, such as simulated uses

Exhibit 9.1

Positioning Advertising Copy Testing (PACT)

Good copy testing will utilize these (PACT) criteria.

1. Provide measurements that are relevant to the objectives of the advertising.
2. Require agreement about how the results will be used in advance of each specific test.
3. Provide multiple measurements; single measurements are generally inadequate to assess the performance of any advertisement.
4. Base the research on a model of human response to communication, e.g., reception of a stimulus, understanding a stimulus, and responding to the stimulus.
5. Allow for consideration of whether the stimulus (the advertisement) should be exposed more than once.
6. Recognize that a more finished advertisement can be evaluated more soundly and that any alternative messages to be tested should be in the same phase or degree of completion.
7. Provide control to avoid bias of the context of the advertisement exposure.
8. Account for basic considerations of sample selection.
9. Demonstrate validity and reliability.

of new product features or pretests of campaign effectiveness for the purpose of comparison with later posttest studies. Copy testing can apply to proposed messages in any medium: print, broadcast, online, or mail.

A number of large advertising agencies have agreed on precepts for Positioning Advertising Copy Testing (PACT) to provide specific criteria for good copy tests. These are shown in Exhibit 9.1.

Copy testing is a mix of research and creative message development. Copy testing can be diagnostic in its approach, ascertaining, for example, the ability to attract attention, if the message is linked to the brand name, or whether audience members are motivated to buy and use the advertised item. A number of nonverbal measurements can also be used, trying to determine whether a message may operate below the consciousness level of the audience members; this kind of emotional impact can often best be tested using qualitative methods. Other copy testing approaches, such as measuring physiological reactions to messages, sorting pictures, tracking eye movement around a layout, and various attempts to link message recognition, recall, and sales, are quantitative techniques, not qualitative.

MEDIA TRUST

Americans' trust in the mass media has been slipping in recent years, and now fewer than one-third of the populace say that they generally trust the mass media. The trust levels have fallen furthest and fastest during national political campaigns. If audiences do not believe what they see and hear in the news, their trust of commercial messages, in advertising and public relations, must also suffer, perhaps even more.

As with the other research applications that have been discussed here, media trust can be studied using both qualitative and quantitative methods. In qualitative research, it is essential to go beyond simple ratings and rankings and delve deeper into what kinds of messages are believed and which are not believed, why this lack of trust exists and why it has expanded, and what the media could do to increase audience trust. Again, panels, focus groups, personal and in-depth interviews, and field studies may be appropriate qualitative approaches.

MEDIA RELIABILITY

Similar to media credibility and media trust, media reliability studies explore whether the media themselves are reliable. These studies do not involve only the reliability of the news and commercial messages carried by the mass media, but also whether the media cover all important issues instead of ignoring some items or covering up information that might harm a political party, an advertiser, or a public figure.

As before, media reliability can be studied by quantitative methods and qualitative methods, and qualitative approaches would involve in-depth interviews, panels, focus groups, field studies, and other methods that allow for follow-up questions, probing questions, and flexible interview schedules rather than set lists of choices to be checked off or ranked.

QUALITATIVE RESEARCH METHODS

In discussing the various applications of qualitative research in public relations and advertising, we have mentioned personal interviews, in-depth interviews, panels, focus groups, field studies, and similar research methods. Now we can discuss these specific research methods as they are applied in qualitative research.

PERSONAL INTERVIEWS

As the name implies, personal interviews are those that take place directly between individuals. That does not necessarily mean that these interviews are face-to-face; personal interviews could be conducted by telephone or over the Internet. Also, a personal interview could be with a group of respondents as well as with only one respondent.

Interviews are usually the best approach to use when trying to gather personal reflections such as beliefs, values, and opinions. Because of the lengthy time available and the ability to build up trust with the respondent, an in-depth interview is useful when it is necessary to probe with follow-up questions and with unscripted question-and-answer interviews. Interviews tend to be more flexible than other information gathering techniques and can uncover rich and complex information about the issues at hand.

In-depth interviews are a special type of personal interview. Because they are more intensive, in-depth interviews are usually conducted one-on-one; this approach is also necessitated by the fact that in-depth interviews are often even more lengthy, sometimes running up to an hour or longer. In-depth interviews are good at uncovering latent or hidden issues.

The format of an interview may vary depending on the purpose and on any previous contact with the respondents. It is often best to begin with fairly innocuous questions, perhaps things like "How often do you go grocery shopping?" or similar questions that will likely meet little resistance on the part of the respondent. Then the questions can turn to the direct topic at hand.

If demographic information is sought, especially income data, it may be best to delay that type of question until the end of the interview, after a mutual feeling of trust and confidence has been built. Even then, questions about personal matters, such as income, will sometimes gain a higher response rate when the questions are put into ranges. Instead of asking, "What's your annual income?" the question could be something like "Is your total family income before taxes more or less than $40,000?" Then if the answer is "below," the next question can be "Is your total family income before taxes above or below $25,000?" and if the answer to the first question was "above," the follow-up question can be "Is your total family income before taxes above or below $60,000?" Using this approach and by asking only two questions, the respondents put themselves in one of four categories: below $25,000; between $25,000 and $40,000; between $40,000 and $60,000; and above $60,000. Asking for categories is less threatening and less personal than asking directly for an exact number, and if the responses are to be placed in categories eventually, asking for an exact amount is not necessary. When questioning about income, it is essential to clarify whether a weekly, monthly, or annual income is being sought; many people are paid monthly and do not know the weekly equivalent, but most know their total before-tax income from filing an income-tax return. Distinguishing between individual or family income is also necessary to gain comparable data from all respondents. More information about question formulation is covered in a later chapter.

Some researchers try to disguise the real purpose of the research in an attempt to keep the respondents' responses honest and open, but most qualitative research uses a direct approach that discloses the purpose of the study and the organization for which it is being conducted. Sometimes this information is provided after the research is completed, in case these facts might bias the responses gained.

DYADIC INTERVIEWS

Dyadic communications occur between only two persons, so dyadic interviews are simply one kind of interview setting. Dyadic interviews allow the two persons to get to know and trust each other. Also, spontaneity is possible as the interview leads from one topic to another. The interviewer may have a list of topics to be covered, rather than specific questions to be asked, and ideas and responses are freely interchanged through the use of a dyadic interview.

FOCUS GROUPS

Another kind of interview is the focus group, although it is a very specialized kind of interview. In a focus-group study, a small number of persons will be gathered with an interviewer; most focus-group research has all the persons, respondents and moderator, in the same room, although it is possible to use the Internet with instant-messaging or on-camera capabilities. This moderator asks a variety of questions, often loosely structured to permit the respondents to interject their own views and opinions. The session may be recorded, via audio or video, and sometimes other researchers observe through one-way glass from an adjacent room.

The moderator must try to include all the respondents, and if someone is holding back or seems shy, asking direct questions to that individual may be necessary. The group pressure helps get everyone to contribute. Questions are often general at the beginning of the session and then become more specific as the interview progresses, although still following a general outline or path rather than with specific questions in a certain order.

In public relations and advertising, focus groups are used to uncover hidden opinions and experiences with a product or service or with a generic category, as well as to develop new ideas for campaign themes and appeals. Focus groups are relatively inexpensive. The interview session may last up to a couple of hours, but the responses are immediate so the findings are quick. Because of the small group size, the opinions and information can be attributed only to this group and not projected to a larger population, but it is a common method of gaining insights and ideas.

Projective Techniques

Projective techniques are so named because the purpose is to get the respondents to project themselves into a situation or scenario. This can be a time-consuming technique because normally only one respondent can be questioned at a time. The attempt is to uncover motives, attitudes, opinions, feelings, and beliefs.

There are several specific types of projective techniques.

Thematic apperception tests (TAT) use a picture for which the respondent makes up a story. If the picture is about a specific purchasing or product-use situation, the respondent may be telling his or her thoughts about the product or service or the applications of this item.

Cartoon tests are similar, with cartoon characters talking about a situation and then showing a blank cartoon "balloon" into which the respondent is to interject his or her responses.

Story completion begins with a short tale read by the interviewer, who then asks the respondent to compete the story.

Word association provides only a single word at a time, with the respondent saying the first thing that comes to mind. This technique is believed to bring "top-of-mind recognition" into play in the research process.

Sentence completion is similar, but the researcher provides incomplete sentences and the respondents are asked to finish the sentences in their own words.

Role playing asks the respondent to play the role of another person, in hopes that the respondent will project his or her own feeling or belief into the response.

Exhibit 9.2 shows some uses of these projective techniques. Then in Exhibit 9.3, there are some lesser used but novel projective techniques listed.

Exhibit 9.2

Some Practical Insights into Popular Projective Techniques

Technique	Description
Word association	• Ask consumers to circle the words that they would or wouldn't associate with the brand. • Compare that to other brands.
Storytelling	• Ask consumers to write a brief story about their experience or memories with the brand.
Cartooning	• Develop a situation and ask consumers to fill in the dialogue.

Exhibit 9.3

Some Novel, Lesser Used Projective Techniques

Technique	Description
Emotivescapes	• Use emotivescapes to help consumers tell what their emotions are. • Have them use the product and circle their emotional reaction.
Usability tests	• Give them the product and ask them to try it. • Have them report what they think of it.
Personal diaries	• Ask consumers to catalog what they like to do. • Take pictures of their household and have them try the product.
Obituary exercise	• Ask your consumer to write an obituary for the brand. • Why did it die or what might cause its death?
Listening to others online	• Blogpulse • Technoratti • MySpace • Facebook
Picture storytelling	• Ask consumers to bring in pictures that personify the brand. • Give consumers a disposable camera and ask them to photograph things that personify the brand.
Mystery shopping	• Go undercover and pretend to be shoppers. • Carry a hidden microphone. • Record your observations.

Obviously, because each response is only from a single individual, the results cannot be projected onto a larger population, but projective techniques may provide insights and gain campaign appeal and theme ideas.

ETHNOGRAPHIES

Anthropologists and sociologists have developed ethnographies to describe human interactions and behaviors. Extensive fieldwork is often required to gain this kind of information. And the researchers must maintain their impartiality and not influence the behaviors or relationships in any way. Because of the specific kinds of information sought, public relations and advertising researchers rarely are interested in an ethnographic study of an entire culture or society, but more often only in a certain part or phase of the behavior. Ethnographies require a good deal of time to complete, which

Exhibit 9.4

Practical Applications of Ethnographies

- Story about the product and brand.
- Ethnographic research is a fancy name for observational research. You get immersed in the culture.
- Also can conduct shop-a-long research where you go with the consumer and observe them shopping for the brand.

is a problem for those who work under a deadline in business. Exhibit 9.4 provides some practical insights into ethnographic research.

EXPECTATIONS

Advertising and public relations research may want to determine how to make commercial communications more efficient and effective by exploring the expectations of the senders of the messages as opposed to the receivers of those same messages.

Senders

The senders of commercial communications may be trying to gain attention, impart information, build interest, create desire, and induce actions. The public relations and advertising expectations are inherent in the messages as well as in the communications channels selected for the campaigns, and the research underlying these goals will have those same expectations in mind.

Receivers

Receivers of commercial messages may have completely different expectations. They may want unbiased and clear information, helpful insights, full disclosure of all alternatives available, and suggestions on how to make their decisions pay off in more economical and efficient ways. Obviously, these expectations on the part of the receivers are very different from that of the senders.

Researchers must know on which end of the communication channel they are working, what the expectations are and, if desirable, how to make their research unbiased, fair, and truthful, as well as adequate, valid, and reliable.

SUMMARY

Qualitative research attempts to uncover information to provide a basis for future research as well as for communications insights and prompts. There are many specific aspects of mass communications applications to which qualitative research may be applied. Conducting qualitative research is something of an art that requires practice and experience, in addition to knowledge of the purposes of the research and the limitations of the results.

DISCUSSION QUESTIONS

1. How is qualitative research different from quantitative research? How are they alike?
2. What are the primary limitations of qualitative research?
3. What special contributions can qualitative research make toward successful advertising and public relations campaigns?
4. How can qualitative research contribute to the credibility of a communications source? Concept and copy testing? Media trust and reliability?
5. What are the hallmarks of conducting qualitative research?
6. What traits are required of a good interviewer?
7. What unique contributions can qualitative research make in commercial communications campaigns?

EXERCISES

1. You want to study how consumers of soft drinks (soda) feel about the possibility of purchasing smaller sizes of drinks, for example, 6-ounce or 8-ounce containers. Draw up a list of questions that might be asked in personal interviews.
2. List the topics to be covered in a focus group of employees who work for a local electric utility company, about job satisfaction, job enhancement, salaries, working conditions, and similar subjects.

ADDITIONAL READING

Creswell, J. 2009. *Research design: Qualitative, quantitative, and mixed methods approaches.* Thousand Oaks, CA: Sage.

Marshall, C., and G. Rossman. 2006. *Designing qualitative research.* Thousand Oaks, CA: Sage.

Maxwell, J. 2005. *Qualitative research design: An interactive approach.* Thousand Oaks, CA: Sage.

Morgan, D. 1997. *Focus groups as qualitative research.* Thousand Oaks, CA: Sage.

10 How Qualitative Research Can Enhance Quantitative Research

LEARNING OBJECTIVES

This chapter is intended to help you:

- See that qualitative and quantitative research can help support one another;
- Learn what qualitative research can contribute to the design and conduct of quantitative research;
- Understand that qualitative research can contribute insights into the findings from quantitative research;
- Observe that qualitative research also has great value on its own.

As we learned in the previous chapter, qualitative research is a useful research method for public relations and advertising. In addition to its own values, qualitative research can contribute directly to quantitative research by helping form the foundation for quantitative studies and by providing insights into the information gained from quantitative research. This chapter provides a quick look at how these two major types of research methods can work collaboratively and cooperatively.

Exhibit 10.1 shows a quick comparison of qualitative and quantitative research methods.

PRECEDING QUANTITATIVE RESEARCH

One major goal of qualitative research is to become more knowledgeable about the particular area of study in which you are interested. Quantitative research, in contrast, often begins with research questions and hypotheses, based primarily on a literature search, with little direct information and background into the topic at hand.

Qualitative research offers a sound alternative to trying to hypothesize based only on your own experience and beliefs, especially where there are not many existing studies on which to base hypotheses and research questions. Qualitative research can also lead to new theories, especially when conventional theories do not exist or appear not to apply to the immediate problem or situation.

Exhibit 10.1

Comparing Qualitative and Quantitative Research

Qualitative	Quantitative
Subjective and interpretive	Objective and precise
Helps develop theories	Helps test theories
Depends on context	Free of context
Research questions: What and Why?	Research questions: How many?
During early phases of research projects	Later phases of research projects
Design may emerge as study progresses	Design set in advance
Researcher may not have clear idea of goals	Researcher knows goals in advance
Data as words and pictures	Data as numbers and statistics
Literature review as study progresses	Literature review in advance
Uses observation and conversation	Uses measuring instruments
Sample size not important	Sample size essential
Inductive reasoning	Deductive and logical
Determines which responses are meaningful	Counts responses
Researcher is subjective and involved	Researcher is objective and removed
Researcher is the measuring instrument	Tools are the measuring instrument
Goal is description	Goal is to classify and count

It can be difficult to formulate research questions and research hypotheses without first conducting some qualitative research. The qualitative research provides a foundation of understanding, some insights into the topic, direction for the quantitative study that is to follow, and the depth that is gained only from qualitative research.

Direct contact with the topic, gained through qualitative research, can provide a new perspective as well as a deeper comprehension of the topic. The researcher may discover variables that had not formerly been considered, or may discover some possible relationships between variables that were not previously obvious.

Qualitative research includes systematic exploration of the research topic, along with collecting information, putting the information into some kind of logical arrangement or order, and coming up with apt and complete descriptions of the variables, subject, and possible outcomes of the study. The generalizations that are provided from qualitative research can contribute concepts and ideas, as well as theories, on which to base further research.

The fresh perspective from qualitative research studies can provide new theories and can help you come up with new hypotheses. Eventually, of course, you need to move on to the quantitative research, if that is your original goal, but conducting some qualitative research first will often provide deeper understanding, better research questions, more exact hypotheses, and even directions for the research that had not previously been considered.

In advertising and public relations, it is common to confront a business problem with research that is "quick and dirty," done in a hurry for only one specific purpose. When the research is completed, the findings may be unclear or not statistically significant, or some important, even essential, research areas may be discovered that were not evident at the beginning of the research process. Qualitative research can help overcome these obstacles and make the research more complete, more meaningful, and more accurate. It can also provide more depth.

Adding Depth

Greater depth is especially important and is a unique contribution of qualitative research. If you were to propose a study on the public's opinion of the practice of public relations, you would be unlikely to accomplish anything more than some basic opinion data using quantitative research. To understand the varieties of opinions, the depths of opinions, the possible stability of opinions, and what might influence those opinions to form them into what they are now and how they might be influenced in the future, quantitative research simply is unlikely to suffice. Qualitative research is the solution here.

Qualitative research gives details and insights. Those details may apply only to a very small group of respondents, and the insights may come from only a few individuals, but knowing those kinds of information can deepen your understanding of the product, service, or idea to be sold, help design possible campaign approaches, and predict likely outcomes.

Quantitative research provides generalizations; qualitative research provides specifics. In fact, quantitative research relies on finding information from a sample and projecting the findings onto a larger population. Then some statistical figures will stand for the entire group: the average age, for example, rather than individuals' ages. Quantitative research often formulates the research categories in advance, and every response must somehow fit into these predetermined categories.

Qualitative research, on the other hand, is more basic, without preordained categories. As a result, the results from qualitative data may be more difficult to categorize, but that may not be the best thing to try to do with qualitative results anyway. You need to organize all the raw information that you gain from qualitative research.

The detail that is derived from qualitative research helps you to describe what it is you are studying, in a good degree of detail, using the words and feelings of the respondents rather than those of the researcher. This detailed information can be of great use if you eventually want to conduct quantitative research.

Gaining Insights

In addition to depth, qualitative research can add insights. It lets you see how the respondents react to your questions, rather than just concentrating on their answers. You can uncover ideas that you might never have come up with on your own. You can interview respondents at length, using each response to help you formulate additional lines of questioning.

Imagine the insights that are gained by asking consumers "Why did you purchase that brand of laundry detergent?" or "What do you think of X-brand laundry detergent?" and letting them provide their own range of answers, instead of forcing them to select from a preconceived list of possible responses or trying to fit their original answers into a set of categories that were established before the research even began.

Quantitative research is good at handling large amounts of information and using those data to project some generalizations onto the population or onto the media audience. Qualitative research helps to explore the topic from the perspective of the participant and can uncover rich details that provide insights for eventual quantitative studies.

QUALITATIVE RESEARCH FOR ITS OWN WORTH

Up to this point, this chapter has discussed how qualitative research contributes to quantitative research. Yet much qualitative research is also conducted because it has value on its own, either in addition to quantitative research or if no quantitative research will be used. The results obtained from qualitative research explore the human contexts that are oftentimes complicated and not immediately obvious. They can be used to suggest possible advertising appeals, public relations campaign approaches, and even new uses for the product or service. They may even provide ideas for new products and services. These are valuable contributions that can be gained only from qualitative research.

COMBINING RESEARCH APPROACHES

Finding the best research approach to use is a problem that most researchers face on a regular basis. There is no one best research method for all studies. Different research criteria require different research methods, either used separately or combined into a cooperative effort. Combining research methods may result in a kind of research synergy that produces more and more detailed results than if they were not combined. Qualitative and quantitative methods have different but complementary contributions to the success of research.

The best research design is often a combination of approaches, including both qualitative and quantitative research methods. Especially in advertising and public relations, you can begin with qualitative methods, such as interviews, focus groups, case studies, and even ethnologies, using the findings to provide insights and to provide a stronger foundation for quantitative research to follow. Using only quantitative methods can provide good information but you will have little or no explanation of why things work that way. Using only qualitative designs, you may collect rich information but it is more subjective and cannot be generalized. By combining the two methods, you can delve deeper. Think of it this way: quantitative methods can tell us what works and to what extent, while qualitative methods can tell us how and why it works.

Qualitative studies help generate theories and identify relevant areas of study, for which quantitative studies can be used to test the hypotheses and the relationships between variables. Qualitative and quantitative studies can also be used simultaneously, yet not linked to one another, helping during the process of analyzing the information that was collected and aiding the interpretation of those results, giving us broader findings with deeper meanings than if only one approach or the other were utilized.

SUMMARY

Qualitative research can help formulate quantitative research that is to follow. Qualitative research can add depth and gain insights, which quantitative research might not have been able to do; these insights can then be used in the formulation and conduct of the eventual quantitative research. Qualitative research also has its own value and can provide interesting and valuable information that quantitative research is unlikely to uncover. Combinations of qualitative and quantitative methods may be a good research approach in advertising and public relations.

DISCUSSION QUESTIONS

1. How might qualitative research add depth to the understanding of an audience or consumers?
2. How might this information be used in public relations? In advertising?
3. What kinds of insights might be of value in formulating a public relations campaign? In formulating advertising appeals, copy platforms, and campaign themes?
4. What are the drawbacks of trying to design a quantitative research study without the benefit of prior qualitative studies?
5. How can qualitative research contribute on its own, even if no quantitative research is planned?
6. How can qualitative and quantitative research contribute to the success of each other, whether they are used together or separately but at the same time?

EXERCISES

1. Read a book about the industry in which you are interested: public relations or advertising. In what ways did qualitative research possibly contribute to the writing of the book?
2. Discuss how the concepts of research validity, reliability, and projectability differ between qualitative and quantitative research methods.
3. Think of designing a research study to determine how many units of consumption there might be for a newly developed product or service. How might qualitative research contribute to the goals of such a study?

ADDITIONAL READING

Berg, B. 2008. *Qualitative research methods for the social sciences.* Boston: Allyn & Bacon.

Creswell, J. 2008. *Research design: Qualitative, quantitative and mixed methods approaches.* Thousand Oaks, CA: Sage.

———. 2006. *Qualitative inquiry and research design: Choosing among five traditions.* Thousand Oaks, CA: Sage.

Handling Qualitative Data

LEARNING OBJECTIVES

This chapter is intended to help you:

- Understand how to handle the findings gained from qualitative research;
- Learn how to interpret qualitative research data;
- See how qualitative findings may be presented in a research report.

HANDLING QUALITATIVE DATA

As we learned in the previous chapter, qualitative and quantitative studies can be used simultaneously while not necessarily linked to one another—helping during the process of analyzing the information that was collected and aiding the interpretation of those results, giving us broader findings with deeper meanings than if only one approach or the other were utilized.

In qualitative research, the results are rougher and less refined. In contrast to quantitative research, the categories of responses are rarely predefined and set out in advance. So the task of handling qualitative data involves organizing all of those raw collections of information.

There are many ways to organize qualitative findings. It may be difficult to generalize from such specific responses. Luckily, many times the findings of qualitative research are not generalized at all. Instead, the details are used to generate detailed descriptions about the topic under study.

Sorting various responses into similar categories may be an appropriate step in handling qualitative data, but if the findings are categorized, counted, and statistically analyzed, it becomes an exercise in quantitative research rather than a qualitative study. Qualitative researchers often quote entire sentences or even longer responses from individual respondents, using the subjects' own words to explain and expand on a topic. Several like responses can be grouped and passages quoted from several of them to show a pattern or prevalent feeling.

Qualitative researchers often begin with preliminary scanning of the respondents' responses to find a general theme or outline. They observe patterns provided in the data, then try to organize these patterns into some sort of conceptual framework. At

Exhibit 11.1

Tackling the Qualitative Method–Based Research Report

A research report based on qualitative methods should try to address the following topics:
* Topic of the study;
* From whom or where the results were obtained;
* Justification for conducting the research;
* Justification for using qualitative methods;
* Description of the interviewer's or researcher's training and preparation;
* Description of the contact methods;
* Rigor of the research process;
* How the results were categorized or systematized;
* How the results were interpreted;
* How the results were evaluated;
* How the results are transferable to other settings, groups, or purposes.

that point, additional research may be suggested. The three main stages—data collection, data analysis, and development of theory—may continue to be repeated until a sensible and representative conceptual framework can be developed. One way to tell that this research process is complete is when additional research does not provide new or different information.

Multiple sources may provide corroboration of the initial analysis and conceptual framework. No two sources may provide exactly the same information; in fact, it is unlikely that they would do so. Therefore, the research analyst needs to understand that different sources may provide slightly differing results, yet also realize that similar if not identical response patterns may be pointing in the same general direction and toward the same general conclusions.

The abilities of the investigators are critical to success, so the investigators' training, perceptiveness, intellect, experience, and adherence to research standards all are vital components of successful analysis. It is essential to keep in mind that qualitative studies do not provide specific answers to questions but instead gain explanations and narrative stories.

INTERPRETING QUALITATIVE DATA

Qualitative research usually does not attempt to ask whether people act certain ways or how much they act that way, but rather to ask what and how and why those actions are undertaken. In qualitative research, there is often an attempt to find information that may be undiscovered or seldom reported; this, in turn, helps to identify important concepts, theories, ideas, hypotheses, and variables. Trying to recognize patterns and relationships is difficult but can only be achieved through qualitative studies.

Insights are gained through observations and interviews, which means that the findings will be highly personalized, applying perhaps only to that individual respondent. Because validity is difficult to define and implement with qualitative research, we are often more concerned with credibility of the responses rather than validity. Still, the results must come from systematic observations and competent interpretation. They must match up with reality so they must be credible if not completely consistent. The meaning of the responses must be gleaned by the researcher and provided in readable reports. Thus, those who read and use the results of qualitative research may still be involved in discerning whether the information is relevant and meaningful.

Readers need to read qualitative research reports with a critical eye, assessing whether the research design and data analysis are accurate, complete, and relevant. Was the study designed and conducted in an appropriate manner? Did the research have rigor? Does it make sense? Can it be used to apply to the current situation? What insights can be gained from the research findings? Was the research setting realistic? Were the interviews or observations thorough enough to support the findings and descriptions? How can this research be applied to the problem we face in the upcoming public relations or advertising campaign?

More than one investigator may be employed to collect and analyze the findings of qualitative research. These persons may need to confer with one another to establish similar standards and conclusions. In fact, training the investigators and the analysts is often an important step in qualitative research.

Sometimes a team of individuals may work together on the qualitative research project. It may seem logical to use external reviewers to provide a disinterested and impassionate review of the findings, but because qualitative research requires in-depth interviewing and analysis, external reviews may be too superficial to provide much insight. Members of the research team may check each other's analyses and make sure there are no factual errors or misinterpretations. Such work can be tricky, however, because of the individual nature of qualitative research and the strong role that each researcher plays in the conduct of the study. Matching the findings with existing theory may give more believability to the research, although the theories should be used to analyze the research rather than to guide it, as might be done with quantitative research analysis.

Computer software is available to aid in handling and interpreting qualitative data, but this type of computer analysis does not necessarily provide additional analytic rigor. Instead, computers are simply a tool to record, save, organize, and retrieve the qualitative findings. The investigators, instead of the computers, conduct the analysis and interpretation of the qualitative data as key words are found and recorded, categories are established, and relationships between various findings are discerned. Credibility of qualitative study findings depends on the judgments of analysts that cannot be programmed into computers. For this reason, qualitative interpretation requires well-trained investigators and analysts who utilize creativity as well as strict research standards.

Instead of striving for an adequate number of respondents, as would be done with quantitative research, we try to probe deeply enough to gain in-depth information. A few respondents who are questioned at length and depth may be preferable to a large group of respondents who are asked only superficial questions.

Research analysts may try to challenge the research, even as they are trying to interpret what the findings mean and comparing the findings with other parts of the study or with other existing studies. The researchers may alternate between collecting data and analyzing data, not content until the analysis does not provide any new insights or answers and the findings seem to duplicate or reinforce one another.

Good qualitative research analysis will concentrate on a relatively small number of assumptions, be consistent with what is already known, be expressed clearly and adequately, and suggest possible future paths of related research.

The collection of data in qualitative research should be broad and comprehensive, both in the types of observations and in the extent to which each observation has been examined. Analyzing the qualitative findings may provoke new ideas and suggest additional research, which may encourage additional data collection.

PRESENTING QUALITATIVE RESEARCH RESULTS

A good qualitative research report should be truthful and insightful, and be seen as such even by various readers or other researchers. If the study participants, the researchers and research analysts, the report writers, and readers and external colleagues receive the report and judge it to be accurate and helpful, it may not make the research findings the final word on the subject but it does help establish the fact that the research is a meaningful representation of the phenomenon under study and of the larger world in which it exists.

Qualitative research reports should contain both description and theory. Integrating these facets can be achieved by describing key insights that lead to resulting theories, and backing them with illustrations of the original data findings, such as quotations of responses and even notations of such things as body language, facial expressions, and hesitancy in speech.

The goal of the research report is a narrative account that describes the study and its results, draws theoretical insights and some practical applications. Enough detail should be provided to bring about a realistic image of the research setting and interviewing interactions. Authors often achieve this goal through the use of field notes, transcripts of interviews, documentation of responses, and careful interpretation of what all these things may mean.

The main points should, of course, be clearly supported by the evidence, and adding contextual details will heighten comprehension and deepen understanding. Using examples and referring back to original sources can provide additional understanding of the phenomena that were studied as well as some understanding of how the results were analyzed. Explanation of the findings is often much more detailed in qualitative studies than in other research.

The participants in the research, the research investigators, and the readers of the final research report should all reach similar (although not necessarily identical) conclusions. The result of qualitative research may be to inspire a dialogue between researchers, or to suggest new kinds of research or new paths for study. Although quantitative studies may be intended to reach the final word on the topic being investigated, qualitative research may instead be simply a contribution to some sort of ongoing body of research or to discussion and other communication between researchers interested in the same general or similar topics.

Problems with qualitative research presentations can include such things as unfocused analysis or too much description without categorizing or conclusions. The other extreme is providing theories and conclusions that are not clearly supported

Exhibit 11.2

Questions for Testing Qualitative Theories

If qualitative research leads to new theories, the theories need to be tested. Using these questions may help determine how well the theories reflect the research and how well the theories contribute to the research questions for which the research was originally intended.

1. How well defined is the theory?
2. What minor concepts are contained within the larger theoretical foundation?
3. Does the theory reinforce or conflict with other existing theories?
4. How does the research match with the theory?
5. Are all aspects of the research contributing to the theory, and does the theory reflect all of the research concepts?
6. Do the various parts of the theory work well with one another?
7. Does the theory result logically and naturally from the research, its findings, its analysis, and its interpretation?
8. Does this theory make a contribution to the field?
9. Can this theory be utilized in a practical way with meaningful improvements or effects?

by illustrations, empirical observations, and clear connections between the evidence and the theories and conclusions.

Readers of qualitative studies in advertising and public relations need to determine how well the research fits the situation and how well it suggests new approaches. If the research provides insights into the actions, motivations, and satisfaction on the part of audiences or consumers, it may well be worthwhile even if it is not definitive as the final word on the topic. Qualitative research, after all, can provide insights for the public relations practitioner and possible copy strategies to the advertising copywriter even though the practice is not universal or final. Indeed, in advertising and public relations, doing something differently from one's competitors is often a highly desired attribute and direction, so universal application and acceptance may not only be unnecessary but even undesirable.

Keep in mind that qualitative research is used because it is good at telling inside stories from the participants' perspectives, providing rich details and descriptions that place the results in their everyday human context and setting.

THE ANALYTICAL PROCESS

Now that you have seen the techniques and problems involved with analyzing qualitative research, we can go through the various steps involved. Keep in mind that some experienced researchers may skip some steps or combine two or more steps, and they may even add additional steps to the process.

It is crucial that you conduct good research to start with. Keep track of the questions asked, as well as the answers. Determine and then explain how the respondents were selected, in what settings they were interviewed, how many persons were present (both researchers and respondents), and which questions were established in advance and which were composed during the process. Video or audio recordings will be helpful.

Transfer the questions, responses, and other important information to a written record; a computer is the most common tool for this process. While the transcription is taking place, it may be possible to begin categorizing questions and responses with simple codes such as "Topic 3a" or simple abbreviations such as "QualQs4Demos" as a stand-in for "qualifying questions for demographic characteristics."

Next, put all questions and responses into categories, using the codes entered during the transcription process or making new diagnoses and categorizations. You may have certain categories and characterizations already in mind, but be flexible enough to change or add categories as needed. Be certain that all the items parceled in a category are similar; if they aren't, create new categories or divide the material into subtopics.

You may wish to count the number of responses in the various categories, to see which ones are most prominent and prevalent. However, be careful not to turn the study into a quantitative research project; maintain the character, quality, and feeling of qualitative research.

Now you can begin to interpret the responses. You may see certain similarities among various respondents, or you may see completely different responses. If there are similarities, you may want to discern whether these respondents all had some similar characteristics, such as home locale, age, education, political affiliation, income, or some other factor. Be careful, however, not to read too much into the answers, and do not try to force responses into certain categories or alter the responses to fit a certain pattern or expectation.

Look back at your research objectives and determine whether you have adequate data to answer the question or to apply to the situation under study. If not, you may want to design additional research to add the necessary information. Similarly, determine whether the responses that you have already gathered bring up new questions, either for additional research now or for some future study.

As you categorize and interpret the responses, you may want to begin outlining the research report. What are the most common findings, what new things have you learned, and what responses surprised you? Remember, the results you did not expect may provide the most useful new information.

Write up the research report, and if there is also to be an oral or face-to-face presentation, begin highlighting certain facts and findings that might go into an eventual PowerPoint or similar presentation format.

SUMMARY

Simply categorizing and documenting the results is not desirable with qualitative research. Deeper analysis and interpretation are required. This data handling process requires a great amount of detail, with specific instances cited to support and reinforce findings and conclusions. The final qualitative research report must be a collaborative effort between the investigator, the tabulator, the analyst, and the interpreter. Even the reader of the research report needs to bring understanding and appreciation to make the research meaningful and helpful.

DISCUSSION QUESTIONS

1. If qualitative research does not reach a final conclusion, of what value is it?
2. In how many ways can an advertising practitioner make use of qualitative research?

3. In public relations, how and why does qualitative research make contributions that cannot be obtained from quantitative research?
4. What are the differences between handling qualitative findings, interpreting them, and reporting them?
5. How would a qualitative research analyst decide which data to include in the interpretation and reporting stages?
6. Why is analyzing qualitative data more time-consuming and perhaps more difficult than analyzing quantitative data?

EXERCISES

1. Using the Internet, find a qualitative research study involving the mass media, and observe how the data handling was done.
2. Using the same study, outline an oral presentation of this research and its findings.

ADDITIONAL READING

Corbin, J., and A. Strauss. 2008. *Basics of qualitative research: Techniques and procedures for developing grounded theory.* Thousand Oaks, CA: Sage.

Seidman, I. 2006. *Interviewing as qualitative research: A guide for researchers in education and the social sciences.* New York: Teachers College Press.

Tashakkori. A., and C. Teddlie. 1998. *Mixed methodology: Combining qualitative and quantitative research.* Thousand Oaks, CA: Sage.

PART IV

PRIMARY RESEARCH IN ADVERTISING AND PUBLIC RELATIONS: QUANTITATIVE RESEARCH

12 Empirical Research: Survey Research

LEARNING OBJECTIVES

This chapter is intended to help you:

- Learn some of the basic terms used in advertising and public relations survey research;
- Understand the value of survey research in advertising and public relations;
- Identify different interviewing methods used in advertising and public relations;
- Learn the benefits and limitations of various survey research methods.

Survey research is one of the most popular methods for collecting quantitative data. Surveys are commonly used by advertising and public relations researchers to provide information about populations to clients, government agencies, businesses, nonprofit organizations, and educators. In many instances, the key to success for businesses, agencies, and organizations is knowing what clients or key publics want and what they think. Employers want to identify the attitudes and opinions of their employees. Product manufacturers want to know about customer satisfaction and politicians want to know what issues are important to voters. In most cases, survey research is the best method for collecting this type of information. Researchers conduct surveys when they need new data or when the existing data are insufficient to make intelligent decisions.

The term "survey" is used to describe methods of asking questions to respondents. Surveys are divided into two broad areas: questionnaires and interviews. The survey can range from five questions about a restaurant's service using a pencil and paper questionnaire to more than one hundred questions about your lifestyle in a one-on-one personal interview.

Surveys may be classified as *cross-sectional* or *longitudinal*. Researchers use cross-sectional surveys to collect information and data from a sample of the target market or respondents during a single point in time. Researchers compare the relationships among a set of important variables based on respondents' characteristics. For example, researchers may want to examine the opinions among respondents about political issues based on the respondent's age, sex, race, education, party affiliation, and income.

Longitudinal surveys compare the relationships among a set of important variables at intervals of two months, six months, a year, or even longer.

Survey research is an efficient method for collecting data over broad populations. Researchers may administer the survey in person, by telephone, or electronically. Because of the development of technology and software, some forms of survey research by telephone or electronic methods may be automated with prerecorded messages, instructions, and questions. Automated surveys might be more cost-effective than surveys conducted by human callers.

Surveys are customized to fit a specific research goal. Each question is developed to solicit information to expand our knowledge about an issue, problem, or situation. The information collected from respondents using questionnaires and interviews depends on the purpose or goal of the research. If you do not clearly develop the goal of your research, the data might not contribute to the results you desire. The more specific you are in developing your goals, the easier it will be to collect quality data. Survey information and data are collected using standardized procedures for each question and each survey project. Each questionnaire must be pretested to confirm the accuracy of question formatting, wording, scaling responses, and instructions that lead to the research goals.

Survey researchers collect information from a sample or a number of respondents drawn from a larger target population. Data are collected from this sample so that we may make generalizations regarding behaviors, attitudes, or opinions about the larger target population. Once the generalizations are agreed upon by the researcher and client, the client may then develop communication objectives and tactics in an attempt to influence the attitudes and opinions of target populations. We are inundated daily with hundreds of messages that try to influence or persuade us. Family members, friends, supervisors, employees, media, and special interest groups want us to modify our attitudes and opinions about consumer products, social and political issues, family decisions, and investment opportunities. After campaigns based on survey research data, members of the target publics might be more likely to alter or change their behavior to vote for a specific candidate, purchase a product, join an advocacy group, or increase employee morale.

Some critics of survey research suggest that a survey artificially forces respondents to formulate opinions or provide responses with little opportunity to think about the question, while ignoring the complexity of conflicting views and biases held by respondents. These critics also note that in many studies some survey variables (for example, respondents' religion, race, and family income) do not necessarily predict a respondent's behavior.

Researchers should protect the anonymity of respondents. Individual respondents should never be identified. Reports of the data should be presented in such forms as summaries of numbers, percentages, and statistical tables and charts.

In this chapter, we will discuss the major survey methods used in advertising and public relations. Researchers might use a variety of methods in collecting information or data from a sample of respondents; however, most researchers utilize four major survey methods: telephone surveys, mail surveys, electronic surveys (Internet surveys, e-mail surveys, on-site survey stations), and personal interviews (in-home interviews and intercept surveys). Each method has its advantages and disadvantages.

RESEARCH CONSIDERATIONS

Once you have decided on what you want to know and the sample of respondents you want to survey, you must then employ the survey method that is best for your study. However, there are no simple guidelines in selecting the most effective research method. You must consider the characteristics of your target population such as their level of literacy, possible language problems, and geographical issues. Other concerns include the costs per completed questionnaire, the sensitivity of the requested information, and the deadline for collecting the data.

LITERACY

A self-administered questionnaire must be completed by respondents who can read. In some communities where the education level is quite low, the target respondents may have difficulty in reading and understanding the questions. The questionnaire could contain words and/or technical terms unfamiliar to the respondent. Written questionnaires may not be good survey instruments for children or uneducated adults. Where there is a perceived literacy problem, researchers might want to use a personal interview method or a telephone survey.

LANGUAGE ISSUES

Researchers often assume that a large majority of the population speak or read English. In the United States, there are large populations of people who prefer to speak and read Spanish, French, Chinese, or Italian. If you are aware of these language preferences, you might want to prepare multiple versions of your questionnaire. In some studies, you might read the questions to the respondents in their native language. However, if you conduct a mail survey, it may be difficult to determine the language preferences of the respondents in each household. The key to obtaining quality data from respondents is to provide the questions in a language respondents most prefer.

GEOGRAPHICAL STRATIFICATION

If your target population is a group of employees, then you will have a complete list of your target population. Because you have a complete list of employees, you might decide to use more than one interviewing method. The methods available for interviewing employees are more extensive than a survey of residents in an entire state. To survey a sample of respondents from throughout a state or the nation, you would most likely select a mail, telephone, or electronic interview method. The geographical stratification of your target population will also affect the cost of your survey. The more widely dispersed your target population, the more expensive the survey.

COSTS PER RETURN

Surveys can range from economical to very expensive depending on the target publics or respondents. Researchers might include a large number of questions in the survey to collect volumes of data allowing them to compare responses based on the respondents' demographic variables such as age, race, sex, income, and education. The cost per return is determined based on the return rate of your target population and the value of the information provided by the respondent. While it may be very expensive to conduct one hundred personal interviews compared to mail, telephone, and electronic surveys, the value of the information you receive from the respondents in a personal interview could be far more valuable to you than vast amounts of data from telephone or electronic surveys. Personal interviewers might observe respondents' behavior, lifestyle, and home environment. In many instances, this type of information would be difficult to obtain via respondent comments using mail, telephone, and electronic survey methods.

PERSONAL OR SENSITIVE INFORMATION

Some respondents are reluctant to respond to some types of questions. For example, respondents tend not to provide information about their personal finances, sexual behavior, drug use, mental health, or religious beliefs. Respondents may refuse to comment or provide a response that reflects the mainstream social beliefs of their community. Such information is considered too private and not likely to be shared with a person they do not know. In some cases, this information may be more likely obtained via personal interviews.

DATA COLLECTION DEADLINE

Plan your research in advance so you will select the most appropriate and efficient research method. A deadline to complete a research project should not compromise the research method you choose. There is no such thing as a "down and dirty" quick survey. Inaccurate data is worse than no data at all. Data collection must be completed using acceptable research procedures that yield accurate information. There are some survey methods that will help you collect data more quickly than others; however, the data collection process should be based on the best method to collect accurate data from your target population. Mail surveys and personal interviews will take longer to complete than will telephone and electronic surveys.

QUANTITY OF DATA

You must determine the amount of information you can effectively collect using a particular survey method. Mail and electronic surveys might include more questions than a telephone survey. The personal interview might be more lengthy than other survey methods. Identify the goals and purposes of your research project and calculate the likelihood your target population will complete the questionnaire. What are their interests in the topic of your survey? If respondents are not interested in the topic, they are less likely to participate.

Sampling

You must decide whether a sample of the target population can be identified and contacted. If you wanted to survey females 18 to 24 years of age who have a child less than 10 years of age, how would you identify this target population and how would you contact them? An answer to this question would influence your selection of a survey method. There is no standardized rule for the number of people in a sample. The size of the sample depends on the financial resources and budget allocated to your survey and the number of variables you may want to statistically compare. National political and public opinion polls frequently use samples of one thousand completed questionnaires.

Interviewing Methods

Telephone Surveys

At the present time, the most popular interviewing method is the telephone survey. The telephone survey is a combination of a mail survey and a personal interview. A telephone survey is similar to a personal interview because the interviewer is conducting a personal conversation with the respondent. A telephone survey is also similar to a mail survey because the questionnaire is structured so that one question follows in a sequential order with a list of specific response options. Respondents must answer one question before they proceed to the next question. The respondent is given a list of response options or is asked to respond to the question using a standardized response scale.

Telephone surveys are frequently used in national surveys or when researchers want to survey respondents in small geographically dispersed areas throughout the United States. If your research problem can be answered with only a few questions, then the telephone survey might be the best type of survey. You will be able to collect the data quickly with minimal costs.

Researchers use telephone surveys to collect data for a variety of reasons. For example, researchers conduct consumer awareness or customer satisfaction surveys about consumer products. Telephone callback interviews are used to contact respondents at different time intervals following their initial response to telephone and mail surveys. Callback interviews are important for determining consumer trends and brand loyalty.

A key to collecting quality data rests with the quality of the interviewers. Interviewers must be carefully trained to conduct interviews in a professional manner and to ask questions in a way to avoid interviewer bias. Interviewers should understand the purpose for each question and why the response options are used with each question. They must know the meaning of each word used in the questionnaire and how to explain any question posed by the respondent. Interviewer training sessions frequently include a variety of situations that may occur during the interview. Additional benefits and limitations of a telephone survey are listed in Exhibit 12.1.

MAIL SURVEYS

A mail survey is typically a structured questionnaire that is distributed to a large sample of respondents. The questionnaires are mailed to a sample of a target population and returned by mail after the respondent completes the questionnaire. Because a mail survey is self-administered, the questionnaire must be designed to provide thorough instructions, simply worded questions, and easy navigation from one question to another. There is no source for the respondent to ask questions for clarification. The cosmetic appearance is also important. The appearance of the questionnaire suggests to respondents the importance of the survey and the professionalism of the researcher. The cosmetic factors include the paper, color, print characteristics, page layout, letter from the researcher, and postage-paid return envelope. In many cases, the appearance of the questionnaire will impact the response rate.

Once the questionnaire has been mailed to the sample target population, there is no opportunity for the researcher to make any changes or modifications to the question-naire. Therefore, special attention must be given to every detail of the questionnaire to avoid errors and mistakes. To reduce the number of errors, researchers frequently conduct "pilot tests" of a small sample of respondents prior to printing and mailing the questionnaire. A pilot test will provide feedback about question bias, spelling er-rors, inappropriate response scales, inconsistent wording, duplicate questions, vague instructions, and insufficient space for open-ended questions.

Questionnaires are mailed to two types of target populations: those who have agreed in advance to complete the questionnaire and those who have not agreed in advance to participate. Respondents who have agreed to participate are typically contacted via postcard, telephone, or e-mail seeking their assistance prior to mail-ing the questionnaire. If the respondent agrees to participate, the researcher might offer the respondent an incentive or inducement to participate in the research. For example, the researcher might promise the respondent a cash incentive, a weekend vacation, or a free sample of a product. The return rate is higher among respondents who have agreed to participate in advance than is the rate of return by those without advance contact.

Other respondents who agree to participate in surveys might be members of a "mail panel." A mail panel consists of a large pool of prospective respondents who have agreed to participate in surveys periodically. The researcher will select a sample of respondents from the pool of panel members and then forward them a questionnaire. The return rate of about 80 percent is common among a panel of survey respondents. The panel members are usually compensated with cash for their responses. Commer-cial marketing research companies maintain a list of panel members for a variety of surveys. If there are questions about response clarification, researchers might contact current panel members for more information. Additional benefits and limitations of mail surveys are listed in Exhibit 12.2.

Exhibit 12.1

Telephone Survey: Benefits and Limitations

Benefits

1. Respondents will usually provide longer or more specific answers than will respondents in other survey methods except a web survey.
2. Interviewers may screen participants who may not be the target market. If they want to talk to women, they may request to speak to a woman in the household. They may even ask to speak to the male teen between the ages of 18 and 21 years of age.
3. Respondents can ask the interviewers for clarification of questions.
4. Interviewers can also ask for clarification of responses.
5. More than 90 percent of U.S. households have a telephone.
6. Telephone surveys are usually completed more quickly than other survey methods.
7. A CATI (computer-assisted telephone interviewing) software system allows interviewers to systematically skip questions that do not pertain to the respondent based on their responses to previous questions.
8. The CATI software can tabulate the results of the survey within minutes.
9. Researchers can dial random telephone numbers when they do not have a list of telephone numbers for the target sample. Random digit dialing also provides an opportunity to contact respondents with unlisted numbers.
10. Interviewers may conduct interviews from various locations including their home.
11. Some respondents feel they have more anonymity and confidentiality than in other survey methods. Therefore, they may be more likely to reveal personal information.
12. Telephone interviewers are more easily trained than are personal interviewers.
13. Telephone interviews are more easily monitored than are personal interviews.
14. The elderly and handicapped may be more likely to respond to a telephone interview. They are often lonely and welcome a chance to talk with someone.

Limitations

1. A growing number of young Americans do not have landline telephones. Their primary telephone is a cell telephone with an unlisted number. Therefore, researchers may have difficulty in contacting 18- to 24-year-old respondents.
2. Telemarketers have tended to bias respondents against legitimate researchers. Some telemarketers claim to be conducting research when they start a sales call. Respondents are reluctant to answer phone interviews by screening calls.
3. Telephone surveys are limited to asking questions of respondents. Interviewers do not have the ability to show a product or provide a visual image.
4. Laws limit the time of day that telephone interviewers may contact respondents. Calls may not be placed to a home after 9 P.M.
5. Because of the growing number of working women, interviewers are limited to contacting this popular demographic group to about 6–9 P.M.
6. Daytime respondents are most likely retired, elderly, unemployed, or children.
7. The survey interview is usually limited to about fifteen minutes. It is difficult to get respondents to stay on the telephone for an extended period of time.
8. Interviewers often do not have the time to establish a rapport with respondents.

Not all prospective participants are contacted requesting this participation in the survey. Some researchers send a post card to the respondents prior to mailing the questionnaire. The post card informs the respondents that a questionnaire will be forthcoming and that they will have an opportunity to participate. Reminders are mailed to nonrespondents after about two or three weeks. In many surveys, researchers include a promise that respondents will receive an incentive or inducement when they return the completed questionnaire. Other researchers might include a small cash incentive

Exhibit 12.2

Mail Surveys: Benefits and Limitations

Benefits

1. Mail surveys are among the least expensive per response. Usually the expense to conduct a mail survey is the cost of paper, envelope, printing, and postage. The cost can be about 50 percent of the cost of a telephone survey.
2. Mail surveys can reach a greater population of your target market because they do not require personal contact to complete the questionnaire.
3. Researchers can be very selective in drawing the sample of respondents from a large target population. There are several sources for securing a list of names and addresses. Researchers may purchase catalogs that include thousands of mailing lists.
4. If the researcher uses a random sample of names and addresses, the results may represent the target population.
5. Because there is no personal contact with the respondent, the mail survey is less likely to include personal influence or bias from the researcher.
6. A mail survey is the type of survey you would use when you have the names and addresses of the target population, but not their telephone numbers.
7. The mail questionnaire can include pictures, visuals, CDs, and DVDs for respondents to view. A telephone survey does not have this capability.
8. Respondents completing a mail survey can complete the questionnaire at their convenience. A telephone survey is rather impromptu and could be inconvenient to the respondents. Appointments are usually made for personal interviews.

Limitations

1. Mail surveys take longer than other kinds. You will need to wait several weeks after mailing questionnaires before you can be sure that you have received most of the responses. Researchers usually mail one or two follow-up reminders to nonrespondents.
2. Response rates are typically lower than other survey methods. Many researchers consider a 20 percent response rate as acceptable. If you anticipate a response rate of 20 percent and you want 1,000 completed questionnaires, then you will need to mail 5,000 questionnaires to the target population.
3. Response rates among well-educated populations may vary widely from as low as 5 percent up to 90 percent. However, the best response levels are usually from highly educated people and/or people with a particular interest in the subject.
4. Members of the target population may have physical limitations to complete a mail survey. They could be visually impaired or have dyslexia.
5. Target populations with lower educational and literacy levels tend not to respond to mail surveys. They could have a limited vocabulary, low reading ability, or be illiterate.
6. There is no personal contact with the researcher; therefore, there is no way to ask questions or clarify statements in the questionnaire. The questions must be self-explanatory.
7. Some respondents may read the entire questionnaire before responding to the questions. This could lead to biased responses because the order of questions may be important for eliciting the desired information from the respondent.
8. There is no control over who completes the questionnaire. If you send a questionnaire to the CEO of a large corporation, he or she may not be the person who actually completes the questionnaire. The secretary or an assistant may answer the questions.
9. Many respondents mistake mail questionnaires as "junk mail." Many "junk mail" pieces are thrown away before the recipient even reads the information.
10. Questionnaires distributed through bulk mail could arrive at least a week later than first class mail.

with the questionnaire, such as a dollar bill to motivate the respondents to complete the questionnaire. The advance incentive is used to make the respondents feel more obligated to complete the questionnaire.

ELECTRONIC SURVEYS

Electronic surveys are rapidly becoming a popular method for collecting data. In this section, we will discuss the electronic survey methods of e-mail, Web-based, and on-site stations. Researchers' primary concerns about e-mail and Web-based surveys are the issues of sampling and privacy. There are limitations to electronic survey samples. Samples have not typically represented the target population. Samples frequently come from a list of published e-mail addresses in professional publications, members of professional organizations, businesses, clubs, and universities. Access to the Internet is still more frequent among people who live in urban areas, who have higher incomes and higher levels of education. Therefore, it is not possible to draw conclusions and make generalizations about the population based on the results of the research. Researchers must be as concerned about sampling bias in e-mail and Web-based surveys as they are with telephone and mail surveys. The sample of respondents must represent a larger target population. The sample of respondents will determine the quality of data collected for the study.

Computer and Internet technology allow researchers to collect vast amounts of data inexpensively and quickly. Even though there are some distinct technical differences among e-mail surveys, Web-based surveys, and computer interviews, there are also many similar benefits and limitations. Researchers must design the questionnaire carefully. Electronic surveys are self-administered responses; consequently, there are few opportunities for respondents to ask for clarifications about questions, response scales, or instructions. Therefore, researchers must design the questionnaire for simplicity. The questions must be simple, clearly stated, unbiased, and in a logical order. The response to one question must not influence the answer to the next question.

An *e-mail survey* is either displayed within the e-mail message or attached as a Word document. The researcher has the ability to monitor whether the respondent deleted or opened the e-mail. The e-mail survey does not restrict or prohibit the respondent from changing the content of the questionnaire. The researcher must review the responses for possible changes. Respondents might complete the questionnaire and return the e-mail to the researcher. (This provides an opening for the researcher to establish communication with the respondent.) The survey data are then manually transferred to a data set, recorded, and saved.

Web-based surveys use database technology and an HTML (hypertext markup language) interface. This technology provides the ability to automatically verify and store survey responses. The Web-based survey might include a wide range of textual options, formats, and graphics. Respondents click on the preferred response option and the data are automatically recorded. The software usually restricts respondents from skipping questions on purpose. However, based on a respondent's previous answer, the software may automatically skip questions. For example, if a respondent has not used a specific product, the software will skip questions about the respondent's satisfaction with the product. Video, animation, and color may enhance the questionnaire design. A Web-based survey has more features than an e-mail survey, and thus is more difficult to design (see Exhibit 12.3).

Exhibit 12.3

E-mail Surveys: Benefits and Limitations

Benefits

1. The distribution of the questionnaire can be global in a matter of seconds.
2. The attractiveness of an e-mail survey is the speed of collecting data. An e-mail questionnaire can collect data from thousands of respondents in one day.
3. Response rates tend to be higher with electronic surveys than with telephone and mail surveys.
4. The cost of developing and distributing an e-mail survey is very small. Once you have developed the questionnaire, the distribution of the questionnaire is at no cost.
5. It is possible for you to attach visuals, pictures, and audio examples.
6. The costs for online questionnaires are more economical than expenses for postage or for telephone and personal interviewers.
7. Online questionnaires may be changed, corrected, or modified more easily than postal surveys.
8. Copying and sorting data are faster than in telephone and mail surveys.
9. Researchers suggest that respondents may answer more honestly with electronic surveys than with paper surveys or telephone interviews.

Limitations

1. A random sample of a target population for the purpose of generalizing your findings is almost impossible. An e-mail list does not represent the whole population. People who have e-mail are different from people who do not have e-mail. Older populations and populations with lower economic and education levels are less likely to have access to e-mail.
2. Respondents often answer more than one time. Multiple responses from the same person do not provide quality data. Most e-mail surveys do not restrict people from responding several times. However, the Survey System's e-mail Module will only accept one reply from each e-mail address.
3. Some respondents will provide two responses to a question when the question requests only one.
4. Many e-mail surveys are treated like spam messages. People typically dislike unsolicited e-mail messages. So that respondents do not delete your survey, you may want to notify them in advance that you are sending a questionnaire on a specific date.
5. E-mail surveys do not have the ability to automatically skip questions or to randomize questions or response options. If respondents are to skip questions based on their previous response, you must include written instructions within the context of the questionnaire.
6. E-mail surveys are limited to simple questionnaires with a simple questionnaire design.
7. Electronic responses are not truly anonymous. Researchers know the respondents' e-mail addresses.

Web surveys are becoming more popular among researchers. The major advantages of the Web survey are speed, cost, and flexibility. However, a Web survey has the same limitations of sampling the population as e-mail surveys (see Exhibit 12.4).

On-site survey stations enable people to enter self-administered responses on computers in public places. Respondents enter their answers directly into a computer using a keyboard or a touch screen. Computers are typically installed in malls, trade shows, offices, airports, or any location with access to many people. For example, a mall researcher might want to know about consumers' shopping habits, such as their store preferences, number of times they have shopped during the past month, other malls they have shopped, and demographic information about them. Travelers in airports may respond to questions about their frequency of travel, destinations, demographic information, and airline preferences. People in all locations might be quizzed about their opinions regarding social and political issues.

Some researchers set up a Web page survey that is accessed via the computer. The computer configuration at the site location might vary depending on the technology

Exhibit 12.4

Web-based Surveys: Benefits and Limitations

Benefits

1. Distribution of and responses to Web-based surveys are very fast.
2. Web-based surveys can prevent people from completing more than one questionnaire. Researchers often restrict access to the Web page by requiring a password or by putting the survey on a page that can only be accessed directly without links to it from other pages.
3. A researcher can collect thousands of responses within a few hours.
4. The cost of developing a Web-based survey is very minimal.
5. Web-based questionnaires can automatically utilize complex question skipping techniques and randomizations of questions. Other survey methods must include skipping instructions within the context of the questionnaire.
6. Web-based questionnaires can enhance the design of questionnaires through the use of colors, fonts, visuals, and other formatting options not possible in most e-mail surveys.
7. Researchers suggest that respondents tend to give more honest answers to questions about sensitive and personal issues compared to responses given by a person or on paper.
8. Researchers suggest that people provide longer answers to open-ended questions on Web page questionnaires than they do on other kinds of self-administered surveys.
9. Contacting large samples of a target population does not cost more than contacting smaller samples.

Limitations

1. A random sample of a target population for the purpose of generalizing your findings is almost impossible. A list of possible respondents does not represent the whole population. People who have Internet access are different from people who do not have Internet access. Older populations and populations with lower economic and education levels are less likely to have access to Internet service.
2. People can easily terminate their responses in the middle of a questionnaire. Respondents tend not to complete a long questionnaire as they would in a personal interview.
3. You often have no control over who replies. Your survey may pop up on numerous computers when someone is simply browsing the Internet. They may or may not be part of your sample. Therefore, it is important to restrict access to the Web page by requiring a password or by putting the survey on a page that can only be accessed directly without links to it from other pages.
4. Because of the open nature of most online networks, it is difficult to guarantee anonymity and confidentiality.

used in the survey. Each computer might accommodate three or four terminals for simultaneous use. The computer might be linked directly to a mainframe computer for data storage.

The on-site station has the same questionnaire design benefits as a Web-based questionnaire. The on-site stations may include a wide range of textual options, formats, and graphics. Respondents click on the preferred response option and the data are automatically recorded. As in the Web-based survey, the software usually restricts respondents from skipping questions on purpose. However, based on a respondent's previous answer, the software may automatically skip questions.

On-site survey respondents are known as an available, convenient, or volunteer sample. An available sample is a collection of respondents who are readily accessible. They do not necessarily represent a true sample of the population. Therefore, conclusions about the data collected from an available sample must be made with caution and not generalized to the population. The data may bias the results of the

Exhibit 12.5

On-site Surveys: Benefits and Limitations

Benefits

1. Large amounts of data may be collected in a short period of time.
2. Software may limit the number of respondents in specific demographic categories.
3. Respondents are also more likely to give more honest answers to a computer than to a person or in a paper questionnaire.
4. An on-site survey vitrually eliminates data entry and editing costs.
5. Computers eliminate interviewer bias. Human interviewers may ask questions in a manner that leads the respondent to a specific answer.
6. As with a Web-based survey, on-site survey stations include skip patterns that are accurately followed. The software can ensure people are not asked questions they should skip based on their earlier answers.

Limitations

1. The cost of establishing on-site stations could be very expensive.
2. You often have no control over who replies.
3. Most locations of on-site stations draw people from a specific geographic area or people who visit the location for a specific reason. The characteristics of these respondents may differ from the target population and create a nonrepresentative sample.
4. As with mail surveys, on-site stations may have serious response rate problems in populations of lower educational and literacy levels.

study and lead to inaccurate conclusions about the population. Researchers suggest that respondents differ greatly from non-volunteers. However, available samples can be helpful in collecting exploratory information that could lead to a more valid research method.

Software can restrict the number of respondents with specific demographic characteristics. Screening questions may be placed at the beginning of the questionnaire. The screening questions will determine whether a respondent will continue. For example, if the researcher determines that the population is 52 percent female and 48 percent male, the software might be programmed to restrict the number of female and male respondents to reflect the proportion of the population. The same type of restrictions could be made for respondents based on their age, race, education level, and income.

PERSONAL INTERVIEWS

A personal interview research method is used when the interviewer asks the questions face-to-face to the respondent. Personal interviews might take place in various settings such as in the home, in a business, at a shopping mall, on the street, in the airport, at church, or in a polling place. The location depends on getting access to the target population.

There are several methods and procedures for conducting personal interviews. However, only two methods will be covered in this chapter: unstructured in-home personal interviews and structured intercepts. The personal unstructured in-home interviews discussed in this chapter will consist of mostly open-ended questions posed by the interviewer. These are longer forms of interviews and typically require interviewers to schedule appointments with respondents. For example, interviewers might ask respondents to describe the process they go through in shopping for a new car. In intercepts or structured interviews, the interviewer will interview, select, and approach prospective respondents at random in a public venue. If the respondent agrees to participate, the interviewer usually reads questions to the respondent from a prepared and structured questionnaire that requires responses in quantitative form. For example, the interviewer might ask the respondent to rate the quality of service he or she received in a restaurant. The respondent might rate the restaurant using a scale of one to ten where one is poor service and ten is excellent service.

Personal unstructured interviews are among the most challenging forms of measurement. Personal interviews are the most flexible of the survey methods because they have the greatest freedom in questionnaire length, format, and response options. The interviewer is the key component in successful interview surveys. The interviewer must possess personal sensitivity to comments provided by the respondent and must have the ability to maintain objectivity without influencing the respondent's answers.

In-home interviews are typically conducted in the respondent's home. The popularity of the in-home interview has been waning during the past ten years. Researchers have found that telephone surveys are just as effective in tracking customer awareness, product use, and consumer behavior. However, in-home interviews are excellent methods of research for observations of behavior in the home, use of product in the home, and visual cues of the home environment. The in-home interview is effective when visual cues are important for collecting data or when you need to observe the respondent using a product.

To conduct effective in-home surveys, researchers must locate the appropriate sample of respondents who fit the target population, develop logical and meaningful questions, secure an appointment with the respondent, conduct the interview, record their responses, and draw conclusions about the data. Because the effort required by the survey respondent is less than completing a mail survey, the quality of the data tends to be quite good. Interviewers have the opportunity to give the respondents much flexibility in responding to open-ended questions. Depending on the responses, the open-ended questions are then followed by additional probing questions to collect more information or to clarify or explain more thoroughly the original response.

Intercept surveys are typically structured interviews. The interviewer uses a prepared or structured questionnaire to solicit information from randomly selected respondents in a public place. Intercepts are popular among market researchers because they collect volumes of data in a short period of time at a low cost. Intercepts are typically used in concept, packaging, and product tests. Some researchers use intercepts to collect data regarding respondents' attitudes and opinions on many social and political issues. Because intercepts use an available or volunteer sample of the population, the results are not generalizable. Researchers frequently use intercept data to develop or initiate additional research.

To collect data, interviewers are stationed at key locations in public places with high foot traffic. For example, interviewers might be located at malls, theaters,

Exhibit 12.6

In-home Interviews: Benefits and Limitations

Benefits

1. The respondent has the opportunity to examine, feel, and/or taste a product.
2. You have a much better chance of finding a good representative of your target population than with a mail or telephone survey.
3. During the interview, you can modify the order of questions, skip questions and modify the questionnaire to make data collection more efficient.
4. You can observe the respondent's reactions to your questions.
5. You can observe the respondent using a product.
6. You can build rapport with the respondent. When the respondent is more comfortable with the interview, he or she may be more willing to provide information about sensitive and personal questions.
7. Respondents tend to agree to longer interviews. Some respondents tend to be more willing to talk longer face-to-face than to someone on the phone.

Limitations

1. In-home interviews usually cost more per interview than other survey methods. Travel between interviews increases the cost and time to collect the data.
2. In-home interviews take more time than other survey methods. One interviewer may complete only three or four questionnaires a day. Therefore, several interviewers are usually employed.
3. Training interviewers in personal surveys takes more time, effort, and money.
4. Bias regarding the interviewer may impact the quality of data. The dress, age, sex, and race of the interviewer may cause the respondent to answer untruthfully.
5. Some interviews may be completed only during certain times of the day. If respondents work, they may be available only during evening hours.
6. Interviewers have an opportunity to falsify data.

restaurants, airports, universities, civic centers, and department stores. These venues provide access to a large number of people on a daily basis. In many studies, interviewers are instructed to select a proportion or quota of respondents based on the respondents' demographic profile. For example, if the interviewer is required to complete 20 percent of the questionnaires by 18- to 24-year-old females, the interviewer would approach a prospective female respondent who appears to be18 to 24 years of age. The interviewer would use screening questions to determine whether the prospective respondent meets the age requirement. If not, the interviewer would thank the prospective respondent, explain why she was not chosen, and terminate the interview. The same process would be followed to secure a quota of respondents in other demographic categories.

Researchers must remember that intercept respondents are in public places for a reason. They do not have much time to answer dozens of questions. The list of questions should be short and to the point. If, however, the researcher has a special room prepared to conduct the survey or have the respondent participate in testing products, commercials, or other stimulus material, and there is a monetary incentive, then respondents might be willing to spend as much as thirty minutes in the interview.

Intercept samples are not representative of any large group in terms of demographics, media, buying behaviors, attitudes, or opinions. Respondents are selected to participate because they happen to be in the same location as the interviewer and were perceived

Exhibit 12.7

Intercept Surveys: Benefits and Limitations

Benefits

1. Large amounts of data may be collected in a short period of time.
2. The percentage of respondents who refuse to participate is about 10 to 40 percent.
3. Costs for intercept surveys are inexpensive.
4. The respondent has the opportunity to examine, feel, and/or taste a product.
5. You can observe the respondent using a product or testing copy.
6. Response rates are similar to in-home interviews.

Limitations

1. The selection of respondents is restricted to a convenience or volunteer sampling method. This method of sampling can bias the results of the data.
2. Training interviewers takes time, effort, and money.
3. Bias regarding the interviewer may impact the quality of data. The dress, age, sex, and race of the interviewer may cause the respondent to answer untruthfully.
4. Interviewers have an opportunity to falsify data.
5. Each public location has its own characteristics. These characteristics may differ from the target population and create a nonrepresentative sample.
6. The environment for testing products and other forms of tests is not common. Therefore, the data could be biased.
7. Respondents may complete a questionnaire more than once.

Exhibit 12.8

Survey Methods Characteristics

	Electronic			Interviews		
Features	E-mail	On-site/Kiosk	Web	Mail	Personal	Phone
1. Costs per return	Low	Low	Low	Medium	High	Medium
2. Data collection speed	High	High	High	Low	High	Low
3. Response rate	High	High	High	Low	High	Low
4. Sampling cost	Low	Low	Low	High	Medium	Medium
5. Respondent interaction	Yes	No	No	No	Yes	Yes
6. Interview bias	None	None	None	None	High	Medium
7. Use visuals	Yes	Yes	Yes	Yes	Yes	No
8. Respondent literacy required	Yes	Yes	Yes	Yes	No	No
9. Long questionnaire feasible	Yes	Yes	Yes	No	Yes	No
10. Generalization to population	No	No	No	Maybe	Maybe	Maybe

to fit some type of profile. They might be randomly selected by some method; however, they are not a true random sample. Respondents were available and they volunteered to participate. Therefore, as with on-site surveys, conclusions about the data collected from an available sample must be made with caution and not generalized to the population.

SUMMARY

Survey research is a common practice among advertising and public relations practitioners. Surveys typically provide descriptive data that are collected quickly and economically. The survey research method depends on the purpose of the study and the budget allocated to the research. Respondents might complete survey questionnaires by providing the answers to an interviewer or completing the questionnaire themselves.

A telephone survey is fast and economical but includes opportunities for interviewer bias. Telephone surveys also require multiple callbacks. Mail surveys tend to take more time to administer and are less economical than telephone and electronic surveys. Mail surveys can be quite visually appealing and interesting. Electronic surveys may be distributed to respondents via e-mail or be posted on the Web. They are self-administered, usually very fast and economical, and frequently include visuals. However, electronic surveys are limited to respondents who have computers or knowledge of using computers. Personal interviews have higher response rates, provide opportunities for respondents to ask questions, and include probing questions. However, data collection is slow and the cost per completed questionnaire is higher than other survey research methods. Each method has its benefits and limitations in making generalizations of the data to a larger population.

DISCUSSION QUESTIONS

1. What should researchers consider before selecting the best interviewing method?
2. Discuss the benefits and limitations of electronic surveys in determining respondents' concerns about the local ecology.
3. Discuss the best interviewing method to determine respondents' media use habits.

EXERCISES

1. List the benefits and limitations of using a telephone survey to determine respondents' opinion about the following topics:
   a. Voter preference for two presidential candidates.
   b. Respondents' job satisfaction.
   c. Brand awareness for female athletic shoes.
2. List the benefits and limitations for using a mail survey to determine local respondents' opinions about the following topics:
   a. Customer satisfaction with a local bank.
   b. Teaching sex education in local high schools.
   c. City ordinance for smoke-free restaurants.
3. Explain the limitations for using Web-based surveys.

ADDITIONAL READING

Alreck, P., and R. Settle. 2004. *The survey research handbook.* Boston: McGraw-Hill/Irwin.
Babbie, E. 1990. *Survey research methods.* Belmont, CA: Wadsworth.

Bradburn, N., and S. Sudman. 1988. *Polls & surveys: Understanding what they tell us.* San Francisco: Jossey-Bass.

Cooper, D., and C. Emory. 2006. *Business research methods.* Chicago: McGraw-Hill/Irwin.

Dillman, D. 1978. *Mail and telephone surveys: The total design method.* New York: Wiley-Intersciences.

Groves, R., et al. 2004. *Survey methodology.* New York: Wiley.

Rubenstein, S. 1995. *Surveying public opinion.* Belmont, CA: Wadsworth.

Salant, P., and D. Dillman. 1994. *How to conduct your own survey.* New York: Wiley.

13 Sampling

LEARNING OBJECTIVES

This chapter is intended to help you:

- Know the differences between probability and nonprobability sampling;
- Learn when and how to select the best sampling method;
- Learn the definition of key sampling terms;
- Identify sampling biases.

Good Meats, a company that distributes steaks and ground meat to grocery stores in ten states, discovered that some of its meat came from cows with the "Mad Cow Disease." A thorough examination by government investigators revealed only two cows used in processing meat had this disease. For the next two months, steak and ground meat sales were down in many of the stores that purchased meat from Good Meats. A public relations researcher wanted to measure the image of Good Meats among people in these ten states. A survey is an acceptable method for measuring shoppers' image of Good Meats. Obviously, it would be impossible to survey every person who shopped in the stores where Good Meat products were sold. The cost would be too high and it would be difficult to get a good population frame. Therefore, the public relations researcher decided to survey a sample of the shoppers in each state. How might a researcher draw a representative sample of these consumers who shopped in stores located in these ten states?

Advertising and public relations researchers want to know what people think, how they behave, what they purchase, how they spend their time, and what they value. There are several research methods that might provide valuable data to researchers. However, most researchers do not have access to every person in a target population. It would be almost impossible to contact every person in a state, county, or city. Therefore, researchers rely on acceptable sampling methods of key target populations to survey and draw conclusions about the entire target population based on the responses from the sample. Before you select a sample from a population, answer five questions. These five questions will guide your sampling method and data collection procedures.

1. What do you want to measure? Do you want to measure attitudes, opinions, behaviors, awareness, or preferences?
2. Do you plan to use only one survey or do you plan to survey the respondents again at a later date?
3. Who has the information you need to collect?
4. Will you define your population in terms of demographic information, geographical location, or unique characteristics?
5. How accurate must the data be? If your sample size is too small, the data will be less accurate. Probability samples are generalizable to the population, while nonprobability samples might result in rough estimates or approximations.

The sample is the group of people you want to participate in your research, however, not everyone in your sample will participate. The people who will actually participate in your research represent a subset of the population. Researchers are constantly reminded that the sample of people must reflect the characteristics of the population from which the sample was selected. They want to generalize the data collected from a sample of respondents and conclude that the sample represents the entire population. Sampling procedures primarily determine the generalizability of your research.

In this chapter, we will discuss probability and nonprobability sampling methods. Probability sampling methods include random, stratified, and cluster. Nonprobability sampling methods include quota, convenience, purposive, and snowball. We will also discuss surveys that use a census. Census is a survey method that includes all of the members of a population. A census might be used to survey all members of a church, organization, club, or class.

A major advantage of a probability sampling method is the researcher can state the sample represents the target population to a given degree. Sampling error is the term advertising and public relations researchers use when they calculate the degree that the sample might differ from the population. The larger the sampling error, the less likely the sample possesses characteristics similar to the population. In a nonprobability sampling method, the sampling errors cannot be determined and the conclusions of the research do not have generalizability.

There are two very logical questions about sampling target populations. What is a population and how many people should be selected to represent a sample of the population? The answers to these two questions are included in the following four sections regarding populations, units, frames, and sample sizes.

POPULATION

The target population is typically identified by the researcher. The researcher usually relies on logic and experience to define the population based on the objectives of the study. The group whom you want to learn certain facts about or wish to generalize your data is called the population. For example, if you want to market a new line of jeans to young females, you might decide to survey females 14 to 24 years of age. These females would be your target population. Or, you might want to know the image of your company among suppliers from whom you purchase raw material. In this study, your

Exhibit 13.1   **Population of Urban Voters in County**

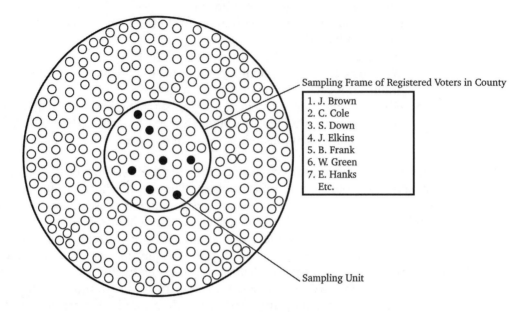

Sampling Frame of Registered Voters in County

1. J. Brown
2. C. Cole
3. S. Down
4. J. Elkins
5. B. Frank
6. W. Green
7. E. Hanks
   Etc.

Sampling Unit

suppliers would be your target population. Here is another example: College recruiters tend to target junior and senior high school students. This group contains the largest number of prospective students who most likely will attend college. Therefore, the college recruiters' target population would be junior and senior high school students.

You most likely will not find a complete and accurate listing of every person in your population. If you did have a complete and accurate listing, you probably would not be able to contact or conduct a survey of each person in your population. The costs and the time to complete the study would be prohibitive. Therefore, you must view your population as two possible groups. One group includes the entire population identified by the researcher as the theoretical population. This is the entire population you would like to survey, while the other group, the accessible population, includes the population that will actually be accessible or available to survey. The accessible group is a sample or subset of the theoretical population. Hence, you will need to select a sample or subset of the theoretical population to survey. Before you conduct your survey, you should carefully define the target population.

SAMPLING FRAME

A sample is a portion of the population you wish to study, while a sampling frame is the list of people you select for your sample. These are the people selected from your accessible population. For example, if you were surveying registered voters, you might develop a list of registered voters who voted in the last presidential election. A list of registered voters is available from the county government. The list of registered voters is your sampling frame for this survey.

Most organizations have a list of its members. For example, if you were to survey members of the American Association of Retired Persons (AARP), you would secure a list of its members. The list of AARP members serves as your sampling frame for this research project. However, before solidifying your survey research plans, check the source of your prospective list of members to determine whether the organization will allow you to have access to its membership list. Names, addresses, and telephone numbers of some organizational memberships are confidential. If the sampling list includes fewer than two hundred names, many researchers decide to survey every member. Country clubs, universities, and local service clubs such as the Lions Club usually survey all of their members. This is called a census survey.

Advertising and public relations researchers might want to conduct a telephone survey of residents in a particular metropolitan area. They select names from the current telephone book for that respective metropolitan area. In this case, the sampling frame is the telephone book. However, if you want the results of your study to be generalizable to the entire population, a telephone book is not a good source for selecting a sampling frame. Many residents do not list their phone numbers, they move out of the metro area after the telephone book is published, or they may have just moved into the metro area. This matters only if the people who are not listed in the phone book differ systematically to the sample you select to survey.

Sampling Unit

After you have identified and secured your sampling frame, you are ready to draw a sample using one of the sampling procedures discussed later in Chapter 14. The individual member selected from your sampling frame is called a sampling unit. Once the sampling frame has been defined, you begin the process of contacting the individual sampling units. Survey sampling units provide the data you collect for analysis. Sampling units are typically people. In other surveys, the researcher selects a sample of people according to their specific characteristics such as age, race, income, or sex. Yet, in some studies, you might identify your sampling unit as households, census blocks, residential areas, adults, students, families, schools, organizations, clubs, businesses, or political parties. For example, if your sampling unit is schools, a secondary sampling unit might be teachers. In this example, both the schools and teachers are considered to be sampling units. You would select a sample of schools as your primary sampling unit and then select a sample of teachers as your secondary sampling unit. In this case, the secondary sampling unit, teachers, will provide the data you collect for your study. The same is true for households. Your primary sampling unit could be households; however, all households are not the same. Some households have single residents, some are couples only, and others include children. Therefore, the secondary sampling unit might be 18- to 35-year-old males within each household.

Advertising and public relations researchers might prefer to define the sampling unit quite specifically. For example, if you want to determine the proportion of male students interested in participating in intramural football or basketball leagues, a sampling unit of college students could be defined as full-time, male students only.

This definition would exclude part-time students and females. More specifically, a sampling unit of families might be defined as spouses with a child less than twenty years of age living in the household. The major consideration for identifying and selecting a sampling unit is to determine from whom you want information and what are their characteristics.

Sample Size

Advertising and public relations researchers want to generalize their research to a target population. The survey sample size is a major factor that determines accuracy of the generalizations of your data. The larger the sample, the more likely the data are accurate for making generalizations. Therefore, in the design stages of the survey, researchers try to determine methods for securing random samples as large as possible, but not too large. There is a point when the sample size will result in the value of diminishing returns. In other words, a sample of 1,000 may not yield any additional accuracy than a sample of 500. Where are they located and are they easily contacted? How do you get them to participate and are they interested in the topic? You might find that it is easier to get people to participate in a survey about their preferences for political candidates than it is to get their participation in a survey about their shopping habits. In most advertising and public relations surveys, researchers cannot afford the costs of sampling an entire or large population. The size of the sample depends on the homogeneity of the population and the complexity of the data analyses.

By determining the homogeneity of the population, you are actually deciding how much the sample is different from or similar to the population. The more homogeneous the population, the more likely you might draw a smaller sample. The less homogeneous the population, the more you will need to draw a larger sample. For example, if you are interested in measuring female responses on a topic and your population is 90 percent female, you would say that the sex of your population is very homogeneous. However, there might be other characteristics among these females that would cause them to be different. The female population could be quite different in age, race, education, shopping habits, religion, political affiliation, and income.

The complexity of the data analyses also influence the size of the sample. If you are interested in the responses of females only, you might report their responses as the number of times the females answered "yes" and the number of times they answered "no" to a specific question. You also might report the percentage of females who responded "yes" and "no." This is called descriptive statistics. In this example, you might draw a smaller sample from your population. However, if you want to report the number of times they answered "yes" or "no" according to their race and age, you need to draw a larger sample to include more females in each category of race and age. The age of the respondents might be grouped into six different categories: 18–24, 25–34, 35–44, 45–54, 55–64, and 65 and more. Your sample would need to be larger to get an adequate number of responses from females representing each age category. As the number of categories increases, the size of your sample also needs to increase. The basic problem of examining subcategories of the data is that you are effectively reducing the sample size of the number of people in each of the subcategories. By reducing the sample size, you increase the uncertainty of inferences and generalizations that can be made about members in the subcategories.

Researchers who survey a sample of a national population desire large random samples. The sample size of a national survey typically runs from 1,000 to 1,200 people. Random samples of this size provide enough data for the researcher to conduct a detailed analysis of the data among several categories. For local and regional surveys, the researcher often samples only a few hundred people. Most local and regional surveys are limited by the costs allocated to the study; therefore, a random sample may consist of 400 to 500 people.

PROBABILITY SAMPLES

Probability survey sampling is based on a randomly selected sample of units from a population. In probability sampling, each member of the target population has a known chance of being selected, there are clearly defined selection procedures, and the sampling error can be determined. You should strive to select sampling units without any bias or predetermined method that shows favoritism. Data from a probability sample are used to make generalizations about the characteristics of the entire population. By randomly selecting sampling units, researchers can calculate each sampling unit's probability of being selected, thus giving the study more credibility. The most common probability sampling methods are *random, stratified, systematic,* and *cluster.*

RANDOM SAMPLING

Random sampling is the most straightforward form of drawing a probability sample and is the most desirable kind of survey method. Each sampling unit or member of your target population has a known chance of being selected. For example, if you were to select between two sampling units, you could flip a coin or draw a name on a piece of paper from a bowl. While these two methods are simple examples of randomly selecting a sampling unit, these methods would not work with hundreds of sampling units or members. An acceptable random sample determines the validity and reliability of your research, making it possible for your conclusions to be generalizable. There are various methods for drawing a sample from small and large populations. Here are some examples of drawing a *simple random sample.*

Suppose the president of Pay More Insurance (PMI) wants to measure customer satisfaction with PMI. PMI has twenty thousand customers (the population). The president wants to develop a self-administered survey and mail a questionnaire to each customer. However, he decides that the costs for printing and postage to each customer are too expensive. He decides to draw a random sample from the list of customers (sampling frame) and mails a questionnaire only to those customers. The president determines that a sample of five hundred customers (sampling units) would give him a representative and homogeneous sample of the population and be cost effective. What is the best method for randomly selecting these five hundred customers or sampling units?

The marketing director of PMI, Miss S. Curves, assigns all of the customers a

Exhibit 13.2 **A Simple Random Sample**

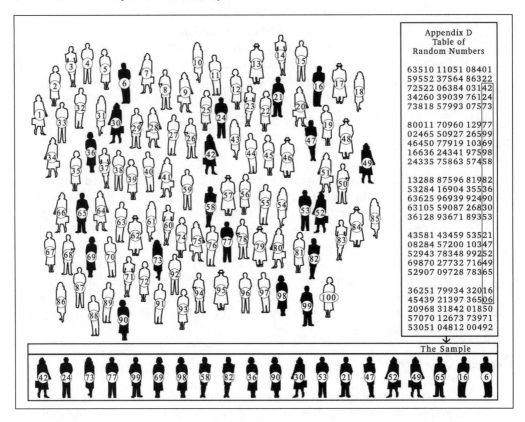

number. She then uses a computer program to randomly select five hundred numbers between 1 and 20,000. The five hundred numbers randomly selected by the computer were matched with the numbers assigned to PMI's twenty thousand customers. Each customer has an equal chance of being selected to receive a questionnaire.

A table of random numbers (in the Appendix) might be used as an efficient method for selecting a simple random sample from a small sampling frame of two hundred people or less. For example, Make Us Well (MUW) is a nonprofit organization of physicians who provide free medical service for children of indigent guardians. To receive the free medical care, children must be five years of age or younger. The local county wants to provide financial support for MUW. One county commissioner suggests that the county conduct a survey of the one hundred physicians who volunteer their time to MUW to determine the organization's most pressing needs. The commissioner suggested that a number be assigned to each volunteer doctor. A *table of random numbers* is used to select twenty physicians to survey. The researchers decides to use the last two numbers in the second column beginning with the fourth number from the top. Twenty numbers are selected. The numbers selected in the table of random numbers are matched with the numbers assigned to each physician.

Suppose researchers for the Super Electronic Store (SES) of Greensville were to determine why people shop their competitors. They want to conduct a telephone survey using a sample of the 200,000 people who reside in Greensville (the population). After a brief discussion, the researchers determine that they cannot use the telephone directory as a sampling frame, because the directory includes the names of people who have just moved into Greensville, lists people who are no longer residents, and does not include people with unlisted numbers. Therefore, they choose to use a random digit dialing method instead of the telephone directory and determined that they need to draw a sample of five hundred numbers.

Random digit dialing is an automated procedure that randomly assigns numbers to telephone prefixes established by the telephone company. Random digit dialing is a good random sampling method when there is no sampling frame. The researchers select all of the telephone number prefixes assigned to Greensville. The automation system randomly assigns the final four numbers to the prefix and dials the number. For example, Greensville might have six prefixes, 784, 946, 554, 631, 774, and 598. The automated system selects each prefix and randomly assigns the last four numbers to generate a telephone number: 784–5598. The 5598 numbers are the random numbers assigned to the 784 prefix. If the number is disconnected or is assigned to a business, the system replaces the final four numbers with four new randomly selected numbers. There is no system bias to influence the selection of the telephone number. Many researchers purchase a list of telephone numbers from companies that specialize in providing telephone numbers of populations that match the researchers' needs. These numbers are screened to eliminate the ones that do not match the target population.

STRATIFIED SAMPLING

Advertising and public relations researchers use *stratified sampling* procedures when they want to measure opinions or attitudes of subgroups within a population. These subgroups might be divided by various demographic variables, such as age, sex, race, and income. These homogeneous subgroups are called *strata* of a population. Members of each subgroup or stratum share at least one common characteristic such as age, sex, race, or income that is mutually exclusive of the other strata characteristics. For example, members of a population might be divided into strata by their age. Population members who are age 18 to 24 years might be placed in one stratum, members 25 to 34 years in another stratum, and so on. Each stratum would have a unique and mutually exclusive age characteristic. If you want two strata based on the respondent's sex, they would be placed in either the male stratum or the female stratum. While demographic variables may be the most common strata, you also might group the population by the number of years they have worked for a company, college student classification (freshmen, sophomore, etc.), job classification (managers, nonmanagers), geographical region (New York, Texas, California), or political party affiliation (Republican, Democrat, independent, or other).

The stratified sampling method requires that researchers possess a list of every population sampling unit and the relevant characteristic about each sampling unit used in establishing strata. For example, if you were to develop strata according to the sampling unit's age, you must have a list of the population that also includes each

Exhibit 13.3

Proportionate Stratified Sampling

Sample Size = 200 Parents

Hispanic = 35%	African American = 35%	White = 25%	Asian = 5%
70 parents	70 parents	50 parents	10 parents

unit's respective age. If you developed strata based on the sampling unit's income, you need a list of the population and each sampling unit's respective income.

A stratified sample controls the number of sampling units assigned to each stratum. The number of sampling units assigned to small and large strata might ensure that you have an adequate sample size for each stratum from which you will select your sample. The strata or sample size you draw does not have to be the same. If every sampling unit in your population were similar in age, then a small sample would be adequate for your study. For example, a large proportion of college students will range from 18 to 22 years of age. In many surveys of college students, you may not need age strata. However, if the ages of your population vary widely, then you might need to group your population according to a range of ages. If you have 20 sampling units in one stratum whose age ranged from 18 to 24 years and another stratum of 50 sampling units whose age ranged from 35 to 44 years, you might decide that a sample of 10 sampling units from the younger age stratum and 15 from the older stratum would likely represent your stratified sampling needs.

There are two methods of stratified sampling—*proportionate stratified sampling* and *disproportionate stratified sampling*. Proportionate stratified sampling ensures representation of each strata in proportion to the population. A random sample may or may not result in an equal representation of your sample. For example, if you were to survey 200 parents about eliminating competitive sports in elementary schools, you might want equal parent representation corresponding to the students' race or ethnicity. Suppose the student population in your school district is 35 percent Hispanic, 35 percent African American, 25 percent white, and 5 percent Asian. You would develop strata by student race and then select your sample to have the same proportions as the student population. You would list and group all of the parents by their respective race or ethnicity.

How would you select these sampling units? You might randomly select 820 parents or about a third of the 2,400 parents in the district. These 820 parents will serve as your population. However, this sample most likely will not represent the population proportionally (35 percent Hispanic, 35 percent African American, 25 percent white, and 5 percent Asian). Your sample might include more of one race than another. For example, of the 820 parents in your sample, you might have 280 Hispanics, 245 African Americans, 225 whites and 70 Asian parents. These are your respective strata.

Each stratum is now an independent population and the sampling frame for each race. You might choose from among several methods for systematically selecting your sample. If you used one of the simple random sampling methods, you would call your sample a *stratified simple random sample.*

Exhibit 13.4   **A Stratified, Systematic Sample with a Random Start**

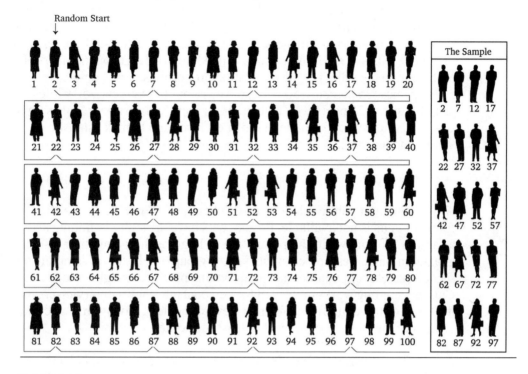

Exhibit 13.5

Disproportionate Stratified Sampling

Sample Size = 200 Parents
• 50 Hispanic parents
• 50 African American parents
• 50 White parents
• 50 Asian parents

A representative random sample of the 200 parents representing the population would include 70 parents from the 280 Hispanic parents (35 percent), 70 parents from the 245 African American parents (35 percent), 50 parents from the 225 white parents (25 percent) and 10 parents from the 70 Asian parents (5 percent). Therefore, in this example, you would have systematically selected a proportion of parents from each respective stratum (70 Hispanics, 70 African Americans, 50 whites, and 10 Asians) representing the population (70 Hispanics, 70 African Americans, 50 whites, and 10 Asians).

To systematically select 70 Hispanics, divide the number of sampling units in the Hispanic stratum (280) by the number of Hispanics you want to select (70). The calculation results in the number 4. This is the number you use to select every fourth name in your sampling frame from the Hispanic stratum. The distance between each name on a list is called a sampling interval. We randomly select a beginning point on the list and then select a sequence of names with a sampling interval of 4 until we have selected 70

Hispanics. The same procedure is followed in selecting a proportionate sample for each of the remaining stratum. Each stratum might have a different sampling interval.

A *disproportionate stratified sampling method* intentionally varies the proportion of respondents among the strata. By using the same example listed above, the researcher might use a simple random sampling procedure to select equal numbers of units from each stratum regardless of the population proportions. For example, you might select 50 Hispanics (25 percent), 50 African Americans (25 percent), 50 whites (25 percent) and 50 Asians (25 percent). The benefit for using a disproportionate sample is to ensure that you have enough members in each stratum to make statistical comparisons among the four strata.

Cluster Sampling

Advertising and public relations researchers use *cluster sampling* when a sampling frame of units is not available. Researchers have difficulty in finding and identifying a sampling frame when the population is large or the population resides in a wide geographic area. Researchers might survey groups or clusters of sampling units such as schools, cities, communities, hospitals, voting precincts, neighborhoods, and counties. Cluster sampling works quite well for personal interviews. Interviewers might reduce the time for traveling from one interview to the next, saving time and money.

Cluster sampling should meet at least four criteria:

1. The physical boundaries should be clearly defined and identifiable.
2. The clusters should be located in close proximity to one another; otherwise, costs will soar.
3. The number of people in each cluster should be limited. This will aid in minimizing the number of people in the sampling frame.
4. The researcher should know the size of the cluster prior to selecting the sample.

Suppose you want to conduct a national survey of people about crime in their cities. It is not practical to survey every person in the United States. Therefore, you might use cluster sampling to survey units within randomly selected clusters. Cluster sampling involves at least a two-stage process and as many as five stages in some studies. To select a sample for your national survey, you might randomly select several cities throughout the nation (stage one), then randomly select several blocks of houses within each of the cities (stage two), randomly select a cluster of houses within each of the blocks (stage three), prepare a sampling frame (stage four), and, finally, randomly select adult members of each house for the interview (stage five). You would use one of the random sampling methods to select each of the sampling units. Every household in a city belongs to a block and every city block represents a number of households. The number of sampling units (households) within each cluster could be different. Not all city blocks include the same number of households; therefore, you cannot control for sample size.

The random selection of the various clusters is an attempt to include sampling units in your study that represent the total population. You must strive to select a sample that has characteristics similar to the population. You might reduce the validity of your research if

Exhibit 13.6 **Random Selection of Various Clusters**

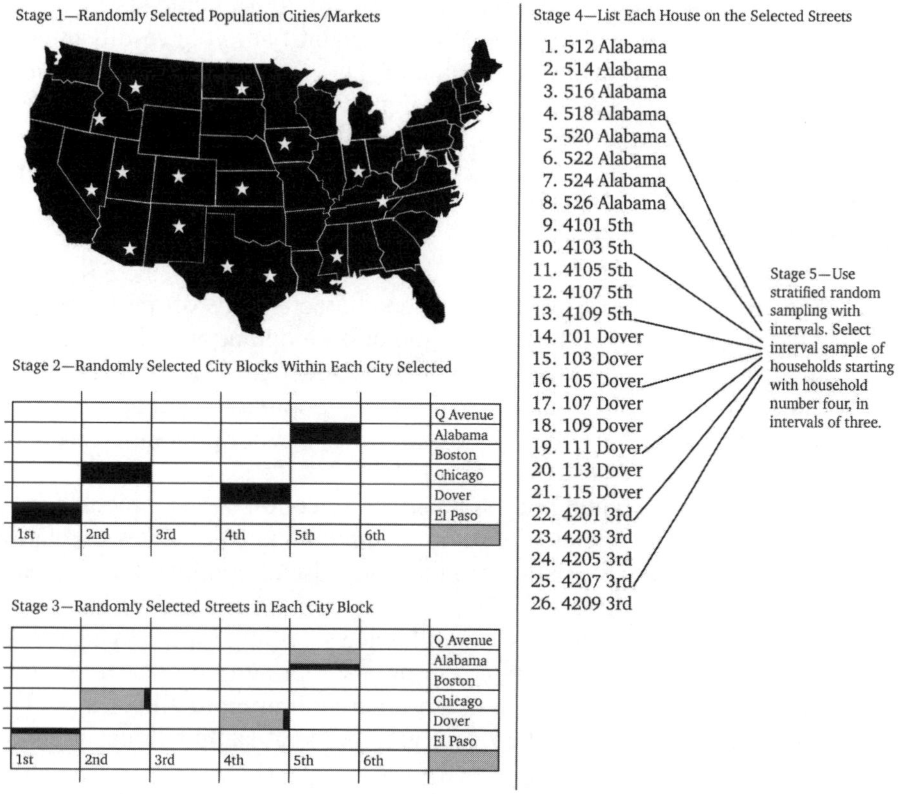
Stage 1—Randomly Selected Population Cities/Markets
Stage 2—Randomly Selected City Blocks Within Each City Selected
Q Avenue
Alabama
Boston
Chicago
Dover
El Paso
1st
2nd
3rd
4th
5th
6th
Stage 3—Randomly Selected Streets in Each City Block
Q Avenue
Alabama
Boston
Chicago
Dover
El Paso
1st
2nd
3rd
4th
5th
6th
Stage 4—List Each House on the Selected Streets
1. 512 Alabama
2. 514 Alabama
3. 516 Alabama
4. 518 Alabama
5. 520 Alabama
6. 522 Alabama
7. 524 Alabama
8. 526 Alabama
9. 4101 5th
10. 4103 5th
11. 4105 5th
12. 4107 5th
13. 4109 5th
14. 101 Dover
15. 103 Dover
16. 105 Dover
17. 107 Dover
18. 109 Dover
19. 111 Dover
20. 113 Dover
21. 115 Dover
22. 4201 3rd
23. 4203 3rd
24. 4205 3rd
25. 4207 3rd
26. 4209 3rd
Stage 5—Use stratified random sampling with intervals. Select interval sample of households starting with household number four, in intervals of three.

the sampling units within clusters do not reflect homogeneous characteristics similar to the population. People within the same neighborhood tend to be very homogeneous on many opinions, attitudes, and demographic variables; therefore, they may be very different than other sampling units within other neighborhoods of the city. It is better that you include many small clusters in your sample rather than a few large clusters. Smaller clusters will more likely produce broader sampling units that represent the population. You must review and evaluate each of the clusters for its homogeneity to the population.

CENSUS SURVEY

A *census survey* includes every sampling unit in a population. Obviously in a census survey, there are no sampling procedures and no generalizablity issues. Because you have contacted every person in your population, your findings will represent the population. While you may think that a census survey would be the best survey method and it would eliminate all issues of sampling bias and errors, it is not practical to conduct a census survey of large populations. The U.S. government attempts to conduct a census of its population every ten years. The cost of completing this census survey is several millions of dollars. Even after all the time and money spent on this national survey, there are issues with nonresponses and incomplete questionnaires.

Suppose you wanted to survey a population in a town of 10,000 residents. You might get the same results with a simple random sample survey. If you draw a representative sample of 400 residents, the validity of your results might be just as high as a census survey and cost much less. The cost efficiency of a survey is often based on the cost per completed questionnaire. Even a census survey does not guarantee that every sampling unit will respond. Many sampling units in the population will not complete and return the questionnaire or allow you to conduct an interview.

SAMPLING BIAS

Sampling bias might occur when the characteristics of the random sample are different from the characteristics of the entire population, when the sample size is too small, and when the sample is not homogeneous. The characteristics of the sample must reflect the same characteristics of the population and be large enough to address differences in variability. As the variability of your population increases, the sample size must also increase.

A researcher should not influence the selection of a sample in any way that would violate a random selection of sampling units. There is an inverse relationship between sampling bias and the validity of the research. As sampling bias increases, the validity of the research decreases.

There are several factors that influence sampling bias. Any factor that increases or decreases the probability of selecting a sampling unit relative to other units creates sampling bias. Nonresponse is a problem common to all surveys. Typically, nonresponse is encountered when no one is home at sample households or when survey subjects refuse to be interviewed.

Exhibit 13.7 includes a list of factors that produce sampling bias.

NONPROBABILITY SAMPLES

The difference between probability and nonprobability sampling is an assumption that in probability sampling each member of a population has a known chance of being selected, while in nonprobability sampling each member does not have a known chance of being selected. In probability sampling, the researcher strives for randomization in the selection process. In nonprobability sampling, the researcher arbitrarily selects sampling units. The reliability of probability sampling can be determined, while the reliability in nonprobability samples cannot be estimated.

There are situations in which researchers are not able to select a probability sample of a population. If you were to survey people who visit a shopping mall, there would be no available list of customers. You could use a telephone survey and screen respondents who have shopped at the mall, but the costs and time to conduct the study might be prohibitive. What proportion of the population shops at the mall? You may find that only a small percentage of residents stop at the mall. Therefore, you would use another method for selecting a sample of mall customers. You would use a nonprobability sample. Many researchers use nonprobability sampling methods to obtain a sample because they are inexpensive and easy to administer. Nonprobability sampling methods also are used for

Exhibit 13.7

Sampling Biases

1. Some respondents are more accessible than others. Respondents who are more accessible might have characteristics that differ from the characteristics of the population. They are more accessible because of the time of day the survey is conducted or they are geographically more convenient.
2. Interviewers might have a tendency to select respondents who are more like themselves, such as social status, race, age, or dress.
3. In personal interviews, respondents might select a cluster of homes in a neighborhood that differ from the population. Respondents who live in the same neighborhood might be very similar in their opinions and behavioral characteristics.
4. Respondents selected from a list might not be representative of the population. Names listed in alphabetical order may have several names that begin with the same letter resulting in under-selection of respondents representing the population.
5. Respondents who volunteer to participate in a survey might differ from the population.
6. Respondents who refuse to participate or who terminate the survey might cause underrepresentation of sampling units with similar characteristics.

questionnaire testing and during the preliminary development stages of a questionnaire. However, nonprobability sampling methods do not involve randomness and, therefore, the sample might be biased.

QUOTA SAMPLING

Quota sampling is conducted in similar ways as a stratified sampling method but without randomization. Quota sampling is the most common form of nonprobability sampling used by advertising and public relations researchers. Many advertising and public relations researchers use quota sampling to conduct telephone surveys because it has the potential for satisfying specific demographic proportions of a population. There are no unique criteria for selecting sampling units; therefore, sample size is determined by the number of sampling units a researcher desires for meeting a quota of each sampling stratum.

The researcher identifies the population and determines the sampling strata of the population. The researcher establishes the proportions of the strata and then selects a specific number or quota of sampling units who meet a predetermined profile. The researcher might decide that the respective strata would include 40 percent white, 40 percent Hispanic and 20 percent African Americans. When the researcher completes the quote for each strata, he or she does not collect additional data from representatives in that particular strata. Quota sampling dictates that the number of people selected match the racial proportion in each stratum.

Another researcher might decide to select a sample of people based on their sex or gender. Suppose an interviewer at a mall wants to determine shopping habits of 100 female and 50 male mall shoppers between 20 and 30 years of age. An interviewer selects shoppers estimated to be between 20 and 30 years old. The first question is a screening question inquiring about the respondent's age. If the respondent indicates that he or she is between 20 and 30 years of age, the interviewer would complete the survey. Once the researcher completes the quota of questionnaires, he or she does not collect additional data from representatives in that particular target population.

This quota system of selecting respondents is quite easy and efficient; however, the sample does not mean that these 100 females and 50 male shoppers are representative of all female and male shoppers 20 to 30 years of age.

Convenience Sampling

Convenience sampling is another nonprobability sampling method used during the preliminary research stages to collect general information about the research topic. This information might be used to conduct other types of probability sampling research or to draw conclusions only about this sample of respondents—usually customers, clients, or students. Convenience sampling is typically conducted where large numbers of people congregate or pass by a particular location. You might find large numbers of people at shopping malls, schools, churches, athletic events, or conventions.

Researchers use convenience sampling in exploratory research. Some researchers attempt to randomly select respondents through some sampling procedure; however, a convenience sampling method does not have the properties of randomization. For example, university researchers frequently ask students enrolled in their classes to participate in surveys. Even though students within the class may be randomly selected to participate, they are not randomly selected from the population of all university students or those enrolled in any university. Many classes are populated by a majority of freshmen and sophomores, while other classes are populated by a majority of juniors and seniors. Therefore, conclusions based on surveys of college students are not generalizable to all college students.

Conclusions that researchers draw from a convenience sample are limited; however, the conclusions might be accurate when the populations are homogeneous. For example, you might conduct taste tests in a grocery store. You might station interviewers throughout the store with a tray of food samples. The interviewers would ask shoppers to taste the food samples and complete a questionnaire about the food's taste, appearance, texture, or other qualities. The questionnaire also might include questions about the respondent's shopping habits.

Purposive Sampling

Purposive sampling is used when researchers have identified specific characteristics of a population that match quite well with the purpose of the research. Some people are more qualified than others to provide accurate answers about some topics because of who they are or what they have done. You will save a lot of time, money, and effort when you select respondents who have the expertise that corresponds with the purpose of your study. For example, if you are seeking information about why a respondent purchased a specific product, has been elected to public office, been involved in an auto accident, or served in the military, you would select only qualified respondents with that specific experience. To study the quality of health care and insurance service for people involved in automobile accidents, logically, you would interview only people with this experience. They are qualified to answer the questions related to the purpose of your research.

A political exit poll is an example of purposive sampling. Pollsters might identify precincts that have historically voted for the winner of a particular race. However, in

Exhibit 13.8 **Snowball Sampling**

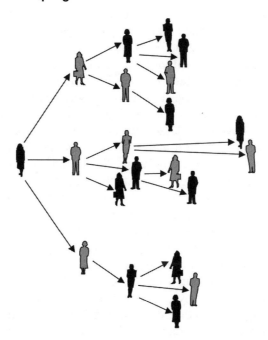

some polls, researchers may randomly select the precincts. Researchers constantly update and review the voting patterns of voters in these key precincts. Interviewers are stationed at these precincts to ask voters for whom they voted.

The purpose of an exit poll is to predict the winner of the political race before the polls close and the votes are counted. These pollsters might also combine purposive sampling and quota sampling to make these predictions. For example, if 60 percent of the voters at these key precincts who voted in the last election were males, the pollsters would set a quota of 60 percent of the respondents in their exit polls to be male.

A purposive sampling method also is ideal for pretesting questionnaires to determine problems with the questions or response scales. You also might want to study responses from easily identifiable small subsets of a larger population before conducting a survey of a large population. These small subsets of respondents might include clients, customers, faculty members, or PTA members. Data collected in the pretesting stage is valuable in conducting focus groups and in-depth surveys.

SNOWBALL SAMPLING

Researchers use a *snowball sampling* method when the characteristics of the population are rare and the information from the members of the population is quite valuable. Snowball sampling identifies members of a population with particular knowledge and/ or experience. It depends on a system of referrals and recommendations similar to a chain letter. A few prospective respondents are asked to identify people they know with unique characteristics that match the purpose of the research. For example, if you want to interview survivors of cancer, parents of children with reading disabilities, military veterans, people who support a controversial city issue, or people who participate in marathon races, you may find more people with these experiences by using a snowball sampling method because people tend to know people like themselves.

Your initial sample might be a small group of ten to fifteen people who meet the criteria for being selected. You would approach members of this small group of prospective respondents and seek their cooperation. Cash incentives are typically given to the participants. The choice of the initial contacts is critical to the study. After the respondents have completed the survey or participated in some form of qualitative research, you then solicit their assistance in identifying other people they know with similar experiences or knowledge. The initial members will be the key for securing referrals and identifying additional prospective participants. Cash incentives also are given to the participants who make referrals. The researcher might give the respondent $20 for each name and contact information up to three names. The researcher might also stipulate that two of the referrals must be in different towns.

This is how the snowball works. If 12 people participate in the initial research and you can secure two referrals from each participant, you have added 24 more prospective participants to your study. Suppose that 20 of the 24 referrals participated in the second round of surveys, you will have completed 32 questionnaires (12 original participants plus the additional 20 participants). Of the 20 participants in the second round, 18 participants each provided names of two referrals or a total of 36 new prospective participants. Thirty of the new referrals agreed to participate. You then would have completed a total of 62 questionnaires (32 second round participants plus 30 participants in the third round). The snowballing effect would continue until you achieved the number of respondents you desire for your study.

Building a network of prospective participants will reduce the time and cost of contacting respondents and collecting data. The snowball sampling method works well with audiences that are difficult to contact. For example, you might find that you achieve a better response rate with a snowball sampling method when selecting a sample of respondents representing homosexual or homeless people. The response rate is typically quite high. However, the time to conduct a snowball sample might be longer with than other sampling methods and the opportunity for bias is quite high. You might expect the snowballing method to run from six weeks to six months. It will take time to interview one group of respondents and contact additional prospective participants. Sampling bias is common. Participants who provide referrals to the researcher will talk to the people they refer and possibly influence their comments and responses.

SUMMARY

Survey sampling is the foundation for conducting valid research. There are several sampling methods that might be successfully used with any single study. The purpose and breadth of the research will determine the sampling method most appropriate for your research. Sampling members of target populations is economical and efficient; however, sampling procedures are not easily accomplished and errors in the sampling process might create bias resulting in invalid data.

Survey methods are classified as either probability samples or nonprobability samples. In probability sampling, each member of the target population has a known chance of being selected. Probability sampling methods include *random, stratified,* and *cluster.* The results of research using probability sampling are generalizable to the population. In nonprobability sampling, people in the target population do not have a known chance of being selected. Nonprobability sampling methods include *quota, convenience, purposive,* and *snowball.* The results of research using nonprobability sampling are not generalizable to the population.

Researchers follow specific procedures in drawing a sample from a population. They must first define the target population they plan to survey. The target population includes the people the researcher wants to interview. Researchers then develop a list of prospective respondents called a sampling frame. A sample is selected from the sampling frame. Each person selected from the sampling frame is called a sampling unit. A sampling unit is the person who is contacted to complete the survey and provide the information used by the researcher.

DISCUSSION QUESTIONS

1. Discuss the limitations of random digit dialing. When would you most likely use random digit dialing in advertising and public relations research?
2. When would you most likely use proportionate and disproportionate stratified sampling methods?
3. Explain the differences between probability and nonprobability sampling methods.

EXERCISES

1. Use the table of random numbers (see the Appendix, p. 313) and select a random sample of six students in your class.
2. If you were to survey a population in seven major metropolitan cities about crime rates in their respective neighborhoods, which probability sampling method would you use? Why?
3. Define and give an example for the terms listed here.
   a. Sampling frame
   b. Sampling unit
   c. Sampling interval

ADDITIONAL READING

Herek, G. 2009. A brief introduction to sampling. http://psychology.ucdavis.edu/rainbow/html/fact_sample.html.

Magnani, R. 1997. FANTA-2 Publications: Sampling guide. Food and Nutrition Technical Assistance II (FANTA-2) Project, December. http://www.fantaproject.org/publications/sampling.shtml.

Policy Hub. 2008. What is sampling? In *The magenta book.* Berkshire, UK: Policy Hub, National School of Government, United Kingdom. http://www.nationalschool.gov.uk/policyhub/evaluating_policy/magenta_book/chapter5.asp.

American Association for Public Opinion Research. http://www.aapor.org/mapor.

14 Measuring Instruments

LEARNING OBJECTIVES

This chapter is intended to help you:

- Learn how scales of measurement are used in survey research;
- Identify the different scales of measurement used in survey research;
- Understand when to use the appropriate measuring instrument in survey research;
- Learn to design scales of measurement for survey research.

Advertising and public relations researchers use survey research to *explore, describe,* and/or *explain* a variety of concepts, attitudes, and behaviors. The purpose of *exploratory* research is to examine something new. You strive to learn more about a new product, new concept, new political issue, or a new procedure for doing something. However, exploratory research rarely yields solid answers that might be used to describe an entire population. Exploratory research results in statements of generalities that usually lead to additional and more formal data collection research methods. *Descriptive* research utilizes observation techniques for data collection. A marketing survey might describe the process consumers follow in purchasing and using a product. The researcher usually practices scientific rules of observation to increase data accuracy. Therefore, the results might be generalizable to a larger group of consumers. Researchers also conduct surveys to *explain why* people do the things they do or why they develop a certain attitude about an issue. Most research studies have elements of all three characteristics.

MEASURING INSTRUMENTS

Scientific inquiry requires careful planning and execution so the researchers can understand certain concepts, attitudes, and behaviors. Researchers can study individuals, groups, and organizations. The various components of analysis might include their characteristics and orientations. Researchers are interested in how respondents answer questions according to their personal, demographic characteristics—*sex, age, marital status, education, income,* and *race.* Or, they might be interested in respondents' orientations—*attitudes, beliefs, prejudices, values,* and *predispositions.* An important ingredient of scientific inquiry in survey research depends on the quality of the measuring instruments. The measuring instruments (questionnaires are the instruments in survey research), must produce accurate, reliable, and valid information.

Reliability in survey research is the degree of consistency of measuring responses as long as there are no changes in the characteristic being measured. For example, when you step on the bathroom scale to measure your weight, you expect the scale to provide the same reading if you step on, step off, and then step on again. If the scale indicates that your weight is the same each time you step on the scale, you might say that the scale used in measuring your weight is reliable. Researchers strive to develop questions and scales of measurement that are reliable. We say that our scales have reliability when we measure the same respondents repeatedly using the same measuring instrument (questionnaire) and we get the same or similar results. However, reliability does not guarantee that the data you collect are accurate.

There are several methods for measuring or testing reliability. The two most frequently used methods are *test-retest* and *split-half.* In the test-retest method, researchers record respondents' answers to questions at one period of time and then record responses from the same respondents using the same questionnaire three to four months later. If the responses are similar and do not vary significantly, researchers say the measuring instrument has reliability. In the split-half method, the researcher randomly divides questions dealing with the same topic into two groups and compares the responses. For example, if you had twenty questions about respondents' prejudices toward hiring female executives, you would randomly divide the twenty questions into two groups of ten questions. Each group of questions should provide a good measurement of prejudices concerning women executives. If the two groups of ten questions yield major differences in the responses, then you might have a problem with the measuring instrument's reliability.

Researchers say that scales of measurement have *validity* when the scales measure what they are supposed to measure. In the example about the bathroom scales, you expect the scales to measure your weight but not your height. Scales of measurement depend heavily on the question being asked and the information you seek from respondents. The question and the scale must complement each other. However, researchers realize that questions and scales might have reliability without validity. Depending on the question, respondents might repeatedly provide the same answer to the same question. That does not mean that their responses are accurate or truthful. For example, you might survey respondents about their use of tobacco. If some of the respondents were told not to use tobacco because of some health issue they experience and they used tobacco anyway, the respondents could lie and say they don't use tobacco or they could underreport their use of tobacco. If you called them three months later, they might continue to lie and underreport their use of tobacco. Their responses could be consistent from one survey time to another. In this case, the responses could be reliable; however, the measurement of their responses would not provide valid data.

The three most frequently used methods for measuring or testing validity are *content validity, face validity,* and *construct validity.* Content validity is basically a judgment of validity by qualified researchers who are experts in methods of research. The researcher might seek assistance from other researchers to review each question

Exhibit 14.1 **Reliability and Validity**

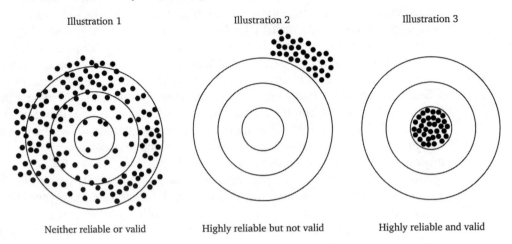

Illustration 1	Illustration 2	Illustration 3
Neither reliable or valid	Highly reliable but not valid	Highly reliable and valid

and determine whether the questions relate to the full meaning or dimensions of the concept being measured. The experts might review literature of previous studies to identify the various aspects that make up the concept. What influences or affects the concept? Do the questions in the questionnaire capture the complete or full range of possible effects? If the experts agree that the questions address the concept being measured, then the questionnaire has been judged to have content validity.

Face validity is a term used when researchers inspect the questions and determine that "on the surface" or "on face value" the questionnaire is measuring what it is supposed to measure. The measure has validity if the researcher decides that the concept is being measured more than any other concept. Suppose you were measuring the driving habits of teenagers, you might determine that driving speed, number of speeding tickets, and number of accidents are factors in measuring safe driving. By reviewing all the factors involved in good driving habits, you might decide that the measuring instrument includes questions about the factors associated with good driving habits and, therefore, has face validity. However, face validity alone does not provide solid evidence of measurement validity. Researchers must assume that responses from survey participants are true. We accept these self-reports as factual information. Because respondents are self-reporting the information, they might tend to underreport the information.

Construct validity is a method used to illustrate that a measurement is similar, related to, or associated with other variables of a theory. Suppose you want to measure employees' level of satisfaction with their jobs. You develop a measurement that includes questions about employee responsibilities and supervisor relationships that contribute to job satisfaction. For example, what factors contribute to a person's job satisfaction? Are there emotional criteria for determining job satisfaction? Is an employee's salary a factor in determining job satisfaction? Do safety standards contribute to job satisfaction? Is there a relationship among any of the factors that measure job satisfaction? You might decide that salary is a major factor in determining employees' job satisfaction. A measurement of job satisfaction might reveal that 60 percent of the respondents are satisfied with their jobs and 40 percent are not. If you find that respondents in both groups are equally satisfied with their salary, then salary would not be a construct in measuring job satisfaction and, therefore, would seem to challenge the validity of your measurement. However, if you found that a very large proportion of the "satisfied" employees are also satisfied with their salary and a large proportion of the "dissatisfied" employees are not satisfied with their salary, then you might conclude that salary is a valid construct in determining job satisfaction.

DATA COLLECTION FORMS

Advertising and public relations researchers use a variety of forms to collect data. Researchers might use questionnaires with specific formats to conduct surveys via mail, computers, e-mail, telephone, and kiosks. Some of the surveys are self-administered while in other surveys interviewers might read the questions to respondents. Barcode scanners and Scantrons also are used to enter survey data electronically. However, all of the forms have one common characteristic—data are systematically recorded on the forms designed for each respective research project.

QUESTION FORMATS

Researchers typically construct two forms of questions. One form is the *open-ended question* and the other is the *closed-ended question*. In the open-ended question, the researcher asks a question and the respondent provides an answer using his or her own words. No limitation is placed on the respondent's answer. In the closed-ended question, the researcher asks a question and the response options are limited to a finite list of responses. The respondent must select only one of the response options. However, most questionnaires include a response of "other." The "other" option allows respondents to provide an answer that is not included in the original list of options. Both of these types of questions have benefits and limitations. Researchers must determine the type of information they want to collect and develop the type of question that best provides the most accurate information.

OPEN-ENDED QUESTIONS

Open-ended questions are ideal for determining a variety of responses without response option limitations. What do people really think about the questions? When researchers want to explore other possible responses, an open-ended question is a good exploratory method for seeking new and different information. For example, some pollsters might include this type of question. "What is the most important problem you face today?" This type of question gives the respondent much more flexibility in answering questions and including information the researcher might not include in a list of responses. This question allows the respondent to provide his or her opinions about economic, education, health, and neighborhood safety issues. In the closed-ended question, the researcher might ask, "Which of the following economic problems are of most concern to you?" The researcher then would provide a short list of economic problems. Therefore, the list of responses might limit the respondent's answers.

Open-ended questions are often followed by more open-ended questions. For example, after a respondent provides the answer to the question listed above, the most important problem facing the respondent, the researcher could ask: "Why is this problem a concern to you?" Or the researcher could ask: "How might this problem be solved?" These types of questions give the respondent opportunity to provide many difficult comments. Some of the respondents might provide information that the researcher had not initially considered.

The major limitation to the open-ended question is the difficulty in coding or grouping responses into meaningful categories. To analyze and form some conclusions about the data, similar responses must eventually be grouped together. Researchers might make errors in grouping similar responses. Open-ended questions typically take participants more time to complete; therefore, the researcher might include fewer questions in the survey. Respondents also tend to give little or no response to open-ended questions. They may not know how to answer them and may not be able to conceptualize response categories.

CLOSED-ENDED QUESTIONS

A *closed-ended question* relies on a limited or fixed number of response options, and respondents must select one of the answers from the list of options. There are no options for respondents to create their own response. For example, one question might ask, "About how many times, during the past six months, have you visited a dentist?" You might list response options as "none, once, twice, three times, four times, five or more, and don't know/don't remember." You will notice that these response options are inclusive. This list of response options includes all possible answers a respondent could give. Here is another example: "Did you vote in the last presidential election?" The response options could be listed as "yes" or "no," "don't remember," or "refused." Again, these response options are inclusive. There are no other response options to consider. Many questions seeking a respondent's demographic information are typically closed-ended. "What is the highest level of education you have completed?" The response options could be "none, less than high school, some high school, completed high school, some college, college degree, some graduate education, graduate degree, don't know/refused." These response options also are inclusive.

Closed-ended questions are much easier to manage than open-ended questions. They also provide data that are easier to analyze. A respondent selects the appropriate answer and the answer is recorded. The researcher then tabulates the responses and statistically analyzes the data. However, respondents might also experience frustration with the limited number of responses. Sometimes respondents feel forced to respond to categories that do not include a response they want to provide. In some questionnaires, the researcher might list "other" as an option. The "other" response option is intended to provide an opportunity for the respondent to include an answer that is not listed. Many polling companies prefer to use closed-ended questions. Most scales are created for closed-ended questions.

Closed-ended questions must include response options that are mutually exclusive. This means that when you list the response options to each question, each response option must be exclusive of the other answers. Respondents must be able to select an answer that stands alone from all of the other answers. For example, the following age categories are mutually exclusive: less than 18 years of age, 18 to 24 years; 25 to 34 years; 35 to 44 years; 45 to 54 years; 55 to 64 years; and 65 years and older. These age categories are also inclusive. The list of age categories will include the respondent's age and only one age category will be selected.

SURVEY DATA

After data are collected, researchers conduct a thorough analysis of the data and draw conclusions about what the data mean. In some studies, researchers report the number of respondents who selected a specific answer to each question. They might report the data as a percentage of all of the responses to a specific question. For example, researchers might report that of the 850 respondents in a telephone survey of registered voters, 610 respondents preferred candidate Smith over candidate Brown. In this example, the researchers might also report that about 72 percent of the registered voters who responded to this question preferred candidate Smith.

Researchers also might report the mean scores of responses. For example, if respondents were asked to rate their favorite movie on a scale of one to seven, with one being poor and seven being excellent, the researcher might represent these ratings with a mean score. If you know the mean score for each movie, then you can rate them in order of preference. Maybe the mean score for one movie is 5.7, while the mean score for another movie is 4.6. The movie with the highest mean score is the most preferred movie. Some researchers might want to compare these two mean scores by respondents' gender, age, race, and/or income. How did males rate the movies compared to ratings provided by females? In this example, researchers would use special statistical formulas to determine whether an observed difference between male and female mean ratings reflects a population-level difference. Some of these statistical comparisons can be made with only specific types of data. Certain statistical formulas use only numbers and percentages, while others use mean scores. Therefore, to determine the appropriate data analysis, researchers must know the type of data used in each scale of measurement. Researchers typically use four scales of measurement: nominal, ordinal, interval, and ratio.

NOMINAL DATA

The lowest scale of measurement, from a statistical point of view, is a nominal scale. In a nominal scale, data are simply placed into categories or classes without any order, value, or structure. The classes or categories are listed so that all possible response options are mutually exclusive and collectively exhaustive. For example, if you asked a respondent to list his or her sex, you would provide three possible answers: male, female, and refused. You would assign a number to each of the response options. The number you assign to each of these response options serves as a numerical "identification" of the respondent's sex. You might assign the number one to "male," the number two to "female," and the number three to "refused."

Q: What is your sex or gender? Please place a check mark beside the appropriate answer.

1. ____ Male
2. ____ Female
3. ____ Refused

Nominal scales of measurement have no specific order and no answer is more important than another. Therefore, you might actually reverse the order of numbers in the response options and report the same results. The number three could be assigned to "refused," the number two to "male," and the number one to "female." The numbers used to identify the classes and categories of responses are arbitrary labels assigned to response options. Nominal data do not have characteristics of order, distance, or origin. No mean scores may be calculated from nominal data. What would it indicate if the mean scores for respondents' sex was 1.4? The mean score has no value to the researcher.

Another example of nominal scales of measurement would be categories that describe respondents' demographic information such as age, race, and level of education. You might categorize age into groups of ages. However, if you asked respondents their age, without these categories, then age becomes ratio data. The respondent simply records his or her age in years without a listing of age categories. Ratio data will be covered later in this chapter.

The scale listed here is a nominal scale; however, it also has the characteristics of an ordinal level of measurement.

Q: Which category of ages listed below best describes your current age? Please place a check mark beside the appropriate answer.

1. ____ Less than 18 years of age
2. ____ 18–34 years of age
3. ____ 35–44 years of age
4. ____ 45–54 years of age
5. ____ 55–64 years of age
6. ____ 65 years of age and older
7. ____ Refused or don't know.

Nominal scales of measurement also might include response options for a respondent's brand of automobile, college attended, favorite brand of hair spray, favorite brand of toothpaste, state of residence, city of residence, and political party affiliation. Any question with response options of "yes," "no," "don't know," and "refused" is a nominal scale of measurement. However, to enter the data, researchers arbitrarily assign a number to each of the response options so the responses can be accurately tabulated.

While cross-tabulations with a chi-square are more advanced statistical programs used to analyze nominal data, researchers typically report nominal data as the number of respondents who select each of the response options (frequency), the percentage of each response option as a proportion of all responses (percentages), and which response option was selected most frequently (mode).

ORDINAL DATA

Ordinal scales of measurement provide an order of attributes or characteristics. Ordinal data report the order or rank of responses from the smallest to the greatest, best to the worst, or first to last. Ordinal data provide opportunities for researchers to define attributes or characteristics in an ordered sequence. For example, if you were running a race, there would be one runner who finishes first, one second, one third, and so on. If you were running a mile race, you could win by ten seconds ahead of the second place finisher. Yet, the second place finisher could be ahead of the third place finisher by only one second, but the order they finished would suggest that one individual finished first, one second, and one third. So the distance between each of the top three runners might not be the same, but they would complete the race in an order of first, second, and third. The same type of ranking occurs in most sporting events and other types of competition. One team is the top rated team and others follow. However, the distance or the spacing between each of the teams or individuals in a race may not be uniform. There is no uniform or objective distance between any two points on a subjective scale. In team sports, the first team could have a record of twelve wins and one loss. The second place team could have a record of eight wins and five losses and the third place team could have a record of seven wins and six losses. The first team is far ahead of the second place team, but the second place team is only one win and one loss ahead of the third place team.

In ordinal scales of measurement, researchers may report the number of respondents who selected each of the response options and/or report the number as percentages of the total number of responses. Because only order is implied, ordinal scales of measurement determine central tendencies of mode and median statistics. The mode is the response option that is selected most frequently and the median is the middle response along an ordered continuum or list of all responses.

A *Likert scale* is one of the most popular ordinal scales of measurement typically used by researchers. It measures respondents' level of agreement or disagreement with a *statement*—not a question. Respondents cannot agree or disagree with a question. The Likert scale is an ordered, one-dimensional scale from which respondents choose one option that best represents their opinion. However, some researchers will modify or customize the Likert scale for specific research projects to collect interval data. Other Likert-type scales will be discussed later in this chapter.

In an ordinal scale of measurement, the responses have an order or a systematic sequence from a strong level of disagreement to a strong level of agreement. There is a continuum from one extreme to another. For example, the illustration in Exhibit 14.2 asks respondents to indicate their level of agreement with characteristics of a restaurant.

Additional questions could be included in the restaurant survey to cover all characteristics of food, service, and facilities that measure excellence. However, in the examples in Exhibit 14.2, the statements do not describe "why" a respondent was or was not pleased with the service or food. The data in an ordinal scale will only measure whether respondents were or were not pleased with the food or service. Additional questions would need to be developed to determine "why" respondents were or were not satisfied with the food or service.

The number below each response option in Exhibit 14.2 is used as an example for

Exhibit 14.2

Ordinal Scale of Measurement—Example

Please select your level of agreement with the following statements about our restaurant.

Q: I was pleased with the service.

Strongly disagree	Somewhat disagree	Neither agree nor disagree	Somewhat agree	Strongly agree
1	2	3	4	5

Q: I was pleased with the quality of my food.

Strongly disagree	Somewhat disagree	Neither agree nor disagree	Somewhat agree	Strongly agree
1	2	3	4	5

data entry purposes only. The number representing each response option is arbitrarily assigned to the response option. The numbers might be reversed without affecting the value of the scale. If a respondent selects "somewhat agree," the number 4 listed below the response option is entered into the computer or spreadsheet to represent the response of "somewhat agree." In many scales, the numbers would not be included on the questionnaire. The appropriate number representing the response selected by the survey participants is identified at the time of data entry. Even though the numerical difference between the rating of "strongly disagree" (option 1) and "somewhat disagree" (option 2) is equal to the difference between the rating of "somewhat agree" (option 4) and "strongly agree," (option 5), we cannot say the difference in overall levels of agreement between the first and second levels of agreement equals the difference in the fourth and fifth levels of agreement. The terms are only indexes of measurement. The survey is measuring the response option or level of agreement that is most preferred by respondents.

A Likert scale also may be used with a series of statements listed in a horizontal fashion (Exhibit 14.3). This example is called a Horizontal Likert scale. Respondents would read each question, select a number that corresponds with their level of agreement to the statement, and record the appropriate number beside the statement. The numbers listed in this Likert scale are arbitrarily assigned to the response options to identify the respondent's level of agreement with each statement and should not be used to calculate the sum or mean for each of the statements.

A *forced-ranking scale* is used to determine respondents' preferences for products, brands, or political candidates. In example Exhibit 14.4, respondents are asked to rank their preferences for golf clubs. Respondents would place the number 1 beside the brand of golf club they prefer the most, the number 2 beside their second choice, and so on.

INTERVAL DATA

The standard survey rating scale is an interval scale. An interval scale is a linear scale of measurement in which the distance or interval between all the integers along the

Exhibit 14.3

Horizontal Likert Scale

Please select a number from the scale listed below that matches your level of agreement or disagreement with each statement. Write the number on the corresponding line to the right of the statement.

Scale

1 = Strongly Agree
2 = Agree
3 = Neither Agree nor Disagree
4 = Disagree
5 = Strongly Disagree

1. People who burn the American flag should be put in prison. _____
2. The United States is spending too much money on the war in Iraq. _____
3. Democracy is not the best form of government for some countries. _____
4. Demonstrations against the war in Iraq are mainly publicity stunts. _____
5. The United States should withdraw all military personnel from Iraq. _____
6. The United States should use nuclear weapons against Iraq. _____

1. The Obama stimulus package has benefited the banks in my town. _____
2. The Obama stimulus package has created more jobs in my town. _____
3. The United States has a better economy with Obama than with Bush. _____
4. Former President Bush's economy plan was better than President Obama's. _____
5. The Dow Jones/stock market should be under the federal government's control. _____
6. President Obama's health plan is good for all Americans. _____

Exhibit 14.4

Forced Rankings

Please rank each brand of golf driver listed below in your order of preference. For your most preferred brand of driver, place the number 1 in the blank space located on the left hand side. For your second most preferred brand of driver, place the number 2 in the blank. Continue to rank each brand of driver until you have filled all of the blanks.

_____ Callaway
_____ Cleveland
_____ King Cobra
_____ Nike
_____ Ping
_____ TaylorMade
_____ Titleist

scale is equal. Thus, the distance or interval is the same along a continuum from the extreme point at one end to the extreme point at the other end. The days of a week might be viewed as an interval scale.

Researchers report the frequencies and percentages of responses to nominal and ordinal scales of measurement, while interval data might also be reported as frequencies and percentages plus mean scores. Therefore, researchers conclude that interval scales of measurement provide stronger data. Researchers might compare mean

Exhibit 14.5

Examples of Semantic Differentials

The semantic differential listed below uses a scale of 1–7.

Q1: Please check the appropriate space below that reflects your opinion about the quality of your college education.

Good								Bad
	1	2	3	4	5	6	7	

Q2: Please check the appropriate space below that reflects your opinion about the quality of your college education.

Good								Bad
	+3	+2	+1	0	−1	−2	−3	

Q3: Please rate political candidate Smith's character. (Honesty would be only one of several characteristics.)

Dishonest								Honest
	1	2	3	4	5	6	7	

scores of one group of respondents (male) to the mean scores of another group of respondents (female) using statistical tests called the t-test, analysis of variance, and factor analysis. A t-test compares two mean scores, while analysis of variance and factor analysis compare three or more mean scores.

The *semantic differential* is an interval scale that uses pairs of adjectives in a simple way to measure respondents' attitudes about a multitude of topics. Researchers use semantic differentials to measure respondents' attitude development and change about mass media programs, occupations, political parties, organizations, religions, and local governmental and educational issues. A semantic differential measures people's perceptions or reactions to stimulus words and concepts. Respondents are asked to rate their perceptions of concepts using bipolar scales of adjectives. The semantic differential can be used with adults or children from a variety of cultures and societies. Examples of simple semantic differentials are illustrated in Exhibit 14.5. These three examples include only one pair of adjectives. However, at least eight pairs of adjectives are typically used to measure a concept.

In selecting adjectives, certain procedures should be followed to maximize the relevance of the data and to make it meaningful. The standard and essential procedure for selecting the adjectives is to conduct a pilot study from a sample of respondents. The respondents should list the most common adjectives they use to describe the concept you are measuring. Once the relevant adjectives are selected, the researcher must then determine the antonyms for each adjective. Some antonyms seem to be quite obvious. For example, the antonym for entertaining might be boring. Other antonym examples might be impatient for patient, uneducated for educated, unkind for kind and unreliable for reliable. Researchers must develop a list of adjectives for each study. Depending on the target audience, the meaning of adjectives for measuring the same concepts could be different.

After you have selected the bi-polar adjectives you will use in your study, you must develop response options. Some researchers prefer a five-point scale, some a seven-point scale and others a nine-point scale. While the number of response options may vary among researchers, most prefer an odd number of options. They want a central or neutral position for respondents who have not developed a definite attitude about the topic. The five-point scale is perceived to have a narrow window of assessing attitude and the nine-point scale is too broad to grade evaluations. Respondents often become confused and lose their perception for rating concepts when they have more than seven rating options. Therefore, the seven-point scale is the most preferred scale of measurement.

A simple semantic differential may be used to measure your opinion about the quality of education you received at your college (Exhibit 14.5, Q1). You would select the number along the scale that represents your opinion about the quality of education you received. A rating of 1 would suggest that your education was very good, while a rating of 7 would suggest that the quality of education you received was very bad. If you select a rating of 4, this means that you are neutral about the quality of education you received.

Some semantic differentials use a central zero to illustrate neutrality. An example of a central zero for neutrality is listed in Exhibit 14.5, Q2. Typically, the central position marked 0 is labeled "neutral," the 1 positions are labeled "slightly," the 2 positions "quite," and the 3 positions "extremely."

Respondents might be asked to rate a political candidate on a number of personality features. The candidate's honesty could be measured using a semantic differential scale. The scaling form might include a scale similar to the one in Exhibit 14.5, Q3.

Respondents might indicate whether they think the candidate is extremely honest or dishonest by marking the respective spaces at the extreme ends of the scale (1 or 7), or whether they have not formed an opinion by marking space number 4, a neutral position between the two extremes. You might develop a list of adjectives that are synonyms and antonyms of honesty. Instead of asking respondents to rate honesty on one scale, you might ask respondents to rate several characteristics that are related to honesty.

The semantic differential scale in Exhibit 14.6 consists of eight pairs bipolar adjectives or characteristics that might describe a customer's opinion about two competing hotels. To avoid any bias, the adjectives or characteristics are randomly listed so that the negative or positive adjectives are not always on the left-hand or right-hand side of the scale. Respondents are asked to select one of the seven categories that best describes his or her views about the customer's experiences at hotels. Response values are usually assigned a 1 for the extreme negative adjective and a 7 for the extreme positive adjective. However, the order of these numerical assignments might be reversed. To determine the overall attitude about the object, the researcher sums the responses for each adjective pair and calculates a mean. In Exhibit 14.6, the mean score for each pair of adjectives represents the respondent's view of the object being

Exhibit 14.6   **Semantic Differential—Measuring Hotel Experiences**

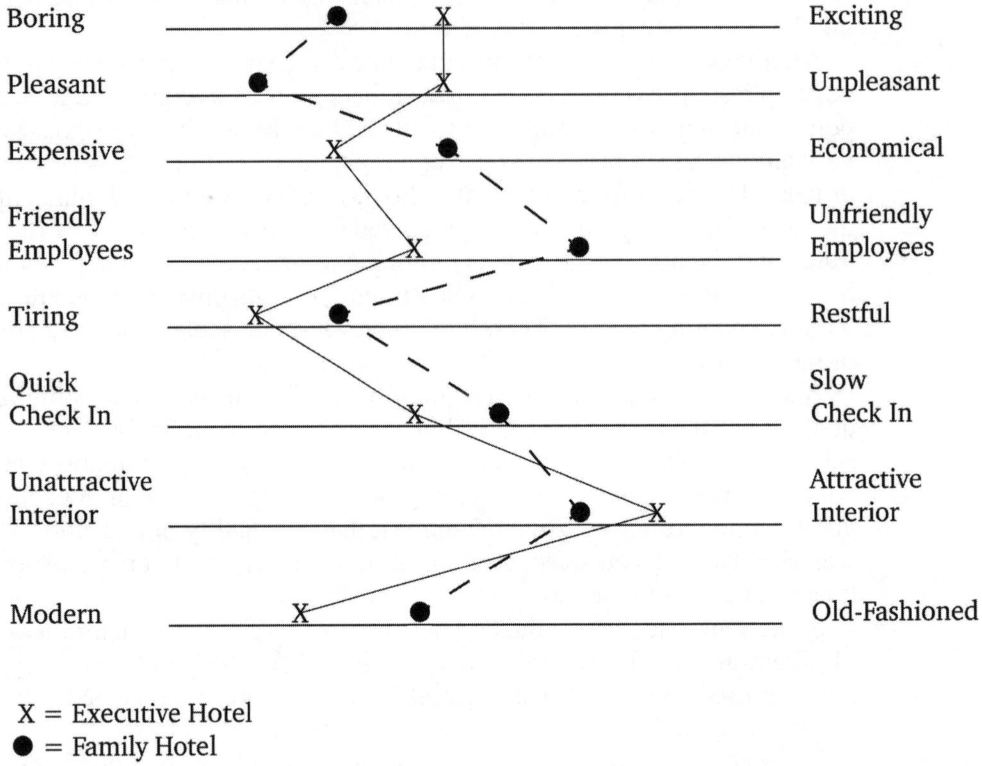

X = Executive Hotel
● = Family Hotel

evaluated. However, before summing the responses, the researcher must reverse the individual scale items when necessary so that each scale lists the values of the response options from positive to negative or from negative to positive for all response options in the same order. The solid dot and "X" are pictorial representations of the mean scores for each adjective pair for each hotel.

Another good example of an interval scale is the thermometer scale for temperature (Exhibit 14.7). The thermometer scale has equal distances on its scale that represent equal differences in temperature, but it does not have a true zero. Researchers using the thermometer scale must not assume that a temperature of 30 degrees is not twice as warm as one of 15 degrees.

In the behavioral sciences, such as advertising and public relations, a true interval scale of measurement is used very rarely. Many researchers use a Likert-type scale to develop modified ordinal scales of measurement that might be used as interval scales of measurement. Researchers suggest that the response options in the examples (see Exhibit 14.8) are equidistant between each integer and should be treated as interval data. Therefore, marketing researchers use this Likert-type scale to measure interval data. In this example, researchers wanted to measure respondents' opinions about neighborhood safety. They used a "Likert-type" scale. The difference between a

Exhibit 14.7 **Thermometer Scale**

Please mark an (x) on the line beside the thermometer that best describes how you feel about the quality of health care you received in the hospital. The lowest line is poor and the top line is excellent.

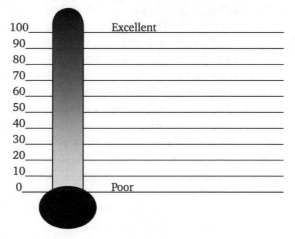

Exhibit 14.8

Likert-Type Scales (Linear)

Please rate your level of agreement with the following statements. If you strongly agree with the statement, select a number on the scale on the far right side and write the number in the blank beside the corresponding statement. If you strongly disagree with the statement, select a number on the scale on the far left side. If you feel that your agreement is between the extremes, select a number from the center of the scale.

Rating Scale

Strongly Disagree	1	2	3	4	5	6	7	Strongly Agree

1. I feel safe in my neighborhood at night.   _____
2. I am afraid to answer the door at night.   _____
3. I do not walk in my neighborhood at night.   _____
4. There is less crime in my neighborhood than in other neighborhoods in my city.   _____
5. I think police should patrol my neighborhood more frequently.   _____

score of 2 and a score of 3 would represent the same difference in opinion as would a difference between a score of 6 and a score of 7.

RATIO DATA

A ratio scale of measurement is the highest level of measurement; however, ratio scales are not often used in social research. A ratio scale of measurement is very similar to the interval scale of measurement, and some researchers even label both interval and ratio scales of measurement as continuous scales. The best way to explain or compare interval and ratio scales of measurement is to look at temperature. The Centigrade scale has a zero point but it is an arbitrary point. The zero is selected because that is the point that water freezes. Therefore, zero in the Centigrade scale of measurement is not the absence of temperature but a temperature or point where water freezes. The Fahrenheit scale has an equivalent point of freezing at 32 degrees. The Fahrenheit scale also has a zero point but it also is not without temperature. The temperature is low, but it does have some level of temperature. So, even though temperature looks as if it would be a ratio scale, it is an interval scale. The single major difference between the two scales is that a ratio scale has a true zero point. The simplest examples of ratio scales of measurement are height, weight, age, and length. Height, weight, age, and length all have a characteristic of zero measurement. Therefore, you are allowed to make statements and comparisons of ratios among ratio scaled variables. When comparing ratio data, you might state that a person six feet tall is twice as tall as a person who is three feet tall. Or, you might conclude that someone who weighs 200 pounds is twice as heavy as someone who weighs 100 pounds. This ratio holds true regardless of whether the object is being measured in meters, feet, or yards.

SCALE COMBINATIONS

Some scales combine the features and characteristics of different scales. The *fixed-sum scale* uses some characteristics of nominal, ordinal, and interval scales to report the proportions of responses from a list of options. For example, you might ask respondents, "Of the last 10 times you ate a hamburger, how many times did you eat one of the hamburgers listed below?" The total number of times you ate one of the hamburgers must total 10 (Exhibit 14.9). The data can be reported as percentages by dividing each value listed beside the respective hamburger by 10. The percentages should total 100 percent.

The *multiple-rating list* is another scale of measurement that combines characteristics of different scales. The multiple-rating list includes a list of product or service features and interval scale characteristics (Exhibit 14.10). The researcher might list a number of features on one side of the questionnaire and ask respondents to rate the performance or value of each feature using an interval-type scale. In this example, respondents have just shopped at a department store and are asked to rate the various areas of the department store for cleanliness, and so forth, using a scale of one to seven, where a rating of one means the feature is very poor and a rating of seven means that the feature is excellent. The responses from all survey participants might then be summed and a mean score calculated for each feature or characteristic.

NONVERBAL SCALES

All of the scales we have discussed have included verbal and numeric characteristics. Some market researchers may need to survey young children who do not read well or members

Exhibit 14.9

Fixed Summed Scale

Of the last ten times you ate a hamburger, how many times did you eat a hamburger at:

McDonald's	_____ times
Burger King	_____ times
Wendy's	_____ times
Dairy Queen	_____ times
Sonic	_____ times
Whataburger	_____ times
Total =	10 times

(Please make the total equal 10.)

Exhibit 14.10

Multiple Rating List

Please rate each area of a department store listed below on the area's cleanliness, product displays, staff friendliness, and product variety. Select a number from the scale and write it in the corresponding blank space. (Place a zero in the blank space if you don't know.)

Scale

Don't know	Very Poor						Excellent
0	1	2	3	4	5	6	7

	Cleanliness	Product displays	Staff friendliness	Product variety
Children's Clothes	_____	_____	_____	_____
Men's Clothes	_____	_____	_____	_____
Women's Clothes	_____	_____	_____	_____
Kitchen Appliances	_____	_____	_____	_____
Jewelry	_____	_____	_____	_____
Furniture	_____	_____	_____	_____

of a target population who are not literate in the researcher's native language. In other situations, some prospective survey respondents might be illiterate and not able to read very well. Therefore, researchers must develop additional methods for collecting data for this target population. *Nonverbal scales* of measurement are typically used to collect data from children and respondents with little reading ability or poor language skills.

Nonverbal scales might include pictures of drinking glasses filled with water, happy faces, stairs, or ladders (Exhibit 14.11). The scales usually have five variations of the picture representing different levels of feelings, opinions, or preferences. Each picture represents a feeling or an opinion from one extreme position of a continuum to the other extreme position. The pictures are assigned a number from one through five with the number three representing a neutral position. The pictures represent ordinal data along a continuum from less to more or from low to high.

Exhibit 14.11   **Nonverbal Scales—Picture and Graphic Scales**

Happy and Sad Faces
A. Please mark (x) on the face that best describes how you feel about your job.

Bottle Scale
B. Please draw a circle around the bottle that best describes how you feel about your career opportunities. The empty bottle means there is no opportunity for you.

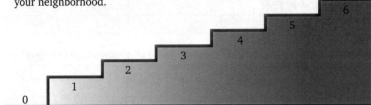

Stair-step Scale
C. Please mark (x) on the stair-step that best describes your opinion about the crime in your neighborhood. The lowest stair-step means there is no crime in your neighborhood and the top stair-step means the crime is very high in your neighborhood.

Advertising and public relations researchers most often read the questions to respondents and then ask them to select one of the figures in the nonverbal scale that best represents their feeling or opinion. For example, if a respondent selected the face with a large frown, the respondent would disagree with the statement or would have a negative opinion about the topic, item, or issue. If the face with a big smile were selected, then the respondent would agree or have a very positive attitude about the statement, topic, or issue. A face with no expression would represent a neutral position. The same analogy represents the drinking glasses with water. If the respondent chose the glass that is filled, he or she would have a positive opinion about the topic. The glass that is empty represents a negative position.

Researchers arbitrarily assign numbers to each picture. The corresponding numbers for each respective response are summed and analyzed for each picture. The responses for each picture are reported as ordinal data such as frequencies, percentages, and modes.

SUMMARY

Advertising and public relations researchers use survey research to *explore, describe,* and/or *explain* a variety of concepts and behaviors. The measuring instruments must produce accurate information that is reliable and valid. *Reliability* in survey research is the degree of consistency of measuring responses as long as there are no changes in the characteristic being measured. Researchers say that scales of measurement have validity when the scales measure what they are supposed to measure.

Researchers might construct two forms of questions. One form is the open-ended question and the other is the closed-ended question. In the *open-ended question,* the researcher asks a question and the respondent provides an answer using his or her own words. A *closed-ended question* relies on a limited or fixed number of response options and respondents must select one of the answers from the list of options. Some market researchers may need to survey young children who do not read well or members of a target population who are not literate in the researcher's native language. In these cases, researchers use nonverbal scales.

Researchers typically use four scales of measurement: nominal, ordinal, interval, and ratio. The lowest scale of measurement, from a statistical point of view, is a nominal scale.

A nominal scale simply requires the placing of data into categories or classes without any order, value, or structure. Ordinal scales of measurement provide an order of attributes or characteristics. Ordinal data report the order or rank of responses from the smallest to the greatest, best to the worst, or first to last. The standard survey rating scale is an interval scale. An interval scale is a linear scale of measurement in which a certain distance or interval between the integers along the scale is equal. A ratio scale of measurement is very similar to the interval scale of measurement with the major difference between the two scales being that a ratio scale has a true zero point.

DISCUSSION QUESTIONS

1. Discuss why it is important to know when to use different scales of measurement.
2. Discuss the advantages of using interval scales of measurement rather than nominal scales of measurement.
3. If you use data that are not valid in a new advertising campaign for a furniture store, what are some problems you might experience?
4. Identify and explain four examples where data might have reliability but not yield valid data.

EXERCISES

1. Create three closed-ended questions to record respondents' demographic information.
2. Create two Likert scales of measurement and statements to measure respondents' opinions about water conservation.

3. Create a nonverbal scale of measurement not used in this text to measure customer satisfaction for a restaurant.
4. Create a semantic differential scale of measurement with six pairs of adjectives to measure respondents' opinions about a new car.

ADDITIONAL READING

DeVellis, R.F. 2003. *Scale development: Theory and applications.* 2d ed. Thousand Oaks, CA: Sage.
Punch, K.F. 2003. *Survey research: The basics.* London: Sage.
Spector, P.E. 1992. *Summated rating scale construction: An introduction.* Newbury Park, CA: Sage.

15 Question Wording

LEARNING OBJECTIVES

This chapter is intended to help you:

- Learn how to avoid bias in questions;
- Understand how and when to use structured and unstructured questions;
- Learn how to develop simplicity in word selection;
- Learn how to collect accurate information from respondents;
- Learn how to list and group questions.

The purpose of a survey is to collect accurate and valid information from a sample of a population. The instrument used to collect this information is a questionnaire. The quality of the questions used in the questionnaire determines the accuracy of the data and information. Questions are formed by using a series of words in a sequence that survey participants easily understand. Questions must be constructed so the respondent provides information accurately and concisely. To collect accurate information, you should carefully review and pretest the questionnaire for word selection, question development, question order, grouping questions, and branching questions.

QUESTION DEVELOPMENT

The data collected in a survey are only as good or valid as the questions used to obtain the data. Objectives should be written for each questionnaire and each question must contribute to the objectives of the questionnaire. Researchers typically discuss the objectives of the research and then conduct a brainstorming session to explore question alternatives and options. Each question included in the survey must be evaluated and considered in terms of its relationship to the objectives of the survey and other questions. What do you want to know? What is the purpose or objective of your research? Do the questions contribute to the purpose of the research? Each question you consider must be reviewed, evaluated, and refined to meet the objectives of the survey. Review the questions for clarity and simplicity. Even if a questionnaire has been used in a previous survey, the questions should be reviewed and evaluated for your current study. There is no guarantee that the questions used successfully by respondents in previous studies will be understood by a sample of respondents in future studies.

If the questionnaire is divided into different segments, write objectives for each segment of the questionnaire. For example in advertising research, the questionnaire might measure the brand awareness of a product in one segment, use of the product in a second segment, and respondent demographic data in the final segment. In public relations research, the questionnaire might be constructed to measure respondents' opinions about the use of their local taxes to build a new animal shelter in one section, the types of pets they own in another section, and their demographic information in the final section.

WORD SELECTION

The perceived meaning of words can vary among people based on their ethnicity, geographical region, sex, age, nationality, and education. The words you use in a question are the key elements to maximizing data validity and reliability. An example of reliability occurs when every respondent understands a question so clearly that he or she gives the same answer each time the question is asked. Do not assume that respondents know everything about your topic. For example, registered voters may not know the names of all candidates running for various state offices. Therefore, you must determine the respondent's knowledge about the candidates before you ask specific questions about the candidates.

Word *nuances* and *ambiguities* affect the accuracy of the data. Words should be selected with great care. To a great extent, the words you include in a question will determine or influence the response. Use words that seem to have universal meaning and keep the question simple. For example, the following question could cause respondents to answer differently. How frequently do you dine in a restaurant? The question does not specify a consumption period—daily, weekly, or monthly—and it does not define restaurant. Some respondents may consider McDonald's and Burger King as restaurants, while other respondents might not consider these eating places as restaurants. They may assume that a restaurant is a place where a waiter comes to your table and takes your order.

Researchers try to avoid using modifying adjectives and adverbs. Adverbs such as *often, occasionally, seldom, sometimes, rarely,* and *usually* are used in developing questions but do not have a universal meaning among respondents. What is the frequency associated with *often, occasionally, seldom, sometimes, rarely,* and *usually?* Is "often" twice a week or four times a week? These adverbs also are used in some scales to measure and categorize responses to questions. They should be used with caution. The following adjectives do not have universal definitions among respondents: *few, hardly, large, lots, most, majority, minority, many, numerous,* and *several.* Do we agree on the definition of these words? If someone stated that only a "few" people attended the concert, would that mean 1,000 people or 5,000 people? It would depend on the venue of the concert. If 1,000 people attended a concert held in a high school gym, it would most likely be a crowded facility. However, if 5,000 attended a concert in Madison Square Garden, we might suggest that only a few people attended.

Researchers want questions to sound conversational. In some questions, you might want to relax *grammatical standards*. The question could sound too formal or academic. For example, "who" might be appropriate in many instances instead of "whom." "With whom did you go?' is technically correct. However, a better-worded question that sounds more conversational and simple would be "Who went with you?" Here is another example of sounding too formal. "What is the frequency of using your automobile as transportation for traveling to your primary place of employment in the last month?" A more simply worded question would be "About how many times in the last 30 days have you driven to work?"

Avoid *double negatives*. A question that uses double negatives is one that uses two negative words within the same sentence or a series of statements. For example, "Don't you agree that teenagers less than 15 years of age should not drive?" If the respondent replies with an answer of "no," does that mean that the respondent does not disagree or that the respondent thinks that teens less than 15 years of age should be allowed to drive? Remember that the question should be worded so that respondents will know exactly what you are asking.

Double-barreled questions ask two questions but allow only one answer. Look for questions that include the words "and" and "or." These two words are keys to identifying double-barreled questions. For example, "Do you think that the United States should have sent troops to Iraq and should continue its military presence there?" One respondent might answer "yes" to the first question. That would mean that one respondent might agree that the United States should have sent troops to Iraq. A "yes" by another respondent might mean that the United States should continue its presence in Iraq. However, that does not mean that the first or second respondent agrees with both questions. One respondent might have an opinion that the United States should have sent troops to Iraq but should not continue its military presence. Another respondent might believe that the United States should not have sent troops to Iraq, but since the United States did send troops, it should continue its military presence. A simple method for correcting double-barreled questions is to develop two questions instead of one.

A *leading question* influences the respondent's answer by suggesting that there is a more preferred answer to the question. The respondent may find it difficult to disagree with a statement made by someone in authority or one that reflects negatively on the respondent. A leading question might influence respondents to give inaccurate information because they do not want to admit something about themselves that could be viewed negatively.

Survey research is usually sponsored by a company, corporation, individual, or organization. They might want to include questions about their products or services that will result in specific responses. If the research results are positive, they often disseminate a summary of the study to the media or use it in advertising campaigns. They want consumers to believe that the population has a positive opinion about the product or service. For example, "Don't you agree that Sally's Facial Lotion makes you look years younger?" Respondents are led to believe they should agree with this statement. If respondents are users of Sally's Facial Lotion, they are less likely to say that the lotion does not work because they would be using it with no obvious benefit.

Here is another example of a leading question: "Don't you tend to agree that Councilman Smith has more credibility than does Councilman Jones?" There are two major problems with this question. The first part of the question suggests that the respondent should agree that Councilman Smith has more credibility and the word "tend" suggests you might agree without having to take a strong position on credibility. The second problem is the use of the word "credibility." What is credibility? Is credibility about one issue or is this a question about the councilmen's character?

Prestige bias influences responses by suggesting that a well-known person or organization supports one opinion rather than another. For example, a sports celebrity or the U.S. Supreme Court might state an opinion as an authority on a subject. "The U.S. Supreme Count has ruled that a woman may go to a doctor to end a pregnancy at any time during the first three months. Do you favor or oppose this ruling?" A reference to the U.S. Supreme Court might influence a person's opinion because of its reputation as an authority.

A *loaded question* is more subtle than a leading question. The loaded question usually includes a statement about the reason for doing something. For example, "Do you believe that we should recycle plastic containers to save the ecology?" The question is phrased in a way that the respondent who responds negatively would appear to oppose saving the ecology. When the question includes a statement about the benefit or reason for doing something, you should review the question to eliminate the reason. Here is a more objective way for stating the question. "Will recycling plastic containers improve the ecology?"

Loaded questions might also include emotionally charged words such as deadbeats, wife beaters, criminals, or drunk drivers. "Do you agree that drunk drivers involved in a car accidents should have their driver's licenses revoked?"

An *over-demanding recall question* asks respondents to recall something over an extended period of time. The researcher might assume that respondents have the ability to recall information from a time, an event, a behavior, or an experience that occurred a long time ago. For example, "How many cups of coffee did you drink last month?" If you don't drink coffee, the question is quite reasonable. However, if you have several cups of coffee throughout the day, the question requests the respondent to estimate the number of cups of coffee. Also, are all cups of equal size? Or another question, "How many times did you and your spouse date before you got married?" Very few of us could accurately recall this information. Instead of saying they "don't know," the respondent is likely to give a number which may or may not be accurate.

QUESTION ORDER

The order of questions might create questionnaire bias. A question included in the questionnaire during the early stages of the interview might influence the respondent's answers to questions later in the survey. Interesting and simple questions are listed at the beginning of the questionnaire. A respondent may question how his or her responses will be used. By listing the interesting and simple questions at the beginning, the respondent is more likely to be convinced that he or she is capable of completing the questionnaire.

Simple and interesting questions build respondent momentum and confidence to continue. Respondents completing a self-administered questionnaire might scan the first few questions to determine whether they have any interest in completing the questionnaire. If they are not interested, they will not complete the questionnaire and your response rate will decrease. List questions in a logical order so that you present questions seeking general information first followed by questions seeking more specific information. For example, a simple question could inquire about the respondent's qualifications to participate. You might want to survey only a male in the household between the ages of 18 to 35 years with a child, registered voters, users of specific products, or working women. Here is another example: You might ask questions about the problems related to teen pregnancy before asking respondents to identify problems or issues faced by teens. Respondents will be more likely to name teen pregnancy in a subsequent question about issues or problems teens face than they would have without having seen teen pregnancy mentioned in the previous question.

More difficult or sensitive questions are included later in the survey and minimize the respondent's frustration and anger. Difficult or personal questions might cause the respondent to feel threatened or become frustrated and terminate the survey. Personal and confidential questions about the respondent's religion, political preferences, bank accounts, and income should be placed toward the end of the survey. Questions seeking demographic information about the respondent are classified as sensitive questions.

A simple method for asking sensitive questions is to develop categories of responses. For example, you might ask respondents to select the income category that best describes their annual income—"less than $10,000, $10,000 to $24,999, $25,000 to $39,999, $40,000 to $59,999, $60,000 to $74,999; or $75,000 or more." The categories you select for sensitive questions will depend on the audience you are surveying. If you know the sample is likely to be lower income respondents, then you will create more income categories in the lower income range. If you know the sample is likely to be higher income respondents, then you will create more income categories in the higher income range. Response categories to questions regarding age and education might be created using similar methods.

In a telephone or personal interview survey, the researcher reads the questions to the respondent. The researcher gives the respondent his or her name, explains the purpose or topic of the survey, and describes how the respondent was selected. In self-administered surveys, the introductions include information about the topic of the survey, how the respondent was selected, identification of the researcher or company conducting the survey, and instructions on how to complete the questionnaire. In a mail survey, the researcher includes a letter providing instructions about when and how to return the completed questionnaire. Electronic surveys will include information about when the questionnaire should be completed. In all surveys, the introduction should be brief, simple, and clearly stated.

GROUPING QUESTIONS

The questionnaire typically is divided into three parts: introduction, body, and conclusion. Each of these parts has a specific function and contributes to the validity of the questionnaire. The body of the questionnaire includes the questions for collecting information or data. The number of questions included in the body of the questionnaire will vary depending on the purpose of the survey and could range from as few as fifteen to as many as one hundred. For longer questionnaires, it is necessary to group questions into sections. By grouping the questions, you simplify the answering process for respondents.

Questionnaires usually include multiple sections of instructions and questions. Questions may be grouped together by topic, scale type, or a combination of both. Any of these methods is appropriate for collecting valid data. The method you choose will depend on the purpose of your survey and your target population. Respondents can more easily follow instructions and provide accurate information when questions are grouped together. Questions are arranged in an order and grouped much like a conversation. When you talk with someone, you might talk about several different topics in your conversation; however, most of your conversation will focus on one topic at a time. Questionnaires that group questions tend to have a higher response rate.

An advertising survey questionnaire might be divided into several topics. For example, the topics might be about the respondent's *awareness* of a product or *purchasing behavior,* the respondent's *image* of the product, the respondent's *lifestyle,* and the respondent's *demographic* profile. By grouping questions, respondents are more likely to follow the logic of the questions. By grouping questions, interviewers save time when the interviewer reads the questions to the respondent and researchers save space for self-administered printed questionnaires. For example, you might group questions that measure a respondent's awareness of a specific product brand. "What are the brand names for X product?" "What are other brands for that product?" Another section could group questions that measure the respondent's purchase behavior. "Have you ever purchased brand X?" "What brand do you purchase?" "If the store stocked only one brand of product X, what brand would you prefer?" Questions about the image of the product could be grouped into another section. "Which brand is the most durable?" "Which brand is the most economical?" A fourth section might include questions about the respondent's lifestyle. Lifestyle questions may seek information about the respondent's recreational activities, frequency of travel, and restaurant preferences. The final section may include questions about the respondent's age, sex, income, education level, and race.

Researchers should provide instructions and explanations at the beginning of each section. For example, a statement preceding a section might state: "For the following section, please tell me whether you are aware of or familiar with the following products and brands." Similar statements might be couched in appropriate language for each additional section.

Questions also might be grouped according to their scaling techniques and result in the same benefits as those for grouping questions by topic—ease of following questions, time saved in responding to questions, and space saved in self-administered or printed questionnaires. Each time you change scaling techniques, explanations and directions must be provided to the respondent. Therefore, it is practical and efficient to reduce the frequency of explaining the scaling methods, group similar scales together within a section, and provide a format that is easy for the respondent to follow.

Researchers might use multiple types of scales in one questionnaire to measure responses. Some questionnaires may include Likert scales, semantic differential scales, ordinal scales, interval scales, or several other scales for measuring responses. For example, you might want to measure respondents' level of agreement or disagreement with a series of statements. In this case, you would use a Likert scale. "Please indicate your level of agreement with each of the following statements. We will use a scale of one to five, where one means that you strongly disagree with the statement, two means you disagree, three means you neither agree nor disagree, four means agree, and five means that you strongly agree with the statement." Some researchers include a "Don't Know" response option. As you can see, if you had to read this statement for 10 to 15 statements scattered throughout the questionnaire, you would consume a lot of time and the respondent may become confused about which scale to use.

Researchers also might group questions using both grouping methods—topics and scaling techniques. Within one section of the questionnaire, you might include questions to measure a respondent's use of a product. For some questions within that section, you might decide that questions should be grouped according to topic. You might group several questions about the performance of the product such as its durability, the frequency of use, how the product was used, and others who used the product. Then questions might be grouped by the scales you use to measure the respondent's level of satisfaction with the product. For example, you could use a Likert scale with a series of statements about the respondent's level of agreement with these statements and about the respondent's level of satisfaction with the product. View the questionnaire as an outline to move from one section or group of questions to another so that the conversation flows smoothly without confusion.

BRANCHING OR CONTINGENCY

Questionnaires are designed to move respondents from one question to another. Some questionnaires will include questions to screen or limit responses only to those who are qualified to respond. Qualified respondents are people who have the knowledge to answer questions accurately. The method of skipping certain questions is called *branching* or *contingency questions*. A branching question will branch to another question that is relevant to the respondent. A contingency question is one where subsequent questions are contingent on responses to the first question. Both terms accomplish the same purpose. In this chapter, we will refer to the process of skipping questions as branching.

Branching questions skip forward only and not backward. Electronic and telephone surveys provide skips automatically if the respondent is not qualified to answer subsequent questions. Instructions for the skipping process in self-administered questionnaires might include two types of instructions. Depending on the respondent's answer, the instructions might state that the respondent should skip only one question. For example, the instructions following question 10 might direct the respondent to "skip question 11." If the respondent is supposed to skip several questions, the instructions following question 10 might direct the respondent to "Go to question 24."

Exhibit 15.1

Example of a Branching Question

Q10:   Have you purchased a new pair of shoes within the past six months?

( ) Yes
( ) No (If no, go to Question 18)

Exhibit 15.2

Example of a Conditional Branching Question

Q21:   Did you vote in the last presidential election?
( ) Yes
( ) No (If no, skip question 22)

Q22:   If yes, for whom did you vote?
( ) Obama
( ) McCain
( ) Others

There are two types of branching questions: conditional and unconditional. Respondents answer subsequent questions based on the condition they were qualified to answer the questions. For example, a conditional branching question might state, "Have you purchased a new pair of shoes within the past six months?" If the respondent has not purchased a new pair of shoes, then you would instruct the respondent to skip all of the questions that might relate to the respondent's process of making decisions about which stores to visit and the types of shoes he or she purchased.

The same process of skipping questions might be used in a survey about political races. "Did you vote in the last presidential election?" The next question might ask the respondent for whom he or she voted. Therefore, if the answer was "No" the respondent did not vote, then he or she would not answer the next question.

Branching also might be used with other measurement scales. For example, the question in Exhibit 15.3 includes a list of fast-food restaurants the respondent might select with "Go to" instructions. If the respondent chose McDonald's, he or she would then "Go to" question number 15.

A respondent's rating on an interval scale might include instructions to "Go to" other questions based the rating he or she gave to a specific question. For example, the question in Exhibit 15.4 asks respondents to rate their level of satisfaction with the city council.

Unconditional branching will direct all respondents who select a specific answer to go around or branch to a new set of questions. Unconditional branching is a directive to all respondents to a particular question to "Go to" another question. There are no conditions and instructions about "if" you selected a specific response. We will use the example about fast-food restaurants. Respondents who selected McDonald's would be instructed to "Go to" question number 15. After completing questions 15 through 19, respondents would then be instructed to "Go to" question 40. They would

Exhibit 15.3

Example of an Unconditional Branching Question

Q10: Which of the following fast-food restaurants do you most often dine at?

_____	McDonald's	(Go to Question 15)
_____	Burger King	(Go to Question 20)
_____	Wendy's	(Go to Question 25)
_____	Sonic	(Go to Question 30)
_____	None	(Go to Question 35)

Exhibit 15.4

Another Type of Unconditional Branching Question

For the next few questions, I will ask you to rate your overall level of satisfaction with the city council. Please use a scale of 1–7 with 1 being not satisfied at all, 4 represents a neutral level of satisfaction, and 7 being extremely satisfied.

Q15: Please rate your overall level of satisfaction with the city council.

Not at all satisfied	1	2	3	4	5	6	7	Extremely satisfied

Instructions: If the answer to question 15 is less than 4, then go to question 20.

not answer questions 20 through 39 because they refer to other fast-food restaurants. Consequently, respondents who selected Burger King would "Go to" question 20 and then branch to question 40.

Branching techniques are useful survey tools to collect data from the most qualified respondents. However, each branch might cause a certain amount of uncertainty for the respondent. Respondents completing self-administered questionnaires may become frustrated and confused with too many branching instructions and lose interest in completing the questionnaire. If a questionnaire includes numerous branching questions, you may want to reduce the number of branching questions and screen prospective respondents based on their qualifications to respond.

PRETESTING

After developing, reviewing, and refining the questionnaire, researchers might think that the questionnaire is complete. However, what appears to be a good questionnaire could have both major and minor problems when you implement the survey. You should get some external feedback from someone who represents your population. You should pretest the instrument. Pretesting the questionnaire includes testing its format, word selection, question order, instructions, and question simplicity. Examine all aspects of the questionnaire.

There are several ways to pretest your instrument. You might discuss the questionnaire with other research experts. These research experts may identify problems with your questionnaire that they have experienced with previous surveys. Rely on

Exhibit 15.5

Guidelines for Developing Questionnaires

1. Write objectives for each questionnaire, each section of the questionnaire, and each question. The objectives will provide a guideline for including appropriate questions.
2. Review the questions for clarity and simplicity. Every respondent should understand a question so clearly that he or she gives the same answer each time the question is asked.
3. Use words that seem to have universal meaning and keep the question simple.
4. Use the following adverbs cautiously—*often, occasionally, seldom, sometimes, rarely*, and *usually*.
5. Use the following adjectives cautiously—*few, hardly, large, lots, most, majority, minority, many, numerous*, and *several*.
6. Relax grammatical standards. Make the questions sound conversational.
7. Avoid double negatives. A question that uses double negatives is one that uses two negative words within the same sentence or a series of statements.
8. Avoid double-barreled questions that ask two questions but allow only one answer. Look for questions that include the words "and" and "or."
9. Avoid loaded questions. The loaded question usually includes a statement about the reason for doing something. The loaded question also may include emotionally charged words.
10. Avoid leading questions that influence the respondent by suggesting that there is a preferred answer to the question.
11. Avoid over-demanding recall questions. Respondents have difficulty in recalling behavior or events over a long extended period of time.
12. Include interesting and simple questions at the beginning of the questionnaire. The respondent is more likely to be convinced that he or she is capable of completing the questionnaire.
13. The first question should apply to anyone in the same target population and be easy to answer.
14. More difficult or sensitive questions should be included later in the survey to minimize the respondent's frustration and anger.
15. Group questions by topic, scale type, or a combination of both. Respondents can more easily follow instructions and provide accurate information when questions are grouped together.
16. Branching techniques are useful survey tools to secure data from the most qualified respondents. However, each branch adds a certain amount of confusion for the respondent.
17. Pretest the questionnaire. Pretesting elements include the questionnaire's format, word selection, question order, instructions, and question simplicity.

research experts to give you feedback about the types of questions you are considering in your study and how these questions relate to the objects of your study. These experts also possess a wealth of knowledge about word choices, order of questions, response options, and scales.

Another method of pretesting comes from guided discussions or focus groups. A small group of ten to fifteen people representing a sample of your population will complete the questionnaire and then discuss problems they experienced with the questionnaire. They might provide valuable information about the wording of questions and other problems with the questionnaire that restrict or limit the respondent's ability to answer accurately. You should provide a small incentive to these participants.

Some researchers conduct a pilot study to test the questionnaire. Select a small sample of the target population and make the questionnaire available to them via the appropriate method—mail, telephone, electronic, or personal. To increase the response rate, offer a small financial incentive to be paid to the respondents after they complete the questionnaire and discuss their experience with you. You should set a specific deadline for completing a self-administered pilot questionnaire and then telephone respondents at a predetermined time to discuss problems they may have experienced in responding to the questions. You also might provide a space on the questionnaire for respondents to comment about problems they experienced in completing the questionnaire.

SUMMARY

Questions must be constructed so that the respondent provides information accurately and concisely. Review the questions for clarity and simplicity and then conduct a pretest for the entire questionnaire. Even if a questionnaire has been used in a previous survey, the questions should be reviewed for your current study. If the questionnaire is divided into different segments, write objectives for each segment of the questionnaire.

The perceived meaning of words can vary among people based on their ethnicity, geographical region, sex, age, nationality, and education. The words you use in a question are the key elements for maximizing data validity and reliability. Researchers try to avoid using modifying adjectives and adverbs. Adverbs like *often, occasionally, seldom, sometimes, rarely,* and *usually* are used in developing questions but do not have a universal meaning among respondents. The following adjectives do not have universal definitions among respondents: *few, hardly, large, lots, most, majority, minority, many, numerous,* and *several.* Researchers should avoid *double negatives, double-barreled questions, leading questions, loaded questions,* and questions that require *over-demanding recall.*

The order of questions might create questionnaire bias. A question included in the questionnaire during the early stages of the interview might influence the respondent's answers to following questions. Questionnaires usually include multiple sections of instructions and questions. Questions may be grouped together by topic, scale type, or a combination of both.

DISCUSSION QUESTIONS

1. Discuss the factors that might influence respondents' interpretation of words.
2. Discuss the various meanings of the following words: often, occasionally, seldom, sometimes, rarely, and usually.
3. How does question order and grouping affect or influence answers to questions?

EXERCISES

1. Create a double-barreled question for determining respondents' opinion about a hair product. After you have developed the double-barreled question, then create a better question about a hair product.
2. Create a leading question for determining respondents' opinion about the quality of a cell phone. After you have developed the leading question, then create a better question about the quality of a cell phone.

3. Create a loaded question for determining respondents' opinion about the taste of a soft drink. After you have developed the loaded question, then create a better question about the taste of a soft drink.

4. Create conditional and unconditional branching questions for measuring respondents' opinions about licenses for concealed handguns.

ADDITIONAL READING

Alreck, P., and R. Settle. 2004. *The survey research handbook.* 3d ed. Boston: McGraw-Hill/Irwin.

Babbie, E. 1990. *Survey research methods.* Belmont, CA: Wadsworth.

Converse, J., and S. Presser. 1986. *Survey questions: Handcrafting the standardized questionnaire.* Thousand Oaks, CA: Sage.

Fowler, F. 1995. *Improving survey questions: Design and evaluation.* Thousand Oaks, CA: Sage.

Scott, C., et al. 1988. Verbatim questionnaires versus field translations or schedules: An experimental study. *International Statistical Review,* 56, 259–78.

16 | Interviewer Training

LEARNING OBJECTIVES

This chapter is intended to help you:

- Know what to include in interviewer training;
- Recognize good interview techniques;
- Understand issues of confidentiality;
- Understand interviewer biases.

The key to any advertising and public relations survey research project is to collect accurate and valid data. There are several biases that may create poor and inaccurate data. A few of the biases in data collection may occur when the respondent does not provide accurate information; the sample does not represent the target population; the design of the questionnaire is faulty; and the interviewer influences answers. The interviewer is the key person in making sure that data collection is done without bias. Interviewer bias is often a major contributor to data collection problems. In many studies, the interviewer may not be aware of his or her influence on the respondent's answer. It also is difficult to monitor the interviewer for quality control, especially for in-depth or face-to-face interviews. Therefore, it is essential that telephone and intercept interviewers be thoroughly trained for each and every survey interview situation. Each study has unique problems and issues. Even an experienced interviewer should be trained to recognize specific issues that may arise for each survey interviewing project.

Advertising and public relations survey researchers typically choose between two approaches to collect data from target populations. A researcher might hire a research company or conduct the research in-house. These two approaches may be used in collecting data for all types of interview survey methods including telephone, intercepts, and in-home. Both approaches have some benefits and limitations. There are no set rules to decide which approach you should choose. You should choose the approach that will provide the best quality of data for your specific survey purposes.

When you need to conduct an advertising or public relations national survey, a research company might provide the best service. Some survey research companies maintain multiple offices throughout the country. A research company tends to employ field workers and interviewers on a continuing basis. These employees require less time to train because they are experienced interviewers. Research companies might conduct the survey through one office or they may combine resources and personnel in two or more offices to complete the research project more quickly and efficiently. The research company could assign different regions of the United States to different offices located within their respective region.

A major limitation to using research companies is the lack of quality assurance in the data collection processes. Research companies attempt to provide quality service and monitor the work of interviewers; however, some companies are not well managed and they fail to monitor their interviewers. When quality is not monitored, clients often experience difficulty in identifying errors made in the data collection process. Therefore, you may not know that the quality of work is poor and inaccurate. This might result in making costly decisions based on the data.

When you hire a national research company, you should make an on-site visit to inspect the facilities and talk to survey supervisors. You should attend the training sessions for all interviewers and supervisors. It is important that interviewers and supervisors understand the purpose of the survey and the survey research objectives. The more interviewers know about the client and the purpose of the research, the more confident they will feel about their interviewing responsibilities, their data collecting processes, and how they address issues that may arise during the research.

Small research projects tend to be administered in-house. If you conduct only two or three research projects annually, you are most likely to reduce the cost and maintain quality control with in-house interviewers. However, before deciding that you will complete the research in-house, you should determine whether you have the knowledge and the expertise to develop the questionnaire, draw a representative sample of the target population, recruit and train interviewers, monitor interviewers, compile and analyze the data, and write the report. A glitch in any of these interviewing procedures could result in inaccurate data collection that will lead to faulty conclusions.

Interviewers hired for advertising and public relations in-house research interviews are usually hired at minimum wage and on a part-time basis. Part-time interviewers with limited experience will take extensive time and effort to train. Some researchers are compensated per questionnaire they complete. Compensation per interview may encourage the interviewer to cheat and fabricate data or rush respondents to answer. If monitored properly, compensation per completed personal interview method might be the best for in-depth surveys.

IN-DEPTH INTERVIEWS

Advertising and public relations in-depth interviews require extensive planning by the researcher and exceptional interviewing skills by the interviewer. You must determine the purpose and objectives of the survey and secure a representative sample of the target population. The data collected using in-depth interviews are not typically generalizable to the entire population. The respondent selected for an in-depth interview is typically someone who meets specific criteria, such as age, sex, race, product user, or opinion leader. The sample is usually much smaller than in a telephone, mail, or electronic survey. If you want to interview users of a product, then the sample of prospective participants must include only those people who have actually used the product. If you seek information about the quality of health care at a hospital, then only patients of the hospital should be interviewed.

Training advertising and public relations interviewers for in-depth interviews requires much time and effort and must be thoroughly planned and executed. The purpose and objectives of the research must be explained to the interviewer. The more the interviewer knows about the research, the more comfortable the interviewer will be in responding to questions posed by the respondent. Interviewers also should also understand how and why the sample was chosen. Review each question and explain the reason for including the question in the study and the importance of the wording. Explain how the question contributes to the research objectives. Demonstrate how questions should be read and how the response should be recorded. Explain that the interviewer must maintain neutrality during the interview. The interviewer should not interject his or her opinion or judge respondents' answers as being good or unusual.

Once the sample of respondents has been identified, it is best to secure an appointment with the respondents you want to interview. When attempting to secure an appointment with the respondent, you should speak only to the person with whom you will interview. Explain the purpose of the interview and why he or she has been selected. In many situations, the prospective respondent will want to know why he or she has been selected; how did you get their name; how much time will it take to complete the questionnaire; and who will see their answers. Even if prospective respondents do not ask these questions, you should include this information in your explanations. Researchers will typically provide a monetary incentive or inducement for the respondent's participation.

Interviewers must be available to conduct the interview at the respondent's convenience. Sometimes the interviews will be scheduled during early or late evening hours, on the weekends, or at work. These times may not be convenient to you; however, you should not display any verbal or nonverbal behavior that would suggest that you are unhappy with the schedule. You must stress the importance of the research and the respondent's participation.

Interviewers need to dress appropriately for the occasion. A professional appearance is very important in establishing rapport with the respondent. Your dress will communicate to the respondent that you are trustworthy, honest, and professional. You want to establish rapport with the respondent and make him or her feel comfortable when answering your questions.

Each advertising and public relations survey interview is unique and poses different problems, issues, and interpretations. The pace of the interview will vary from respondent to respondent. You must recognize these differences and customize the interview to that specific situation. All interviews have a similar structure or organization. If you want to record the interview, you must request permission prior to the beginning of the interview and the respondent must sign a release stating that the interviewer may record the conversation. During the introduction stage, keep as much eye contact as possible with the respondent. This will increase your rapport with the respondent. The interviewer may review the purpose of the interview, explain how or why the respondent was chosen, and state the importance of the research. The second part of the interview is the "meat" or the purpose of the interview: the question and answer period. During this phase, you should follow the format and structure of the questionnaire with some improvisations for probes and explanations. The conclusion of the interview includes a chance for the respondent and the interviewer to add any additional information that was not covered during the question and answer session and bring closure to the interview. The incentive or inducement, if any, is given at this time.

Interviewers collect responses from participants that might be quite personal or sensitive. Respondents are reluctant to provide personal information about their health, finances, sexual relationships, and religion. Therefore, maintain strict confidentiality.

The questionnaire used by interviewers is typically a combination of structured or closed-ended questions and open-ended questions with additional probing questions. There are several types of probes. For example, you might use a silent probe, an elaboration, a clarification, or a repetition. A silent probe is a technique in which you do nothing at all. Respondents do not like silence in their conversation and, therefore, will add additional information. You may use the elaboration method when you want a respondent to give more information—"Would you tell me more about that?" A clarification comes when you ask the respondent to expand on a comment—"Please explain your comment about not watching television too much." "What do you mean by 'not watching too much' television?" By repeating the statement or rephrasing the statement, the respondent will most likely use additional words to explain or clarify a statement.

In many interviews, you might request quantifiable data using an interval scale and then ask for more qualitative information.

> Q: On a scale of 1 to 10, with 1 being poor and 10 being excellent, how would you rate the quality of nursing care you received in ABC hospital?

The respondent may say that the nursing care would be rated at a 6. You may then ask an open-ended or elaboration probe question.

> Q: Why did you rate the nursing care as a 6?

The respondent may then explain that the nurse did not respond to a call for assistance in a timely manner or was negligent in other areas of health care service. You could introduce additional probing questions regarding comments about calls for assistance and other areas of negligence.

Interviewers must pay attention to the responses and be prepared to clarify the responses with additional probing questions. A benefit of in-depth interviews is the opportunity to include additional questions that add clarity to the data. You might ask several consecutive probing questions about a topic.

When you conclude the interview, record any observation you think is important to the research. Make notes about the behavior of the respondent in response to certain questions and comments. Be sure that the notes you make from observations are clearly identified as your comments and not those of the respondent.

TELEPHONE AND INTERCEPT INTERVIEWS

Advertising and public relations telephone and intercept interviews include many of the procedures used during in-depth interviews. You must conduct an interview that will collect accurate data. Maintaining a consistent high level of attention to the respondent and the questionnaire is difficult for some interviewers. Interviewers are human and at times tend to be distracted or preoccupied.

When training telephone interviewers, advertising and public relations researchers should explain the purpose of the survey, the objectives of the survey, and why the survey is important; they should identify the sponsor of the research and describe the research method. If interviewer trainees know the history of any previous research related to the topic and how this data will be used by the sponsor, they are more likely to understand the importance of each question. Inexperienced interviewers may not understand sampling methods and may not respect the validity of sampling. In describing the research method, explain how sampling works. You do not need to provide a course on research methods; however, a review of good sampling methods will enlighten the trainees about the screening process for selecting respondents.

Interviewers typically screen respondents to match a demographic or product user profile. The target population may be males 18–49 years of age, working females 25–34, home owners 35–64, or anyone 18 years of age who owns a cell phone. The questionnaire will include language and instructions about screening respondents. In telephone interviews, you should screen respondents with adults in the household and not interview children or teens—unless this specific demographic group is the target population. During the initial contact with the prospective respondent, explain why it is important to interview specific target populations. You should explain eligibility criteria to the prospective participant and then confirm their eligibility again before beginning the interview.

When conducting intercept interviews, you must remain neutral in reading questions and avoid communicating any message through your body language or personal comments. It is critical that you avoid communicating your personal opinions and preferences. Do not interview your friends and relatives. They are not good respondents because they are less likely to take the interview seriously, and this may bias the data.

Advertising and public relations survey questionnaires might include several parts or sections of questions. Researchers should review the different parts, explain each question to the interviewer, and explain how the question contributes to the purpose of the survey. There may be some technical terms or jargon used in the questions. These terms should be defined and explained. When you read the question, read the question exactly as it is written. Do not deviate from the order of the questions, do not skip questions unless directed to do so by instructions on the questionnaire, and do not finish or complete sentences for a respondent.

Exhibit 16.1

Key Points in Training Advertising and Public Relations Survey Interviewers

1. Always screen respondents for eligibility to participate. Many surveys will restrict participation by respondents' demographic, social, or behavior characteristics.
2. Explain the purpose of the interview, the research objective, why the survey is important; identify the sponsor of the research and describe the research method.
3. Never interview friends, relatives, or neighbors. They may not take the interview seriously, and this will result in biased data.
4. Read all questions exactly as worded, slowly and clearly. Emphasize words to assist with clarity.
5. Record responses immediately and exactly as they are given.
6. Do not judge respondent's answers or give your own opinions or comments. This may bias the data.
7. Maintain strict confidentiality for all responses.

It is important that all interviewers ask the same questions using the same words in the same order.

Record all responses immediately. For open-ended questions, you do not have to write each word and each sentence verbatim, but you do want to record key phrases and ideas. Always thank the respondent for participating in the survey.

SUMMARY

A researcher might hire a research company or conduct the research in-house. These two approaches may be used in all types of interview survey methods including telephone, intercepts, and in-home. When training telephone interviewers, researchers should explain the purpose of the survey, the objectives of the survey, and why the survey is important; they should indentify the sponsor of the research and describe the research method. Interviewers must remain neutral in reading questions and must not communicate any message through body language, tone of voice, or personal comments. They must read each question exactly as it is written and follow the order of questions listed in the questionnaire.

Questionnaires used by interviewers are typically a combination of structured or closed-ended questions and open-ended questions with additional probing questions. There are several types of probes. In many interviews, you might request information using closed-ended questions and probe for additional information using open-ended questions. Each study may have unique problems and issues. Even an experienced interviewer should be trained to recognize specific issues that may arise for each survey-interviewing project.

DISCUSSION QUESTIONS

1. Discuss the benefits and limitations of hiring a national research company instead of conducting the research in-house.
2. Discuss the types of advertising and public relations research projects that might be best suited for in-depth interviews.
3. How might an interviewer influence data validity and reliability?

EXERCISES

1. Create a list of personal characteristics you prefer for interviewers conducting a mall intercept survey.
2. Create a list of personal characteristics you prefer for interviewers conducting a telephone survey.
3. List at least ten questions you would ask a representative of a national research company to determine whether he or she can collect valid and reliable data.

ADDITIONAL READING

Braverman, M.T., and J.K. Slater (eds.). 1996. *Advances in survey research.* San Francisco: Jossey-Bass.

Fowler, F.J., and T.W. Mangione. 1990. *Standardized survey interviewing: Minimizing interviewer-related error.* Newbury Park, CA: Sage.

Lemay, M., and C. Durand. 2002. The effect of interviewer attitude on survey cooperation. *Bulletin de méthodologie sociologique,* 76 (October), 26–44.

Mangione, T.W. 1995. *Mail surveys: Improving the quality.* Thousand Oaks, CA: Sage.

Schwarz, N., and S. Sudman (eds.). 1996. *Answering questions: Methodology for determining cognitive and communicative processes in survey research.* San Francisco: Jossey-Bass.

Weisberg, H.F., J.A. Krosnick, and B.D. Bowen. 1996. *An Introduction to survey research, polling, and data analysis.* Thousand Oaks, CA: Sage.

17 | Obtaining Accurate Responses

LEARNING OBJECTIVES

This chapter is intended to help you:

- Recognize common threats to accuracy;
- Understand the problem of demand characteristics;
- Be aware of social desirability;
- Be familiar with the problem of nonresponses;
- Comprehend how nonresponse bias can jeopardize results.

THE PROBLEM OF ACCURATE RESPONSES

A regional chain of sandwich stores is preparing a national television advertising campaign. The campaign targets the chain's primary consumer: the urban blue-collar male lunch crowd. The client and advertising agency want to run a test in a single television market, so they buy time for a 30-second spot in several programs on several networks on one evening. They hired a survey research firm to complete one thousand telephone surveys the next night. When the data are analyzed, few people recall the ad, and the campaign is scrapped before it airs. Later, someone notices that almost no urban blue-collar males completed the survey. What went wrong?

The results of a study are only as good as the data that are obtained. If the data are in any way tainted, skewed, or biased, then the results will be inaccurate. And the communications professional assumes great risk planning campaigns around inaccurate research. Error can creep into a study at every single phase, so researchers must be vigilant during every step in the research process. Guarding against every conceivable threat to accuracy is admittedly a tedious process. However, failure to invest time at this stage of the research process almost ensures meaningless data.

Broadly speaking, there are several categories of potential bias when designing research projects. You may end up talking to the wrong people. The people you talk to may be unable to give you accurate responses. Even if your respondents are able to give you accurate responses, they may be unwilling or too uncomfortable to give you accurate responses. If everyone is as likely to hang up on the caller or throw the mail survey in the trash, the problem is minimal. However, patterns that cause nonresponse can introduce significant error to the study.

RESPONSES

Why do you buy what you buy? If you were able to answer that question easily and meaningfully, research in advertising and public relations would be simple, and this book would be about ten pages long. Research is difficult largely because we don't know why we do what we do—which would not be so bad if we would simply admit our lack of insight into our own behavior. But just as nature abhors a vacuum, cognitive scientists say that the mind abhors a vacuum. Ask a person a question about his or her behavior, and a response will quickly bubble up from deep within memory. The relationship between that answer and reality, however, is tenuous at best. Data show that we *all* judge books by their covers, but no one wants to admit to drinking Coca-Cola because of the can or some other trivial reason. Everyone who prefers a brand considers that brand superior to others. Everyone's cola tastes "better." Everyone's detergent gets clothes "cleaner." As consumers, we hold onto these convictions even if blind comparisons do not support our notions.

Does that mean that researchers are simply destined to collect meaningless data? Not necessarily. Great care must be taken to ask questions where the "right" answer and the researchers' intentions are not obvious. With a few notable exceptions, research participants tend to be helpful, and they will usually attempt to provide what they believe to be a helpful answer. When some aspect of a study leads participants to believe there is a desired response, this is referred to as a demand characteristic. If a study has any demand characteristics whatsoever, many respondents will infer the correct answer and attempt to respond accordingly.

Social desirability is another major deterrent to obtaining accurate responses. Respondents do not want to appear shallow, uneducated, easily persuadable, materialistic, conformist, or in any way deviant. Given that so much of advertising and public relations involves fads and broader trends within society, it is difficult to obtain accurate responses even when participants are able to provide them. If people are asked, they will largely report watching public television and never watching pornography. But television ratings and video sales show those self reports to be untrue. It is rather self-evident that any market research involving sexual behavior or personal hygiene may lead to biased responses. Researching these topics requires special sensitivity, and anonymity is always preferred. Even that does not guarantee truthful responses, but more people are likely to be honest when they are not directly accountable for their responses.

The best research in advertising and public relations searches for deep consumer insights rather than merely descriptive data. If you are working for McDonald's, for example, you want to know how consumers make their food choices. You likely want to know what draws them into the store and how you can increase the profitability of the visit. What does it take to convince you to "Super Size" your French fries and carbonated soft drink even though you know it's bad for your health? This is another case where respondents likely cannot tell you what causes them to make such an

Exhibit 17.1

Asking the Right Question

Much research in advertising and public relations focuses on measuring attitudes. How do customers feel about your company? Attitudes can be difficult to measure even when you ask good questions. If you ask poorly designed questions, your likelihood of obtaining an accurate response is diminished.

Your first attempt to write a good question usually will not suffice. Instead you'll need to troubleshoot your first drafts and look for problems with the question. It helps to deliberately try to misinterpret the question. For example, you might be looking for consumer attitudes toward TWIX candy bars. Consider the following Likert scale:

Please indicate your agreement with the statement:

TWIX is my favorite brand of candy bar.

Strongly agree	Agree	Somewhat agree	Neutral	Somewhat disagree	Disagree	Strongly disagree

Do you see anything wrong with that question? Hopefully you recognized that this question cannot stand alone as a single measure of attitudes toward TWIX candy bars. Although you are providing respondents with seven options, really there are only two options here. Either TWIX is your favorite, or it isn't. In the strictest sense, there is no grey area.

Perhaps Snickers is your favorite candy bar, but you really love TWIX, too. How are you to answer that question? If Snickers truly is your favorite, you must respond that you "Strongly disagree." After all, TWIX is not your favorite no matter how much you like it.

In order to measure attitudes toward TWIX, you need to ensure that you're asking just what you intend to ask and nothing more.

Please indicate your agreement with the statement:

I like TWIX candy bars.

Strongly agree	Agree	Somewhat agree	Neutral	Somewhat disagree	Disagree	Strongly disagree

This question is much more likely to elicit a range of attitudes, and it should separate those with intense attitudes from those with relatively mild attitudes. No matter how much you prefer Snickers, if you really like TWIX candy bars, you can answer this question "Strongly agree" without reservation.

impulse purchase, and since it puts them in an unflattering light, they're not likely to pass on what they do know. In these types of cases, a great deal of forethought is required to craft questions that will elicit thoughtful, honest answers. It helps for the researcher to put himself or herself in the shoes of the participant: would you feel comfortable giving a completely honest answer to that question?

RESPONSE RATES

You will learn more about sampling and related statistics in Chapter 28. However, for now you need to know a few basics about sampling in order to understand problems associated with low response rates. Overall, sampling is a way for researchers to make inferences about a large group—usually called a population—without having to study every member of the population. When you're interested in large groups, studying the entire population (called a *census*) simply is not feasible. Despite the fact that you usually will not be studying the population, you want to know about the population. It would be very expensive—and likely impossible—to study everyone who has bought disposable diapers in the past twelve months. Still, if you're a Procter and Gamble brand manager in charge of Pampers diapers, you want to know about this entire group. When you know something about an entire population, such as what percentage of disposable diaper buyers are female, this is known as a parameter of the population. Statistics and proper sampling allow researchers to make reasonable estimates (with some error) about those parameters.

Most sampling techniques, however, are built upon assumptions that are violated by every single advertising and public relations study ever conducted. These statistical tools were not developed for social research. Instead these tools were developed in the so-called hard sciences, where the units of observation are not autonomous, fickle agents, as we humans are. In the hard sciences, it is easy to assume that every member of the population has an equal chance of being selected. This represents a bedrock assumption of inferential statistics, and short of a totalitarian regime, it is impossible to implement with humans.

Imagine a very large jar filled with thousands of M&Ms candies. If you wanted to know the percentage of the M&Ms that are red, for instance, you could simply take a random sample of the candies. In this case, there are no difficulties in random selection. If an M&M is selected for sampling, you simply note the color and write it down. The candy cannot refuse to participate, nor can it screen your observation using caller ID. In cases such as these, sampling estimates are extremely close to what they should be within the given margin of error.

Now let's return to our study of disposable diapers. Even in the unlikely event that we could obtain a list of every single person who had bought diapers in the past year, it would seldom be the case that every individual sampled would be willing to talk to us. In mail surveys, phone surveys, and Internet surveys, a substantial proportion of the population will refuse to participate. Although this is annoying to the researcher, the right to refuse to participate is one of the fundamental principles of research ethics: We never force anyone to participate against his or her will. Unfortunately, as soon as one person sampled refuses to participate, then we must begin to question the generalizability of our data.

There is no perfect answer to what is an acceptable response rate. It continues to decrease over time. One of the most popular research texts in the social sciences states, "A review of published social research literature suggests that a response rate of 50 percent is considered adequate for analysis and reporting. A response of 60 percent is good; a response rate of 70 percent is very good (Babbie 2007, 262)." As nice as these numbers may sound, they merely represent convention. There is no mathematical reasoning behind these numbers.

NONRESPONSE RATES

If people were to randomly refuse to participate, any non-trivial response rate would probably be fine. If refusal were random, then the sample size would simply decrease every time someone refused to participate; however, the sample would continue to look a great deal like the population. Unfortunately, perfectly random refusal is unlikely. Researchers run into problems when there is some unknown *systematicity* underlying willingness to respond. Consider the possibility that males might be more likely to refuse to participate in a survey about diaper buying behavior. Thus, even if the initial sample contained the correct proportion of men, their unwillingness to respond means that they would be underrepresented in the final sample and resulting statistics. The researcher would falsely overestimate the number of women who purchased diapers, and subsequent advertising and public relations efforts would be likely to overemphasize female customers. Men would be less frequently targeted by advertising and public relations efforts, and the efforts at persuasion would never reach them. One very small, very subtle difference in the likeliness to respond could have a significant impact on resulting campaigns. Unfortunately, the variables underlying the likeliness to respond usually are far more complicated than male/female. Instead, an individual's likeliness to respond is apt to be based upon some idiosyncratic combination of psychographic and demographic variables paired with the uniqueness of the particular product and types of question asked.

Given that any response rate less than 100 percent raises concerns, determining acceptable response rates involves more conjecture than science. Response rates continue to drop, and with the growing distaste for telemarketing and "junk mail," every indication suggests that they are likely to continue to drop. A recent study examining response rates found that rates were highest when the respondents' names were not used, when a reminder postcard was sent one week after the initial questionnaire mailing, and a second questionnaire was mailed four weeks after the first (Link, Battaglia, Frankel, Osborn, and Mokdad 2008). All of this effort—and additional printing and postage expenses—generated a response rate of just 40.4 percent. Despite all this work, fewer than half of respondents returned a questionnaire. Although it might seem counterintuitive that not using the name was highest, the response rate in that condition was only slightly higher than when the name was used in similar circumstances (38.0 percent). Using prevailing cost estimates, Link and colleagues estimated that it would cost $70,969 for 1,000 completed mail surveys using these techniques. This is quite expensive for 10 percentage points below what some call adequate.

For random digit dial (RDD) telephone surveys, response rates were lower, and costs were higher. When a second questionnaire was mailed, Link and colleagues found that the mail survey generated a higher response rate than the phone survey in five of six states studied. Telephone response rates varied greatly from 45.8 percent in North Carolina to 29.4 percent in California. They estimated that it would cost $79,578 for 1,000 completed phone surveys, approximately 12 percent more expensive than the mail survey. Other researchers have shown that RDD surveys underrepresent areas of concentrated wealth, areas of extreme poverty, and highly urbanized areas (Johnson, Cho, Campbell, and Holbrook 2006). Corporate researchers must also use caution in not violating do-not-call regulations.

NONRESPONSE BIAS

When comparing respondents with the general population, respondents tend to be better educated and less ethnically or racially diverse than the overall population.

Respondents also tend to be higher in socioeconomic status. All of these systematic differences between willing respondents and the overall population must be taken into account when analyzing data. This mismatch between the general population and the respondents in a study can bias results. In this sense, the people who opted not to respond have created a bias in the data. Hence the name nonresponse bias.

Consider a simple attempt to estimate the annual household income of consumers. The actual average income of a product's customers would tend to be overestimated due to differences among the general population and respondents. If wealthier people are more likely to respond, then the group of respondents for a given survey is likely to include a disproportionately high number of wealthy people. If wealthy and non-wealthy people use the product at equal rates—and wealthy people are more likely to answer the phone to answer the survey—then too many wealthy people will complete the survey. At the end of the day, when the researcher calculates the annual household income of customers, it will be biased toward wealthy people due to the nonresponse of less affluent consumers.

ARTIFICIALLY IMPROVING RESPONSE RATES

It is easy to get caught in the trap of attempting to achieve a seemingly high response rate, even though there is no universally agreed upon definition of a high response rate. Given that any response rate below 100 percent violates the assumptions on the underlying statistical tests, there is no mathematical reason to prefer a 60 percent response rate to 50 percent. Furthermore, research has shown that many attempts to increase response rates skew the characteristics of responders, which can increase nonresponse bias.

One tactic that researchers use to increase response rate is through the use of incentives. Participants are offered something of tangible value in exchange for participation in the study. Although incentives have been shown to increase response rate, there is considerable evidence that they also introduce nonresponse bias. People who would have been willing to participate without an incentive likely will still participate. What differentiates those people who would not have otherwise participated? They are likely to be disinterested in general and also to have little interest in the topic at hand. By including the uninterested, multiple studies have shown that incentives can increase nonresponse bias (Baumgartner, Rathbun, Boyle, Welsh, and Laughland 1998; Roberts, Roberts, Sibbald, and Torgerson 2000). This suggests that researchers would be better off accepting a lower response rather than inflating it with the use of incentives.

SUMMARY

Researchers must be aware of and account for several threats against accurate responses. First, care must be taken to ask questions that are not leading. Questions should be scrutinized so that they do not appear to demand one particular "right" answer from participants. Whenever a sensitive topic is being researched, care must be taken to avoid soliciting socially desirable answers. Anonymity is often beneficial.

Finally, researchers must worry both about the response rate and the factors that led to nonresponse. If different subsets of the sample did not respond equally, these patterns of response may have led to nonresponse bias.

DISCUSSION QUESTIONS

1. What can researchers do to obtain honest answers?
2. What can researchers do to make participants more comfortable answering sensitive questions?
3. How can response rates be increased for mail surveys?
4. How can nonresponders introduce bias to a study?

EXERCISE

1. Go to your university's free speech area with a friend and ten simple surveys about tuition prices. Try to get every tenth person to fill out the survey. Have your friend discreetly record the sex of everyone who walks by. When you have ten completed surveys, compare the sex of your respondents with all of the people who walked by. Do they match?

ADDITIONAL READING

Groves, R. M. 2006. Nonresponse rates and nonresponse bias in household surveys. *Public Opinion Quarterly,* 70 (5), 646–75.

REFERENCES

Babbie, E. 2007. *The practice of social research.* 11th ed. Belmont, CA: Thompson.
Baumgartner, R., P. Rathbun, K. Boyle, M. Welsh, and D. Laughland. 1998. The effect of prepaid monetary incentives on mail survey response rates and response quality. Paper presented at the annual meeting of the American Association for Public Opinion Research, St. Louis, MO.
Johnson, T. P., Y.I. Cho, R. T. Campbell, and A. L. Holbrook. 2006. Using community-level correlates to evaluate nonresponse effects in a telephone survey. *Public Opinion Quarterly,* 70, 704–19.
Link, M. W., M. P. Battaglia, M. R. Frankel, L. Osborn, and A. H. Mokdad. 2008. A comparison of address-based sampling (ABS) versus random-digit dialing (RDD) for general population surveys. *Public Opinion Quarterly,* 72, 6–27.
Roberts, P. J., C. Roberts, B. Sibbald, and D. J. Torgerson. 2000. The effect of a direct payment or a lottery on questionnaire response rates: A randomised controlled trial. *Journal of Epidemiology and Community Health,* 1, 71–2.

18 Data Tabulation

LEARNING OBJECTIVES

This chapter is intended to help you:

- Understand hand and computer tabulation;
- Understand that no one type of tabulation perfectly represents a data set;
- Understand univariate analysis and frequency distributions;
- Recognize bivariate analyses and cross-tabulations;
- Understand multivariate data tabulations.

THE IMPORTANCE OF CLEAR DATA

Many people have heard of the phrase "There are three kinds of lies: Lies, damned lies, and statistics," attributed to Benjamin Disraeli. This phrase certainly is appropriate when numbers are misused to bolster an otherwise unconvincing argument. However, advertising and public relations researchers cannot afford to misuse numbers. The entire purpose of advertising and public relations research is to shed light on an otherwise unclear issue. Using numbers to mislead contradicts this purpose. This type of obfuscation need not necessarily result from malice. Instead, numbers can often prove baffling. Therefore, data must be tabulated and presented both as honestly and as clearly as possible.

HAND TABULATION

Unless your data set is especially small, hand tabulation is likely to be inefficient and time prohibitive. There's a reason that most exams are conducted using bubble sheets: computers are faster and more accurate tabulators. However, if you have a simple questionnaire, and you are looking for a very specific set of data, then hand tabulation may be efficient. If an advertising professor were to ask her students to list their five favorite Super Bowl ads, these data could easily be hand tabulated by a teaching assistant. Each ad could be listed on a master list, and a tally mark could be placed next to the ad each time it was mentioned by a student. This would be far faster than entering the data into a computer.

In a complicated content analysis, it is not uncommon for coders to look at thousands of units. You might content analyze every advertisement in prime-time television for a month or every newspaper story about your company during a given year. In these instances, it is common for individual coders to code the units of analysis using pen and paper. Later these hand-coded sheets are entered into a computer for tabulation.

COMPUTER TABULATION

For most research projects, however, you are far more likely to use computer tabulation. Here the data for each respondent or unit of analysis are entered into a computer program, such as SPSS or Microsoft Excel (see Chapter 29). It is convention for each row to represent a unit of analysis and each column to represent a variable. Data are entered as close to the raw form as possible. Computer programs can recode variables without error while human error is almost assured in recoding large datasets.

In a study of students, for instance, it is common to ask students to list their academic major. The original questionnaire might have given the following options: advertising, journalism, marketing, public relations, and other. If the options were numbered 1–5 on the questionnaire, it is simple for those involved with data entry to enter the correct code. However, if the blanks are not numbered, then there is a greater chance for error if the individual must remember that marketing is always a 3. In this case, it may be advisable to enter the data as "a," "j," "m," "p," or "o." No matter what choice you make, there will be possibilities for error later in the research process. Thus is it advisable to keep data tabulation in mind as the questionnaire or instrument is designed rather than treating it as an afterthought. A properly designed data tabulation code sheet is every bit as important as a properly designed questionnaire.

GETTING A GOOD LOOK AT THE DATA

There is no one way to tabulate data. No matter how data are tabulated, there will be some consolidation and lack of clarity. As you step back, you can begin to see patterns in the data; however, you also will begin to lose sight of micro-level trends in the data. In this sense, data tabulation is about the processing of coming to understand your data rather than simply going through a checklist. Consider the case of exam scores. In introductory college classes, it is common to have an average exam score of approximately 76 percent. Following an exam, instructors usually talk about the overall grades. Students will often hear the average grade and perhaps the number of students who earned As, Bs, and so on. It would be atypical—and likely illegal—for the instructor to discuss individual exam scores, but students often are eager to learn about the trends. The exam score data are tabulated to arrive at these trends.

It is not uncommon to have different instructors teach different sections of the same class. Dr. Smith might teach one section of Principles of Public Relations, and Dr. Jones might teach the other. They might even teach the class at different times in the same room. One day you're headed to class, and you notice that both instructors have posted their exam data on a bulletin board outside the classroom. Would it surprise you if each class averaged a 76 percent on the exam? It's a small coincidence to have the exact same average, but it's still plausible. Then, however, you look at the range of the grades. Dr. Smith had 5 As, 15 Bs, 40 Cs, 14 Ds, and 3 Fs. That's a pretty typical distribution for an exam with a 76 percent average. Turning to Dr. Jones, however, you see an altogether different pattern. There were 0 As, 4 Bs, 70 Cs, 3 Ds, and 0 Fs. Pretty much everyone in Dr. Jones's class earned a C. We hope the performance of these two classes seems entirely different to you. However, you would never have been able to see these differences simply by examining the average grade. Although the average is a common and effective way at tabulating data, it does not show the entire picture. Here we needed to see the range of scores and the frequency (or percentage) of students who received each grade.

THE SINGLE VARIABLE

The simplest form of data tabulation involves a single variable and is often called univariate, meaning one variable. At the most basic level, it is helpful to know how many times each option was chosen for the variable. How many respondents were male and how many were female? How many people strongly agreed with a statement and how many strongly disagreed? We can learn a lot just by the frequency of responses. Therefore, univariate analysis often involves the presentation of a frequency distribution. In order to illustrate this, let's turn to data collected by advertising agency DDB Needham, Chicago, called the Life Style survey. As the name suggests, these data shed light on how Americans live their lives. We have known for decades that the mass media do not influence all Americans equally. Instead, some opinion leaders gain information from the mass media, and those individuals then influence opinion followers through interpersonal communication in a process known as two-step flow. In designing a public relations campaign, for example, it might be more efficient to target these opinion leaders. DDB Needham might have had similar thoughts when collecting the Life Style data. They asked participants to rate their agreement with the following statement using a Likert scale: "My friends and neighbors often come to me for advice about products and brands." Over nine years, approximately 33,315 people answered this question. Thus, we can examine the responses to this single variable. How frequently did respondents agree with this statement?

Exhibit 18.1 presents the data several different ways. Each option in the Likert scale is listed in the first column. In the second column is the coded value that each option was assigned in the statistics program. In the third column, one can see the raw frequencies. Looking at column three, one can see that 1,641 respondents definitely agreed that their friends and neighbors came to them for advice about brands and services. The fourth column shows the raw percentage of respondents who gave each response. This column takes into account all respondents—including the 171 people for whom no response is available. Because we did not collect the data ourselves, we cannot know why that these data are missing. They simply are missing. The fifth column shows the percentage for each possible answer among all *valid* responses. These percentages ignore the missing data. There are relatively few missing responses here, so the valid percent is quite similar to the percent. The final column cumulates

Exhibit 18.1

Advice Sought Regarding Brands and Services

Value Label	Value	Frequency	Percent	Valid Percent	Cumulative Percent
Definitely Agree	6	1,641	4.9	4.9	4.9
Generally Agree	5	4,078	12.2	12.2	17.1
Moderately Agree	4	8,686	25.9	26.1	43.2
Moderately Disagree	3	6,607	19.7	19.8	63.0
Generally Disagree	2	5,850	17.5	17.6	80.6
Definitely Disagree	1	6,453	19.3	19.4	100.0
Total		33,315	99.5	100.0	
Missing		171			
Total		33,486	100.0		

Source: Life Style Data, © DDB Worldwide, Chicago, Illinois.

Exhibit 18.2   **Agreement that Advice Is Sought About Brands, Services**

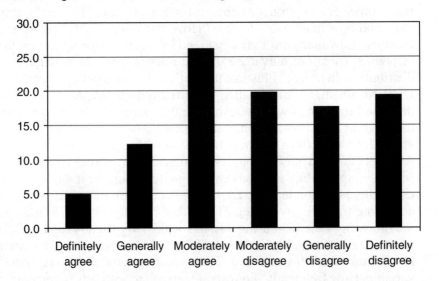

the percents down the rows. In this case, one can see that 43.2 percent of respondents at least moderately agree that their advice was sought regarding brands and services. Fewer than half of respondents consider themselves opinion leaders.

Due in part to the information density of Exhibit 18.1, some audiences may have difficulty quickly deciphering the data contained therein. Therefore, some may prefer to illustrate the data graphically as a figure. Turning to Exhibit 18.2, most readers will be able to quickly see that the pattern of disagreement is stronger than the pattern of agreement. Although the most frequent response (the mode) is "moderately agree," the three next most frequent responses are all disagreements.

Both Exhibit 18.1 and Exhibit 18.2 allow us to examine the frequency distribution of the variable regarding advice about brands and services. And if we arbitrarily select those who either definitely agreed or generally agreed with the statement, then we

Exhibit 18.3

Advice Sought Regarding Brands and Services by Respondent Sex

	Sex of respondent	
	Male	Female
Definitely Agree	4.9%	5.0%
Generally Agree	12.6	11.9
Moderately Agree	25.2	26.8
Moderately Disagree	19.2	20.3
Generally Disagree	17.8	17.4
Definitely Disagree	20.3	18.6
Total	(14,991)	(18,324)

Source: Life Style survey, © DDB Worldwide, Chicago, Illinois.

can conclude approximately 17.1 percent of respondents can be considered "opinion leaders." Technically, those who moderately agreed might also be considered among this group, but how influential can they be if they only moderately agree? In order to focus our public relations efforts, we want to target the most influential individuals. However, these univariate data do very little to help us know *whom* to target. In order to know this, we might want to look at the characteristics of these respondents. Who is more likely to agree with this statement? We might suspect that males and females will answer this question differently.

BIVARIATE ANALYSIS

In this case, we have two variables: respondent sex and agreement. Males and females are subgroups of our overall sample. We can examine their agreement data separately. This is a bivariate relationship. We want to look at how these variables correspond with one another. Although it may seem straightforward to add a second variable, how we tabulate these data requires thought and planning. For instance, consider that 55.5 percent of those who definitely agreed with the statement were female. Can you conclude that women are our opinion leaders? Without knowing the relative proportion of males and females in the sample, that conclusion would be premature. Indeed, 55 percent of our sample is female. In this case, it is far more meaningful to ask what percentage of males and what percentage of females definitely agreed with the statement.

Looking at Exhibit 18.3, we can see that the percentage of males and females at each level of agreement is amazingly consistent. Although the percentages are not perfect matches, 17.5 percent of males and 16.9 percent of females fell within the top two levels of agreement (our arbitrary definition of opinion leadership). These bivariate data allow a better examination of respondents' answers; however, this particular bivariate relationship does not shed much additional light on those whom we should target with our public relations effort. What other variables might make someone more attractive to advice seekers? Perhaps we should consider the educational level of an individual before asking their advice. We can examine this by looking at the bivari-

Exhibit 18.4

Advice Sought Regarding Brands and Service by Respondent Education

	Education Level of Respondent					
	Elementary School	Attended High School	Graduated High School	Attended College	Graduated College	Post-Graduate
Definitely Agree	7.7%	5.9%	4.8%	5.1%	3.9%	4.7%
Generally Agree	8.3	9.5	10.9	13.0	13.3	14.5
Moderately Agree	20.6	24.8	24.8	27.3	27.4	26.8
Moderately Disagree	14.6	18.0	20.0	20.2	20.7	19.5
Generally Disagree	13.8	16.1	17.3	17.0	20.0	18.3
Definitely Disagree	35.0	25.8	22.2	17.3	14.7	16.2
Total	(792)	(2,070)	(11,256)	(9,788)	(4,612)	(4,689)

Source: Life Style survey, © DDB Worldwide, Chicago, Illinois.

Exhibit 18.5

Advice Sought Regarding Brands and Services by Respondent Education

	Education Level of Respondent		
	Did Not Graduate High School	High School Graduate or Some College	College Graduate or More
Definitely Agree	6.4%	5.0%	4.3%
Generally Agree	9.2	11.9	13.9
Moderately Agree	23.6	26.0	27.1
Moderately Disagree	17.1	20.1	20.1
Generally Disagree	15.4	17.1	19.2
Definitely Disagree	28.3	19.9	15.5
Total	(2,862)	(21,044)	(9,310)

Source: Life Style survey, © DDB Worldwide, Chicago, Illinois.

ate relationship between agreement and education. This type of table is sometimes referred to as a cross-tabulation.

The full bivariate relationship is shown in Exhibit 18.4. If we closely consider the table, we can see that there does appear to be a relationship with education and the feeling that one's advice is sought about products and brands. For instance, an individual with only an elementary school education is more than twice as likely (35.0 percent) to definitely disagree as someone with a post-graduate education (16.2 percent). Although these patterns can be seen, the table is extremely busy with six levels of agreement and six levels of education. In order to get a less cluttered picture of our data, we can *collapse* some of the levels of education. For instance, we could collapse those who finished only elementary school with those who attended but did not graduate from high school. We might call these respondents those "did not graduate high school." Likewise we could collapse those who graduated high school with those who attended but did not graduate from college into a single new category titled "high school graduate or some college." Finally, we could collapse the college graduates with those with a post-graduate education and call them "college graduate

Exhibit 18.6

Advice Sought Regarding Brands and Services by Respondent Education

	Education Level of Respondent		
	Did Not Graduate High School	High School Graduate or Some College	College Graduate or More
Generally Agree or Better	15.5%	16.9%	18.2%
Moderately Agree or Disagree	40.7	46.1	47.2
Generally Disagree or Worse	43.8	37.0	34.6
Total	(2,862)	(21,044)	(9,310)

Source: Life Style survey, © DDB Worldwide, Chicago, Illinois.

or more." Exhibit 18.5 shows these collapsed categories and a slighter clearer picture. As was the case before, those with lower education appear to be slightly more "bottom heavy." That is, they appear to have greater percentages toward the bottom of the table. However, even this simpler table is not truly addressing our question of opinion leadership.

Because we're really only interested in those who at least generally agree with the statement, we can collapse categories. That is, we can collapse the two levels of highest agreement into a single category, "Generally agree or better." In addition, we could collapse the middle two categories into a single category, "Moderately agree or disagree." Finally, we can collapse the bottom two categories into a single category, "Generally disagree or worse." By collapsing education to three levels and agreement to three levels, we have greatly simplified our data tabulation, which can be seen in Exhibit 18.6. In addition to being more visually pleasing, this table more directly addresses our question. The percentage of respondents in our "opinion leader" category increases at each level of education. This is also true with our middle group. However, the opposite picture can be seen with the "generally disagree or worse" group. Here, each increasing level of education leads to less disagreement. This suggests that education is an important variable in opinion leadership. We have reason to suspect that our public relations campaign should target the more highly educated.

It is important to make an aside here. Data categories can *always* be collapsed. By measuring education at several different levels, the Life Style survey authors permitted us to collapse these categories. However, should we have needed the finer analysis shown in Exhibit 18.4, such analysis still would have been possible. If the study authors had collapsed the categories for respondents to choose from, we would have been stuck with the broader categories, which might have prevented us from analyzing the data at the level necessary. This goes along with the general rule of thumb to maintain precision for as long as possible.

MULTIVARIATE

With the relationship between opinion leadership and education, we can see the benefit of bivariate analysis. However, the world is a very complicated place. Most

Exhibit 18.7

Bar and Tavern Frequency as a Function of Respondent Sex and Age

	Males			Females		
	35 and under	36–59	60 and up	35 and under	36–59	60 and up
Never visit	27.1%	42.1%	62.2%	36.7%	52.7%	74.4%
Visit at least once in past year	72.9	57.9	37.8	63.3	47.3	25.6
Total	(4,188)	(6,796)	(3,697)	(5,369)	(7,805)	(4,790)

Source: Life Style survey, © DDB Worldwide, Chicago, Illinois.

phenomena cannot be captured with only a single variable. Often times we need to look at three or more variables. When examining and tabulating data in this fashion, we call it multivariate analysis. Although some complicated statistics involve dozens of variables, presenting data in a table usually is limited to three or four variables. Beyond that, tables become too difficult to interpret.

In order to illustrate a multivariate data tabulation, we again turn to the Life Style survey. Although this example is admittedly oversimplified, consider an advertising agency planning a campaign for a new draught beer. Draught beer is almost exclusively served in bars or taverns, so advertising for this new beer likely should be targeted toward those who frequent bars or taverns. For a simple analysis, we might want to see what kinds of people frequent bars or taverns. Once again we might expect to see a difference between men and women. Furthermore, we might expect a difference based upon age. Exhibit 18.7 shows a clear multivariate relationship among the data. To probably no one's surprise, bar and tavern attendance is highest among young males. Among this sample, 72.9 percent of males 35 and under reported visiting a bar or tavern at least once in the past year. Conversely, patronage is lowest among older females. Just 25.6 percent of all females 60 years old and older report visiting a bar or tavern even once during the past year. Young men would clearly be the target of our advertising campaign.

To illustrate the benefit of multivariate tabulation, consider two clear patterns in the data. The probability of bar attendance decreases at each subsequent level of age for both men and women. Furthermore, women are less likely to have visited a bar than men at every level of age. Thus, we gain a better understanding by examining all three of these variables simultaneously. Because we are using percentages rather than raw data, we must be careful how we present the data. By including a final row with the number of respondents in each category, we indicate that we are illustrating what percentage of males 35 or under, for example, have been to a bar or tavern at least once during the past year. Our percentages sum to 100 percent *down the columns.* We could have calculated the percentages differently if we had summed the percentage *across the rows.* The table would look different if we had instead asked, "Of all males who have never been to a bar or tavern at least once during the past year, what percentage were 35 or under?" In this case, the three percentages under "males" and to the right of "Never visit" would sum to 100

Exhibit 18.8

Media Choices as a Function of Respondent Sex

	Males		Females	
	No Cable Television	Cable Subscriber	No Cable Television	Cable Subscriber
Does not read most or all issues of local daily newspaper	22.4%	16.9%	22.3%	16.8%
Reads most or all issues of local daily newspaper	77.6	83.1	77.7	83.2
Total	(3,381)	(5,775)	(4,203)	(7,066)

Source: Life Style survey, © DDB Worldwide, Chicago, Illinois.

percent, and we would include the total number of participants in an additional column to the right.

Let's look at another multivariate table to make sure the concept is clear. Exhibit 18.8 shows the media choices of men and women. Cable subscribers are more likely to read most or all issues of the local daily newspaper. Unlike bar patronage, however, there appears to be no real difference between men and women in terms of media choices. For both sexes, the pattern is remarkably consistent. Only by looking at these three variables simultaneously could we understand that cable and newspaper usage are consistent between males and females. Here the multivariate tabulation provided insight that we could not have gained any other way.

SUMMARY

Masses of data can seem incredibly unclear, but the purpose of data tabulation is to make the data more clear. Whenever tabulating data, decisions should be based upon adding as much clarity and insight as possible. Small datasets can be tabulated by hand, but most data are entered into a software package and computer tabulated. There are many ways that a given data set can be tabulated, and it is up to the researcher to add as much clarity as possible. It is helpful to have a frequency distribution that illustrates the number, or percentage, or people who chose each response. Looking at one variable at a time in this fashion is known as univariate analysis. When looking at two variables at a time—bivariate analysis—patterns can be seen using cross-tabulations. This allows researchers to see whether the response to one question varies as a function of the response to another variable. Finally, tabulating the responses to three or more variables at a time is known as multivariate tabulation.

DISCUSSION QUESTIONS

1. When is hand tabulation likely to be advantageous?
2. What is the benefit of a frequency distribution?
3. How are cross-tabulations used?

EXERCISES

1. Ask 10 people to list their three favorite television shows and tabulate the data in a clear, meaningful way.
2. Ask 10 males and 10 females whether they agree/neutral/disagree with the statement: "There is gender equity in the workforce today." Tabulate the data in a way that will highlight similarities or differences between males and females.
3. Conduct a hypothetical multivariate tabulation for the variables: education level, income, and pet ownership.

ADDITIONAL READING

Holcomb, Z.C. 1996. *Real data: A statistics workbook based on empirical data.* Los Angeles, CA: Pyrczak.

19 | Applications of Quantitative Research

LEARNING OBJECTIVES

This chapter is intended to help you:

- Learn some of the major applications of research in advertising and public relations work;
- Understand how research can aid in the development of mass media campaigns;
- See how research can help you learn more about customers, competitors, and the media;
- Observe how test markets may operate.

Both public relations and advertising operate through the mass media, so it is important to understand how the mass media work. Research can help with that goal, and then go on to help us make our mass media messages more believable, trustworthy, and informative, and to create more effective and efficacious campaigns.

Now that we understand how most quantitative research is conducted, it is time to explore how those research methods can be applied to actual work situations in advertising and public relations. You may also want to look back to the section on qualitative research, because those research techniques are sometimes also used for these real-life applications, especially for source credibility, concept testing, and copy testing.

SOURCE CREDIBILITY

One important application of quantitative research relates to source credibility. How much do the audience members trust us, as senders of messages, to provide useful and reliable information? Remember, source credibility may not refer only to the credibility of the media; in addition, it often refers to the credibility of the sender, whether that is a government agency, a public relations press release, or an advertisement from a retail store. Studies of source credibility often deal with how credible sources may influence selection of a message by an audience member, believability of the message, attitude change, and perhaps even resulting actions.

Exhibit 19.1

An Example of a Source Credibility Questionnaire

Please rate how credible each of these news sources is with "5" being highest and "1" being lowest.

	Low				High
The *New York Times*	1	2	3	4	5
CBS Evening News	1	2	3	4	5
People magazine	1	2	3	4	5
CNN Headline News	1	2	3	4	5
The National Enquirer	1	2	3	4	5
Fox News (cable television)	1	2	3	4	5
ESPN (cable television)	1	2	3	4	5
Time magazine	1	2	3	4	5

Because source credibility can be so subjective, it is difficult to quantify and thus most often is the subject of qualitative research. Nonetheless, it is often quicker and easier to evaluate research findings if they are quantified, so quantitative research is also often employed in source-credibility studies. The questions asked may be similar to, if not the same as, questions utilized in a qualitative study of source credibility; the difference is in how the answers are recorded. In qualitative research, an open-ended response may be sought and the entire answer recorded; using quantitative research, respondents are often provided with numerical scales that have been established in advance to provide some measure of source credibility. A variety of information sources may be listed, and the respondents asked to assign a number from the scale for each one. In that way, the researcher can determine the relative credibility for each information source.

Incidentally, although advertising and public relations do not usually rank at the top of the credibility scales, they often perform better than used-car salespersons, lawyers, or even government officials. Some corporations have very high credibility, while others do not. Even from the same company, some advertisements seem to have higher credibility than others do; there are also significant differences from one brand to another and from one campaign to another.

Content Analysis

Knowing the content of the media is useful for both advertising and public relations practitioners. Learning the characteristics and formats of messages issued by competitors, by highly trusted news sources, by different divisions of your own firm, or of certain generic industries may be very helpful in creating and formatting your own messages.

Suppose you want to examine the press coverage in the local newspaper of your own company and of your major competitors. You might go back through several months of newspaper issues, looking for relevant articles. Then for each article, you might record the date it appeared, the length in words, the section of the newspaper in which it appeared, the type size of the headline, and the placement on the page.

Exhibit 19.2

The Steps Involved in Content Analysis Research

1. Decide what you are looking for and where you will find it.
2. Decide how detailed you want the analysis to be.
3. Decide on how you will define each trait or concept.
4. Decide how to record the existence and the frequency of a trait or concept.
5. Develop rules for recording and coding your traits or concepts.
6. Decide what to do with traits or concepts that marginally meet your definitions.
7. Train assistants or judges.
8. Conduct your research.
9. Analyze your findings.
10. Apply the findings to the original problem or question.

You might even become more detailed, counting the number of positive and negative words used in each article, whether it reported on a specific product or service feature, whether cross-references were made to favorable or unfavorable outside information sources, and even the final impression that was left with the reader; for these latter categories of information, you might use a panel or a group of trained judges to maintain uniformity in judging the available data. Using this information, you could judge how well your firm is being presented to the community and the relative merits of various approaches to releasing corporate news and information.

Similarly, you might want to know how the characteristics of your magazine advertisements compared against those of other firms in your industry. You would go through several issues of selected magazines, counting the number of advertisements, their sizes, placement in the publication, whether color or black-and-white, the size of each advertisement, the use of headlines, photographs or artwork, the headline attractiveness, the benefits being promised, and the action suggested by the advertisement.

Then you could use these data to evaluate your advertising: how well it is set off from competing messages, how well it differs from competitors' placements, and whether there are any obvious improvements that could be made to enhance your magazine campaigns.

Content analysis of other media is a bit more time-consuming. Broadcast announcements are transient and thus are not as available after they appear as are items in print media. They may need to be recorded; otherwise, tracking down past messages may be impossible. Internet information is easily available but tracing through all the links and connections to determine everything that relates to your study could be quite time-consuming, and with the rate of change with online information, it may even be a continuing task.

CONCEPT TESTING

Concept testing is used to evaluate consumer responses to promotional ideas before the campaign is run, during the developmental stages of the campaigns. This type of research can also be used to generate ideas for campaign benefits or themes or to test possible ideas to alter customers' opinions of products, services, or ideas.

As with source-credibility research, concept testing often utilizes qualitative research to explore the nuances of respondents' opinions, but quantitative research makes it easier and faster to evaluate the findings. Using this research application, concepts thought to be workable ideas are presented to customers and then assessed on the degree of purchase intent, percentage of respondents who indicate a likelihood of trial, and the strength of the responses and of opinions on the tested concepts. Sometimes customers are asked to evaluate the promotional concept first, followed by test use of the actual item; then the results are compared to see whether actual experience lives up to expectations. Positioning research also can fall under the rubric of concept testing, with similar concepts evaluated together to compare positions of the product or service attributes.

COPY TESTING

As with source credibility research and concept testing, copy tests often use qualitative research for detailed analyses and in-depth opinion exploration, but quantitative research is again a faster and easier way to analyze the results. Refer back to Chapter 9 and to the exhibit on the PACT copy-testing system in that chapter for more detailed information. Copy tests analyze the written material in a promotional item, such as an advertisement or promotional news release.

Although almost all copy testing occurs before the campaign actually runs, there can be pretests during the early stages of developing the announcements and what are often referred to as posttests after the copy has been written but before the messages are actually produced. Obviously, in this situation, "posttests" is a somewhat misleading term because the research is still being conducted prior to the campaign, not afterward as with most posttesting research.

PRETESTS

In the early stages of developing the creative materials for a promotional campaign, diagnostic measures are often used to determine how well the copy attracts attention, builds interest, ties to the specific brand name, and motivates consumers. Results of these pretests are then used to strengthen the creative execution.

The visual attractiveness and effectiveness of the message development can be measured with eye-tracking equipment, to follow where the reader's or viewer's eye gaze moves while reading or viewing the entire announcement.

POSTTESTS

Copy tests conducted after the copy and the rest of the advertisement has been prepared, but before the campaign appears, are known as posttests of copy. Of course, it is possible to change the copy in an existing campaign, but such alterations are expensive and are usually undertaken only when the campaign is showing signs of weakness or ineffectiveness. Often with posttests of copy, a total score known as a report card is used to try to judge the overall effectiveness of the total advertisement or campaign.

Exhibit 19.3

Applying Copy Testing: Pretests

What can be learned through pretests using copy testing:
1. Are we using the rights words and terms?
2. Did the audience interpret these words and terms in the way we intended?
3. Are the words and terms powerful?
4. Does the copy accurately describe the product, service, or idea?
5. Does the copy utilize the intended audience appeals?
6. What do audience members recall about the advertisement?
7. Does the advertisement feature the brand name and firm?
8. Does the entire message fit together cohesively?
9. Does the copy differentiate us from our competitors?
10. Does the copy introduce unique and positive features?

Exhibit 19.4

Applying Copy Testing: Posttests

Questions that may be resolved through posttest copy testing:
1. Is the message clear?
2. Does the message feature the product, service or idea?
3. Is the message understandable by the intended audience?
4. Is the message legal and moral?
5. Are we stressing the correct appeal?
6. What message are the audience members receiving and remembering?
7. Does the message enhance the image of the product, service or idea, and of the firm?

Nonverbal reactions to promotional messages are often gathered using eye-tracking equipment, galvanic skin responses, and other physiological measurements.

There are no standard measurements for copy tests, so each firm or each researcher usually develops his or her own standards of what constitutes effectiveness and significance. Testing of print media is relatively easy compared to testing broadcast or Internet messaging.

COMPETITIVE SPENDING

Knowing how competitors spend their promotional monies is very useful intelligence for marketers. There are some syndicated research services that provide this information, but many companies, especially small or local firms, are not covered by those syndicated surveys. So it is important to know how to conduct such research yourself.

The first step is to list all the companies whose advertising expenditures you wish to track, along with all the various brand names used by those companies. You will benefit from a general idea of which media and which specific media vehicles are used by your competitors, because it will make your search easier and faster; if you do not have that information, you will need to look through all the logical media and vehicle choices until you discover where the competing messages have been placed. Next, you collect the media and vehicles in which competing messages appeared. It takes some time, but you go through each media vehicle, similar to a content analysis, counting all competitive advertising placements, along with the size of print advertisements or length of broadcast commercials or specifications of Internet and online promotions; you also want to record when each message appeared. Then you can go to media estimating guides, to local-media rate cards or to Standard Rate & Data Service to determine how much each advertising placement is likely to cost; you may also contact the media vehicles directly but they may not be very cooperative unless you, too, are an advertiser with that vehicle. Finally, you add up all the media costs and the number of placements, and then chart the timing of the message appearances. If you do this for all of your competitors, or at least for your major competitors, you will have a fairly good idea of their advertising placements, schedules, media choices, and budgets.

Imagine, however, how difficult it is to track message placements in certain media. In radio, it is necessary to try to listen to all the stations—unless you can convince the stations to provide you with a copy of their station logs, which is not likely. Television is a bit easier because the programming can be recorded for later playback, but it is still necessary to go through all the programs for all the stations and networks. Internet searches are rather straightforward, and print media such as newspapers and magazines can be collected and perused at more convenient times and locations, after the messages appear.

Using this kind of information, you can determine whether you can match your main competitors in promotional spending; if you cannot, then you can determine in which media your messages might appear without being in direct competition in the same media vehicles as your competitors.

MEDIA TESTS

In any promotional campaign that uses the mass media, it is a good idea to test which media and vehicles do the best job of carrying your message, communicating your main ideas, matching with the mood and environment of your message, and gaining effective recall on the part of the audience—and do all this at an efficient cost. Of course, it is a primary concern that the media and vehicles reach the appropriate audiences, but there is much more to be considered.

Most often, messages will be prepared for various media: print, broadcast, and online. Then, within each media type, a series of messages will be prepared, such as 15-second, 30-second, and 60-second television announcements. It is important to keep the message themes and appeals consistent so any audience responses can be attributed to the media and vehicles rather than to the message or appeal. These messages will then be booked on various media and in various media vehicles. It is important to have some tracking mechanism so you will know which inquiries, sales, or other responses are resulting from each vehicle. Most often, some sort of key is inserted in the message, so inquirers will call a certain telephone number or ask for a certain department number, or they will mail a coupon with a code incorporated into it, or they will mail to a certain post office box number or department number. During or after the test, the final step is sorting and counting, to determine which media placements resulted in the greatest responses.

Exhibit 19.5

What You Can Learn through Test Marketing

1. Is the product, service, or idea useful to the intended customers?
2. Is the suggested price right?
3. Who are the best target groups?
4. Where are the best target markets?
5. What attributes are most important to consumers?
6. How can advertising and public relations help promote the item?
7. How can we differentiate our item from competitors?
8. Is the item seasonal?
9. How can we encourage repeat purchases?
10. What messages do we want to send to customers?
11. Will this venture be profitable?
12. When should we launch our campaign?

This kind of test is often repeated at regular intervals, perhaps annually, because audience preferences change and because alterations in the campaign may make it more or less well matched with certain media and vehicles.

TEST MARKETING

Marketing tests are similar to media tests. However, with market tests, rather than testing which media and vehicles are best matched to the messages and appeals, the actual campaign can be tested in a variety of geographic markets to determine where the product or service will sell best. It is even possible to test various products or services against one another to find out which is preferred or which combination of offers will bring the greatest sales and profits.

Marketing tests can be expensive, especially if the entire marketing region is involved, which could include the entire country. For that reason, test campaigns are often introduced in certain test markets that resemble the total population. Most often, markets are selected that offer a wide range of media: radio, television, newspapers, and perhaps even regional magazines or metropolitan editions of national magazines. Test markets should also reflect the general demographic characteristics of the larger population. However, because of the high costs of advertising in the very largest cities in the country, they are usually not used; instead, researchers generally favor smaller communities with more manageable media prices.

The top test marketing sites in the United States include Albany, Rochester, and Syracuse, New York; Charlotte and Greensboro, North Carolina; Nashville, Tennessee; Eugene, Oregon; Birmingham, Alabama; Wichita, Kansas; Richmond, Virginia; and Rockford, Peoria, and Springfield, Illinois. If your campaign will appear only in certain regions of the country, it only makes sense to select test markets from those regions.

Some final points: most often, more than one test market is used in case something unexpected occurs in one of the test areas. Usually, the "old" existing campaign will be tested in half the test markets, as a control, and the new campaign will be tested in the other half of the test markets.

Summary

Knowing how to apply research to real-world situations is just as important as knowing how to conduct the research itself. There are many applications of quantitative research in public relations and advertising. Some of these applications can utilize both qualitative and quantitative research, depending on the time available and the depth of responses that will be sought.

Discussion Questions

1. How could information on competitive spending be used in public relations?
2. What are the advantages of market tests? The disadvantages?
3. What are the advantages of media tests? The disadvantages?
4. What are the limits on the benefits of copy testing?
5. How are concept testing and content analysis similar? How are they different? When would each be used?
6. Is source credibility research more applicable to the media or to the sender of the message?

Exercises

1. Select a local firm and conduct a content analysis of its advertising in your locality.
2. Using your class or another group, conduct a source credibility test of the local mass media outlets.
3. Select samples of advertising copy and use them to conduct a copy testing study.

Additional Reading

Ross, H.L. *How copy testing works: Mapes and Ross copy test validation experience.* Roy Morgan International. http://www.roymorgan.com/resources/pdf/CopyTestingUSA.pdf.

Ambler, T., and S. Goldstein. 2003. *Copy testing: Practice and best practice.* Henley-on-Thames, Oxfordshire: The Advertising Association Economics Committee by the World Advertising Research Center.

McQuarrie, E. 2006. *The market research toolbox: A concise guide for beginners.* Thousand Oaks, CA: Sage.

Birn, R. 2002. *The international handbook of market research techniques.* London: Kogan Page.

20 Experimental Research

This chapter is intended to help you:

- Understand the difference between correlation and causation;
- Appreciate the advantage of control in inferring causation;
- Recognize and control for threats to internal validity;
- Weigh relative benefits of laboratory and field experiments.

CONTROLLING THE CHAOS

Much can be learned by studying advertising and public relations in natural settings without manipulating that environment. Recall from Chapter 4 that studies that observe behavior in natural environments tend to be high in external validity. That is, results obtained in the real world are likely to generalize to the similar situations in the world. But the real world is a chaotic, unpredictable place. You might have an entire team of researchers descend upon a shopping mall one Saturday only to be interrupted by a series of fire alarms at the mall. Similarly, the survey researcher has no control over the many distractions that are likely to confront the survey respondent. How well could you consider your buying habits while one child tugs on your pant leg for a glass of juice and two others quarrel in an adjacent room? Are those survey results comparable to those obtained from a bachelor who lives alone and responded to your telephone survey in complete silence? The truth is that most research techniques offer very little control to the researcher. Experiments, however, are all about control. The experimental researcher typically wants to control every single aspect of the environment except the one she wants to manipulate. This kind of rigorous control is about the only way that a researcher can make any strong conclusion about causation. And at the end of the day, most advertisers and public relations practitioners want to know what will *cause* you to buy more of their products and services—or at least like them better.

FROM CORRELATION TO CAUSATION

Humans are keen observers of correlation. It is easy for us to notice two events that occurred at approximately the same point in time. Think of Pavlov's dogs learning to associate a ringing bell with the presence of food. The dogs did not concern themselves with whether the bell *caused* the food to be present. It sufficed to note that the two events occurred together. We're not so different from those canines, really. Sports fans wear so-called lucky shirts to help propel their teams to victory. Sure, the team did win the last time that you wore that shirt (a correlation), but the chances that the shirt caused the win are pretty slim. Indeed, this points out the danger of a spurious correlation, one where two events co-occur but have no genuine relationship with one another. Although superstitious sports fans may seem silly, most of the time it is advantageous to associate correlation with causation. The toddler who burns her hand on a hot stove need not spend much time pondering whether the stove actually caused the burn. Better to simply avoid the stovetop from now on.

Although this logic suffices for much of everyday life, it is woefully inadequate for the researcher. Causation simply cannot meaningfully be inferred from correlation. When the stakes are low, there is little harm in mistaking co-occurrence for causation. The now antiquated skirt length theory of the economy is an often-cited example. Economists noted largely after the fact that women's hemlines tended to rise during times of economic prosperity and fall during dire times. Did one cause the other? There's not much interest in predicting hemlines, but there's a lot of interest in predicting the stock market. So if you see long skirts on the runways of Paris and Milan, should you speed dial the stockbroker? If the correlation is reliable, and you can profit from trading this way, then causation might not matter much. Yet it does not make much sense that skirts would cause economic cycles. Although one can make the opposite argument, it seems much more likely that some third, extraneous variable is causing a spurious correlation. Perhaps public uncertainty leads both to modest dressing and economic reservations. If circumstances change such that the third variable continues to affect the economy but stops affecting skirt lengths, you could go bankrupt on a buying spree after seeing a parade of short skirts one day.

Basing your persuasion efforts upon correlations is a little more trustworthy than coin flipping or skirt measuring—but not much. Consider launching an advertising campaign for an existing perfume in which each ad lists several tangible, logical benefits of perfume use. Also consider that the campaign not only fails to increase sales, but instead sales actually decrease. Here you have two events that co-occur in time. There is a correlation between the campaign and a decrease in sales. Now consider that you're the executive who must make the call on whether to discontinue the campaign. Do you have enough information to decide? What caused the campaign to fail? Perhaps it is a bad idea to advertise perfume with rational appeals (conventional wisdom would advise against the approach). It is also possible that logical appeals are a great idea, but you picked the wrong ones. Perhaps your appeals were great, but the photograph of the perfume was horrible. However, the possible causes for the ineffective ads extend far beyond your campaign. If you launched your campaign during an economic recession, then it's not very likely that consumers were going to rush to spend money on a luxury perfume. Maybe your primary competitor also launched a major campaign at the same time, but they outspent you on ads by a factor of five-to-one. All of these explanations are possible, and you simply lack the data to decide among them. Instead, you are forced to guess. No amount of speculation will allow you to confidently decide whether the relationship between the ads and sales were spurious or causal.

Experiments represent a different approach. Researchers design experiments specifically in order to be able to make claims about causation. However, in order to know that a given independent variable caused a change in the dependent variable, every other variable must be controlled. This kind of control is easier when human beings are not involved. If you boil distilled water at sea level while holding atmospheric pressure constant, you can expect consistent results around the world. If you vary the altitude while holding the barometric pressure constant, however, you can expect predictable results. At 1,200 feet above sea level, the boiling point is down to 210 degrees Fahrenheit. In Denver, almost 10 degrees have come off of the boiling point. You would expect nearly identical results in Campos do Jordão, Brazil, which is just a few feet higher. Sadly, people are not so cooperative.

CONTROL GROUP

Everyone knows that no two people are alike. Even identical twins are not perfectly similar. Therefore, using people in experiments requires a great deal of thought and planning. A poorly designed experiment is little better than a Magic 8 Ball. Boiling water is not much of an experiment, but it does illustrate some of the inherent challenges with human participants. If you boil a pan of water in Denver at an atmospheric pressure of 29.923 in., then you can expect it to boil at 202.4 degrees Fahrenheit. If you immediately cool the water and boil it again, you can expect the same result. Again and again and again.

Now imagine inviting a 24-year-old female paralegal from Denver to view a banner that your restaurant is planning to display at several event sponsorships in the area. You show her the banner and ask her opinions. Maybe you ask her to rate the banner using a few Likert scales. Then you take the banner away and bring it back. You ask the young woman to again complete the Likert scales. You repeat the procedure a third time. Eventually, you'll have your participant boiling, but in a very different sense than the pan of water. There are many, many problems with simply showing a banner to a participant and gauging her reactions. Different changes in the experimental design can help alleviate some—but rarely all—of those problems. However, because humans are complex, learning machines, no experiment is perfect. Instead the researcher must identify the most important concerns and address those. Other concerns consequently must go unaddressed.

Many concerns can be overcome with a true control group. Just as one group in a medical study gets genuine pills while another gets sugar pills, a true experiment has a control group. If a director of corporate communication wanted to pretest a new speech written for the CEO to deliver, some individuals should hear the speech and some individuals should not. Those who hear the speech represent the experimental group. Those who don't hear the speech represent the control group. If attitudes toward the company differ between the two groups, then we have some reason to suspect that the speech caused the difference. However, the presence of a control group alone does not ensure a true experiment. In order for us to feel confident that our speech (or

Exhibit 20.1

Basic Experiment

Random Assignment	Pretest	Experimental Treatment	Posttest
R	O_1	X	O_2
R	O_3		O_4

any other experimental treatment) caused a difference, participants must be randomly assigned to one of the two groups.

In the classic experimental design, there are two groups, experimental and control. Participants are randomly assigned to one of the two groups, denoted by the letter R in Exhibit 20.1. The dependent variable of interest is observed in the pretest for both groups, denoted by O_1 and O_3. Then only the experimental group receives the treatment, denoted as X. The dependent variable is again observed for both groups, denoted by O_2 and O_4. If the experiment is well designed and successful, the experimental treatment will have caused a difference between O_1 and O_2. That is, the experimental treatment will have caused a change in the dependent variable. However, there should have been no change for the control group because they were not exposed to the experimental treatment. Thus, there should be no difference between O_3 and O_4.

RANDOMNESS

Random is a word that many people use and few people truly understand. The difference between random and arbitrary is lost on most people, but that subtle difference is absolutely crucial in ensuring valid experimental results. In order for assignment to be truly random, each person must have an equal chance of being assigned to the experimental or control groups. This is deceptively simple. An equal chance means that the probability of ending up in the experimental group must be *exactly the same* for every participant. Approximately the same or seemingly the same simply will not suffice.

Readers of this book will accomplish many amazing things in their lives. But they're incapable of randomizing. So are the authors of this book. Instead when we attempt to be random, we are instead arbitrary. We may assign participants without any *seeming* pattern. However, that does not mean that a pattern does not exist. Just as medical doctors might unconsciously assign sicker looking patients to receive the genuine medication, you might assign "better" looking customers to hear the speech or see the event signage.

There are many tools to help researchers overcome their limitations with respect to randomness. When there is exactly one experimental group and one control group, the nearest randomizing device may be as close as your pocket. A quarter works nicely. For lovers of technology, Microsoft Excel has a random number function, as does every major statistical or spreadsheet software application. You can also use dice or numbered poker chips in a coffee can. As long as you use something other than your intuition, you will be better off.

It is important to understand why randomness works. It's not magic, and it's not particularly effective with small groups. The idea is that individual traits tend to vary across the population. If you randomly assign people to two groups, each group will tend to look like the larger population. Each group will also, in turn, tend to look like each other. If you have 200 people, and 100 of them are female, then randomly assigned groups will tend to be 50 percent female. When each randomly assigned group is smaller than about 30 however, you begin to run a risk that the two groups will fail to resemble one another. If you randomly assign five men and five women to two groups, you will get groups with four or five members of the same sex fairly often (for those really interested, it will happen about 18.75 percent of the time). Comparing the results of four men and a woman to four women and a man does not seem very rigorous, and it likely would not be. As the sample size increases, your odds of comparable groups also increase dramatically.

THREATS TO INTERNAL VALIDITY

As outlined above, control is one of the greatest assets of the experimental method. By allowing control over extraneous and possible confounding factors, experiments enable researchers to maximize internal validity. That is, experiments allow much greater confidence that the results obtained were caused by what the researcher expects, and competing explanations can be ruled out. However, several threats to internal validity exist for experiments. Random assignment and the presence of a control group alone are not sufficient to rule out these alternative explanations. In the seminal work on experimental design, Campbell and Stanley (1963) outline nine threats to external validity. Each is a concern, and certain steps can be taken to address these concerns.

HISTORY

Experiments in advertising and public relations often include a pretest and a posttest. That is, we might measure attitudes toward Bud Light before and after the Super Bowl. Since this malted beverage is one of the most frequent advertisers in the Super Bowl, we might expect that attitudes toward the company will improve if the ads were effective. The problem here is that beer ads are not the only thing that happens during the Super Bowl. You might eat food and chat with your friends. Your favorite team might lose. You might get food poisoning from some undercooked chicken wings and spend the entire second half in the bathroom. Every event that happens between the pretest and posttest might affect the outcome and is part of the history. If your favorite team loses the Super Bowl, you might hate *everything* immediately after. So the fact that your posttest attitudes toward Bud Light were hateful may very well have nothing to do with the ads.

A control group helps to solve the problem here. One group of randomly assigned participants does not watch the Super Bowl. Instead they spend the four hours in an all-white room with no television or reading material. Sounds absurd, right? Those poor people would be bored to death and likely not be in a very good mood. This illustrates the fact that there is no such thing as a perfect control group in advertising and public relations. If you have the control group watch a nature video to keep them from being bored to death, they did not watch the Super Bowl. But they did watch something else, and that something else might have led to any differences that you observe. There is no perfect answer. Researchers typically must make a reasonable compromise. It is most common for an innocuous stimulus similar in form but dissimilar in content to be used as a control in a communications study.

MATURATION

Maybe our participants don't get food poisoning, and they don't have a favorite team in the game. No other significant event happens during the game. At the least, however, they are four hours older than when they took the pretest. They probably did not change much during that time, but an experiment conducted over the course of an entire campaign might have some subtle aging effects. Moreover, the participants probably showed up hungry and thirsty and finished stuffed. They may have arrived cold from the January winter and left warm and toasty from having watched beside the fireplace. These subtle changes can have a difference—especially being thirsty in the current case. There are no easy solutions for maturation. Instead, controls should be case specific, such as making sure that participants had eaten and had a beverage before the pretest, too.

TESTING EFFECTS

Recall that our pan of boiling water did not care how many times that it had been boiled. People, however, do change when we ask them questions. For instance, you will probably take an exam for the research course you are taking. Do you think that you might perform better on the exam if you were allowed to take it a second time? This is a reasonable hypothesis. At the very least, you should have gained practice with the questions. Whenever conducting experiments with humans, testing effects are a problem. Both the control group and experimental group are subject to testing effects.

If there is a reason to suspect that testing effects will be problematic, researchers often turn to what Campbell and Stanley (1963) called the posttest-only control group design. In this simplification of the classic experimental design, the pretest is omitted for both the experimental and control groups. Here participants are randomly assigned to one of the two groups, the experimental group is exposed to the treatment, and posttest measures are taken for both groups, denoted in Exhibit 20.2 as O_1 and O_2. If there is a difference between the two observations, then it likely was caused by the experimental treatment. And the possibility of treatment effects has been removed. However, in the posttest-only control group design, one cannot be assured that there were no differences between the control group and the experimental group *before* the experimental treatment.

Solomon (1949) offered a solution to testing effects. Rather than one control group and one experimental group, Solomon proposed using two of each. One experimental group would get the pretest and the posttest, and the other would get only the posttest. The same comparisons can be made with the two control groups. Any effects

Exhibit 20.2

Posttest Only Design

Random Assignment	Experimental Treatment	Posttest
R	X	O_1
R		O_2

Exhibit 20.3

Solomon Four-Group Design

Random Assignment	Pretest	Experimental Treatment	Posttest
R	O_1	X	O_2
R	O_3		O_4
		X	O_5
			O_6

due to testing effects could be observed by comparing the two experiment groups, for example. If there is no difference between the posttest scores for the experimental group that received the pretest, O_2, and the experimental group that did not receive the pretest, O_5, then testing effects are not likely. The same check for testing effects can be made with the two control groups, O_4 and O_6.

Although Solomon's solution is an elegant one, it comes at a high cost. At a minimum, it requires twice as many participants due to the fact that there are twice as many groups. Doubling the cost can strain any research budget. Some researchers have proposed doing away with the pretest altogether. The reasoning is that with random assignment, any differences between the experimental and control groups at the time of posttest must be due the experimental treatment. And if the groups are truly randomly assigned and sufficiently large, then they would have been equivalent on the pretest anyway. For many, this is a convincing argument and an economical means of controlling testing effects.

INSTRUMENTATION

You might be tempted to control testing effects by asking the questions differently during the pretest and posttest. The problem is that one could never know whether the results obtained were due to the treatment or the change in questions. The Solomon design is a far better choice to control testing effects. However, it's not just that the questions—or testing instrument—might change. If you have a different researcher administer the pretest and the posttest, that also represents a possible confound of instrumentation. Likewise, having one researcher exclusively for the experimental group and another for the control group is a danger. You may run into a Jekyll and Hyde problem with one friendly experimenter and one bitter one. A friendly researcher might improve attitudes in only one group. Random assignment of the experimenter would help alleviate this problem. Better yet would be a balanced design where you ensure that each researcher is with the control group half of the time and with the experimental group the other half of the time, for example. However, you must be sensitive to further confounds, such as having Researcher A always with the control groups in the mornings. If Researcher A is cranky in the morning and jovial in the afternoon, you have solved nothing by balancing. An experimentalist never finishes fighting confounds.

STATISTICAL REGRESSION

This is a simple concept with a complicated name. There is a law of averages at work. Over the long term, there is a reason that an average score is an average score: it happens a lot. Therefore, exceedingly high (or low) pretest scores are likely to slide back toward the average during the posttest. Extremely tall parents tend to have tall children, but those children on average will not be quite as tall as the parents. They will be a little closer to the population average. This problem is generally satisfied with sufficiently large sample sizes (see Chapter 28 for a discussion on sample size).

SELECTION

Perhaps you felt that we belabored randomness above, but it is the key defense to problems of selection. If you stray from true randomness, you run the risk of assigning all left-handed people—or blue-eyed people—to the control group. If you're a public relations practitioner with a large account on the line, perhaps you will unintentionally direct those more likely to respond favorably to the experimental group. Any nonrandom selection can lead to selection biases. Random assignment is your friend here.

EXPERIMENTAL MORTALITY

This is not nearly as bad as it seems. In this instance, mortality refers to participants dropping out of the study. The poor soul who gets food poisoning during the Super Bowl might head home at halftime and never complete the posttest. Some people will invariably tire of your questions and simply quit. If this is a random process and the sample sizes are sufficiently large, then mortality is not an especially threatening problem. However, if there is a systematic reason that people are dropping out of your study, there is reason for concern. Perhaps you're preparing a public relations campaign for a major tobacco company, and you want to gauge the results of various tactics. If many of the nonsmokers—but none of the smokers—become offended and drop out after the pretest, you are likely to have skewed results, and the validity of your data will be questionable. Any results obtained may be due to the tactics you tested or mortality, and you will be unable to discern between those two options. This is controlled best by proper planning. Take care to make the experiment not overly burdensome or in any way unnecessarily offensive. Sometimes this cannot be completely avoided, as in a study about the use of sex in advertising. But experiments designed with the participant in mind will be less likely to suffer from problems of mortality.

INTERACTION EFFECTS

This is a somewhat catchall category that suggests that any two of the problems listed about might combine to cause an effect, or one of the items listed above might interact with your treatment. Perhaps your Super Bowl control group gets so bored that they decide to go home early. This is an interaction between the treatment and mortality, for example. Thus, not only must you be vigilant to each of the seven problems listed above, but you must anticipate interactions. It sounds daunting, but proper design can help ensure an excellent experiment with a high degree of internal validity.

LABORATORY EXPERIMENTS

To the experimental researcher, there is no place more wonderful than the laboratory. The laboratory represents the only place where the researcher can shut the door—literally—on the external world and exercise nearly complete control on the environment. Only in the laboratory can we exercise maximal control over the threats listed in the previous section.

If we are interested in the source credibility of various corporate spokespersons, we can record different individuals delivering the same speech. Then when the participant arrives in the lab, she is randomly assigned to see one of the speeches, or no speech at all for a true control group. The spokesperson is the only variable that changes. We can control the lighting, the temperature, the comfort of the chair, and the size of the television. Absolutely nothing will differ other than the speaker, which gives us maximum assurances that any results obtained are due to our experimental manipulation.

The trouble is that although lab experiments tend to maximize internal validity, they usually do so at the expense of external validity. The lab is an extremely artificial place, and the conditions in the lab tend not to resemble any naturalistic setting. In order to make our conditions more like the real world, we must leave the safe confines of the lab for the chaotic and unpredictable field.

FIELD EXPERIMENTS

Experiments in the field allow much more natural environments. We can examine how consumers behave in the market. In many ways, data obtained this way are much more valuable. However, random assignment is much more difficult—if not impossible—in the field. Individuals in a natural setting are subject to far more variables likely to lead to history effects. Fire alarms, competitors' campaigns, and economic changes are all at play in the field. The trade for a naturalistic setting over control is always an impossible comparison. Both the lab and the field have unique advantages, and ideally researchers would combine data from both. One can feel especially confident in results that replicate in the lab and field. The economic and time pressures of advertising and public relations research seldom make this possible, however.

SUMMARY

The primary advantage of experiments is control. By controlling as many variables as possible, the experimenter can often conclude than changes in one variable caused changes in another variable. This causation is far stronger than seemingly similar correlation. With simple correlation, one cannot know which of the variables affected the other—or whether some unknown third variable caused changes in both of the other variables. Even within an experiment, there are several threats to internal validity: history, maturation, testing effects, instrumentation, statistical regression, selection, experimental mortality, and interaction effects. Careful control and consideration can control for these threats. Laboratory experiments provide the greatest control over these threats, while field experiments provide more naturalistic settings.

DISCUSSION QUESTIONS

1. What are some situations where you would insist on knowing causal (rather than correlation) relationships between variables?
2. Are experiments better suited to maximize internal validity or external validity?
3. Which threats to internal validity seem most likely to be troublesome in advertising and public relations?
4. The Solomon four-group design allows experimenters to carefully check for testing effects. However, some have argued that with large sample sizes and true random assignment, the two pretest groups are unnecessary. Explain why this is the case.

EXERCISES

1. Consider that you're designing a public relations campaign to raise awareness about the problem of feral cats in your city. Design an experiment to test the effectiveness of the campaign before it is launched. Discuss your choices with respect to controlling threats to internal validity.
2. Using a database at your campus or local library, search for a peer-reviewed journal article about advertising or public relations that employs an experiment. Based upon what the author(s) state, what kind of experimental design did they use? From reading the article, can you deduce which threats to internal validity the authors felt the need to control?

ADDITIONAL READING

Bradac, J.J. 1983. On generalizing cabbages, messages, kings, and several other things: The virtues of multiplicity. *Human Communication Research*, 9, 181–87.

Campbell, D.T., and J.C. Stanley. 1963. *Experimental and quasi-experimental designs for research.* Boston: Houghton Mifflin.

Lang, A. 1996. The logic of using inferential statistics with experimental data from nonprobability samples: Inspired by Cooper, Dupagne, Potter, and Sparks. *Journal of Broadcasting and Electronic Media,* 40 (3), 422–30.

Lang, A., S.D. Bradley, Y. Chung, and S. Lee. 2003. Where the mind meets the message: Reflections on ten years of measuring psychological responses to media. *Journal of Broadcasting and Electronic Media,* 47, 650–55.

Reeves, B., and E. Thorson. 1986. Watching television: Experiments on the viewing process. *Communication Research,* 13, 343–61.

Shapiro, M.A. 2002. Generalizability in communication research. *Human Communication Research,* 28, 491–500.

21 Experimental Approaches

LEARNING OBJECTIVES

This chapter is intended to help you:

- Recognize common field experiments used in advertising and public relations;
- Understand uses of longitudinal panel studies;
- Understand uses of split run experiments;
- Comprehend advantages and limitations of test markets.

TAKING YOUR MESSAGE INTO THE FIELD

Before a corporation launches a major new public relations effort, executives usually want some indication that it is likely to succeed. Major themes or concepts from the campaign probably have been tested with focus groups, interviews, and even surveys. However, an endless stream of concept testing cannot ensure that a campaign will be effective in the real world. Instead, communication efforts often must be tested on actual consumers in the actual marketplace. These field experiments provide insight into the potential effectiveness of communication tactics. Panel studies allow for careful study of communication effectiveness over time with the same group of participants. Split run tests allow for simultaneous comparisons of different message versions. And test markets allow for smaller scale campaign testing without the risk of a full launch.

PANELS

Britney is leading a team to overhaul employee relations for a major corporation with thousands of employees in dozens of cities across North America. Although her employer once ranked among the top companies to work for, it has fallen out of the rankings in recent years. Morale continues to decrease, and worker productivity also is down. Britney's team of internal relations professionals has designed a series of efforts intended to increase job satisfaction, morale, and ultimately productivity. In addition to tracking these outcomes, the internal relations team worries about the perceived sincerity of the effort. They fear that if their efforts come across as a cheap ploy to placate workers, job satisfaction might decrease even more.

In order to keep a close watch on the campaign, Britney's team has identified 50 employees in each of 10 offices across the country. This group of 500 employees resembles the characteristics of the total corporate workforce. This group will be asked to confidentially report their opinions about the corporation before the effort begins and again every three months for the first year of the campaign. The employees will be given a unique ID number so that their responses can be tracked, but their numbers will not be available to upper management so that the panel participants will feel comfortable giving candid responses. By closely measuring attitudes among this representative panel, the internal relations team hopes to track the effects of their efforts over time. If problem areas arise, the team can take corrective action throughout the year in order to achieve the best possible result for their employer.

Panel studies are quasi-experimental studies that are especially good at detecting changes over time. In a panel study, a group of participants is recruited, determined to match the study's requirements, and studied at multiple points in time. When panel studies are used in advertising and public relations, attitudes, memory measures, and sales data are typically compared multiple times, as changes are made in communications efforts. Because panels study behavior over time, they are a type of longitudinal research. Almost every researcher agrees that more longitudinal research is necessary. However, the relative dearth of longitudinal research is not by accident. These types of studies can be expensive and particularly challenging.

RECRUITMENT

Panel studies vary widely, as it is easy to apply the "same people over time" idea almost anywhere. Participants can be recruited from among current customers, prospective customers, target demographics, and from various publics, such as the internal public described above. Care must be taken during the recruitment process, because mortality—or drop out—can become a serious limitation of panel studies. Some attrition is inevitable no matter how meticulous the recruiting process; however, diligence is required to find reliable participants, especially for panel studies that are expected to stretch over years. Many companies turn to professional recruiting research firms or outsource the panel study altogether. Given the longitudinal nature and the large amounts of data than can be collected, a panel study should not be undertaken without extensive planning. Sometimes the true source of the panel study is revealed during recruitment, but the sponsor's identity usually is concealed when there is a fear that knowledge of the source would bias the results.

INCENTIVES

Researchers have trouble getting participants to complete a single survey for free, and it is extremely difficult to obtain cooperation over time without compensating participants. The types of incentives used vary as widely as the types of panel studies. Sometimes participants are offered free products or services in exchange for their participation, but often they simply are paid for their efforts. The compensation depends upon the tasks required for the research and the relative burden placed upon participants. In every case, both researchers and respondents are continuously reevaluating the cost-to-benefit ratio of the participation and the incentive. If the incentive is too costly, the researcher will have to discontinue. If the incentive is too meager, respondents will drop out.

Data Collection

Due to the variation in panel designs, data collection also varies. Sometimes panelists complete a survey via mail or telephone. Surveys can be used to detect changes in attitude or memory about a corporation or product. Other panels ask participants to record certain behaviors in a diary. Respondents might record their purchases of canned vegetables or carbonated soft drinks. Heads of households might be asked to record consumption patterns for the entire family.

Market research companies increasingly turn to the Internet to collect panel data. Here corporations and universities recruit and maintain panels of respondents. Subsets of these panels can then be contacted on behalf of clients. Often in these cases, the panel is researched over time on behalf of several different clients. Thus, any one study is simply a one-shot survey or online focus group. Yet we still call this a panel because the same respondents are repeatedly contacted by the research firm or university. The advertising department of the University of Texas at Austin maintains such a panel. Each new study typically offers a new incentive to panel members, who are free to participate or opt out of any given study. This practice is extremely efficient because willing respondents do not have to be recruited anew for each successive client. However, this type of panel is susceptible to respondents becoming "professional" participants who learn to be very skilled at answering questions and no longer respond like the general public. In this way, panel participants may fail to be representative of their demographic and psychographic peers.

Technology and database marketing increasingly allow for the use of covert panels. Supermarket scanner data can be used to track purchasing behavior thanks to the widespread use of frequent shopper discount cards. In order to receive discounts on purchases, shoppers divulge their street address and allow a digital record to be kept of their purchases. When combining geographic, demographic, and purchase data over time, readers of this textbook likely have participated in numerous panel studies over time without ever knowing it. Geographic data allow public relations and advertising efforts to be tied to specific changes in purchasing behavior. Demographic data allow for comparison of communication effectiveness by contrasting changes in the purchasing behavior of specific demographic cohorts. Perhaps Mountain Dew's sponsorship of extreme sports events increased sales only in homes with male children between the ages of 9 and 14. ACNielsen Scantrack Services claim to have data from more than 4,800 stores representing more than 800 retailers in 52 large media markets.

ACNielsen is using technology to increasingly refine panel designs. Their Nielsen Homescan Panel project combines survey measures and purchase behavior within households. Portable scanners are used to register every barcode in the household, and then household members are surveyed for their attitudes and information about themselves.

LIMITATIONS OF PANELS

Although panel designs allow unique insight, researchers must be mindful of limitations of panels. As with every research project, the potential advantages of panel studies must be weighed against limitations. Proper planning and careful implementation can minimize possible limitations.

Recruiting and Retention

It is difficult to identify willing and dependable participants who also represent their demographic and psychographic profiles. Dependability and conscientiousness are personality traits that vary, and although individuals who are high in both make excellent panel participants, they may not resemble your target demographic. Complications with recruitment cause many researchers to turn to professional recruiters.

Once a participant becomes an active member of a panel, his or her continued participation is the only way to ensure the success of the panel. Every longitudinal study suffers from mortality, and this must be factored in from the start. The initial panel must be over-recruited to compensate for those who will drop out of the study over its duration. The longer the panel must be retained, the greater the number of participants who must be initially recruited to offset attrition. In the strictest sense, participants cannot be replaced. The benefit of having repeated observations from the same individuals is lost when one dropout is replaced with another individual. This type of research is common, but studying different individuals over time is a cohort study rather than a panel study.

Validity and Reliability

The majority of people asked to participate in a panel will refuse. Thus the external validity of even the first data collection in a panel is subject to debate. The greater the discrepancies between the actual participants and the target group, the greater the worry over the validity of the data.

Testing effects and instrumentation effects also are of concern in panel studies. If participants are repeatedly asked the same questions, they are likely to learn how to answer these questions. By the end of the panel study, the data obtained may be a better indicator of participants' skill at answering the questions than of changes in attitudes or behavior over time. If questions are varied in order to control for testing effects, panel researchers must then be concerned about instrumentation effects. Any changes observed over time may simply be due to changes in the research instrument rather than changes in corporate communications. In either case, the exact same behavior on the part of the respondents might lead to different data, which challenges the reliability of the data.

Undue Attention on the Studied Behavior

Diary studies also present unique challenges to validity and reliability. If participants constantly are asked to record and introspect about their snack food eating, then they are likely to put an undue amount of thought into their snacks. Perhaps this increased thought will lead to healthier snacking—or a decrease in between-meal eating altogether. Likewise, an individual asked to chronicle his use of household cleaners might conclude that he does not clean enough, leading to an increase of purchases. In fact, it might be more troublesome if repeated attention to one's behavior did not in some way affect that behavior.

Overwhelming Data

Panel studies tend to produce a great deal of data, and this quantity is magnified at each subsequent measurement. Novice survey researchers often are surprised by the bulk of paper that amasses when a study begins to be returned. Often no plans have been made to store and archive these documents. For Internet and phone surveys, this is less of a physical problem. However, the digital archive must also be maintained. The data must be preserved and backed up. The people responsible for data analysis must not be overwhelmed by the raw volume of data. Even if sufficient electronic storage exists, many researchers simply are unprepared for the massive data sets that a panel study can generate. If 2,000 panel participants are each asked 100 questions twice a year for 4 years, the study will produce 1.6 million individual responses to be analyzed and tabulated.

Confidentiality

Care must be taken to ensure the confidentiality of participants. Because data must be cross-referenced to individual participants at each administration, anonymous data are not an option. When individuals' responses can be tied to their identities, special care is required. Most panel studies in advertising and public relations will not involve sensitive topics; however, most people would prefer that even their benign buying habits not be shared publicly. For this reason, researchers should devise a plan for handling data in advance.

SPLIT RUNS

Split runs represent a simple yet effective experimental design. In the simplest implementation, two different versions of an advertisement are prepared. Half of the recipients see one version of the ad, and the other half see the other version. The split run, also referred to as an A/B split, is especially powerful when paired with direct-response advertising. When consumers have to return a reply card or telephone a toll-free number, advertisers receive almost instant feedback on which version was more effective.

Given this need to alternate versions, the split run is less easily implemented with broadcast media. It's impossible for a traditional television or radio station to broadcast two different versions of the same ad at once. However, split runs are fairly common among print media. Most large newspapers and magazines can alternate ad versions in every other copy. Preprinted inserts, such as those seen in the Sunday newspaper, can be shipped to the newspaper already alternated. Without ever knowing, half of the readers might get a half-off green beans coupon while the other half get a two-for-one coupon. When the coupons are redeemed by the grocers, then the company will know which appeal was more effective.

SPLIT RUN APPLICATIONS

The split run method is typically used to measure advertising effectiveness. Any number of advertising variables can be clandestinely pitted against one another. Two different background colors can be compared. Does a sports celebrity get consumers to use a soup coupon more often than an ordinary looking consumer? Layouts, typefaces, headlines, rebates, premiums, and illustrations all can be tested using a split run. However, unless there is a direct response to the ad, it would be impossible to know for sure which version of an ad led to a purchase. Consumers have notoriously poor memories, and asking them at the cash register about the ad that they saw would not produce reliable data. If a split run is used to vary the ad in different markets, then that experimental application is better described as a test market rather than a split run. Exhibit 21.1 shows an example of two different versions of the same coupon that could be split run in a direct mail piece. The dry cleaner could see whether the "50 percent" coupon pulled better than the "Buy 2, Get 2 Free" version.

Although not common, split runs can be used in public relations. Different versions of news releases or video news releases can be sent to media outlets across the nation. Researchers can then assess whether one version was more likely to be adopted by the press.

ONLINE SPLIT RUNS

Although television and radio are poorly suited for split runs, the Internet is ideal. Web sites can be programmed to randomly load different versions of an ad, and click-through rates and subsequent purchases can be assessed instantly. More than the banner ad, entire sections of a Web site can load in a split run manner. For example, two different customer complaint pages could be designed. If each were to load randomly half of the time, the final satisfaction of customers could be compared between the two pages. Online pizza ordering is becoming increasingly common, and various coupon offers can easily be tested in split run fashion.

For both advertising and public relations, search engine optimization is becoming increasingly important. Search engine optimization involves customizing Web sites to ensure that search engines—and ultimately potential customers who use them—can find your business. Although there is a science quickly developing around search engine optimization, analytic software allows companies to track which Web pages and keywords lead customers to their Web sites. If a product is featured in two different ways in order to appeal to two different demographics, analytic software can determine which of these approaches drove more search engines and more traffic to the Web site.

Exhibit 21.1   **Split Run Example in Direct Mail Item**

MARKET TESTS

Market tests represent small-scale trials in the actual consumer marketplace. They are common in marketing, where new products, packaging, and promotion are tried out in selected media markets. Market tests also are used to test communications efforts before full-scale campaigns are launched. In this sense, market tests are diagnostic and can be used before funds are allocated for a national campaign launch. Communications professionals research media markets that they feel will represent the nation as a whole. The communications efforts are then launched in these select markets, and outcomes are assessed. In the best case, similar markets are selected to not receive the efforts. These markets represent the control group.

Exhibit 21.2

When Test Marketing Fails

Nothing is guaranteed with fickle consumers. A successful test market means that the ultimate effort is more likely to succeed, but it does not guarantee such success. Pepsi discovered this in the early 1990s with Crystal Pepsi, a cola-flavored drink that was clear like lemon-lime drinks. Consumers responded positively in early test marketing results

According to *Advertising Age,* Crystal Pepsi was test marketed in Dallas; Providence, Rhode Island; and several cities in Colorado. The launch was supported with a multi-platform advertising campaign from BBDO Worldwide, New York, according to *Ad Age.*

Market research drove the clear invention, according to an April 13, 1992, article in *The New York Times.* "Clear has a positive connotation," market researcher George Rosenbaum told *The Times.* "The other drinks have mysterious ingredients."

Despite positive test market results and an ultimate national launch backed by a $40 million advertising campaign, you will not find Crystal Pepsi on shelves today. In September 1993, *Ad Age* reported that Pepsi was lowering sales expectations for the drink and changing advertising strategies. By December 1993, Pepsi was considering reformulating the drink with a citrus flavor, according to *Adweek.* In July 1994, the citrus cola "Crystal" was hitting shelves with "Pepsi" removed from the name, *Ad Age* reported. The new product also failed, illustrating that even successful test marketing and big budget campaigns do not ensure success.

FUNCTIONS

Much is at stake when a national advertising or public relations effort is launched. Although nothing is certain in the unpredictable world of paid persuasion, CEOs typically want some assurance before giving the go ahead. Test markets allow for diagnostic functions in communication efforts. The dissemination of public relations information can be tested before the company goes all in. If one part of a media kit is weak, for example, it can be revised and improved before a national launch.

In the best case scenario, the test markets will predict the program's success. If the communications efforts are wildly successful in the test markets, then one can be reasonably optimistic that the overall campaign will be a success. Upon receiving favorable test marketing data, campaigns usually are launched.

If the data are unfavorable, however, a campaign can be shelved before it potentially fails nationwide. Test marketing communications efforts are not cheap, but the test market is not a failure simply because the campaign is pulled. Withholding a bad campaign may be every bit as valuable as launching a stellar one. The "go/no go" decision is incredibly important, and test markets can help that be an informed decision.

Test markets also can be used to test alternative communication campaigns. Rather than the basic test market/control market design, multiple test markets can be employed. This method is not limited to simply deciding whether to go forward with a campaign. Test markets can be used to decide *which* campaign will go forward. Cost quickly becomes a concern here as multiple campaigns are launched in multiple markets. Given that these are field experiments, actual costs accrue quickly.

Limitations of Test Markets

Perhaps the biggest risk of test marketing advertising and public relations efforts is that you very visibly show your hand to competitors. You are not the only one who will see the relative success of your efforts. Mindful competitors can quickly mimic successes in other markets before you have the chance to. Likewise, if you abandon an ineffective test marketing effort, your competitor also is likely to learn from your mistakes. Whether your test market efforts succeed or fail, you also expose your strategy to your competitors. All elements of surprise are lost when communications efforts reach the actual market. Thus, if the communications efforts are particularly unique, test marketing likely is ill advised.

The investment required for test marketing can be considerable, especially for advertising campaigns. Television, radio, outdoor, and display advertising are expensive, and these costs can seem prohibitive for what amounts to a diagnostic effort. For public relations efforts, the time invested by employees in launching in test markets may be only incrementally less than a national campaign. If the overall strategy is approved, all of the personnel costs will need to be invested again.

Site Selection

The appropriate selection of test market sites represents what is likely the most important decision in the test marketing efforts. If poor choices are made about the actual test markets themselves, any data collected will be meaningless. Foremost, the test markets must be representative of the nation (or region) as a whole. If a market is predominantly blue collar, and you are aiming for an upscale demographic, then it is not suitable for your study. The test markets need to be representative on all key relevant variables, and there is no simple manual to help you know which variables are relevant. This is where it is crucially important to understand the end target of your communications effort. If you truly know to whom your message is tailored, then it should be relatively simple to identify media markets that are representative of that group.

It is always advisable to test in more than one market. If only one market is selected, that market is completely confounded with the campaign. Any changes observed may be due to the public relations or advertising efforts, or they may be due to particular eccentricities of the single market. With only one test market, there is no way to distinguish between the two alternatives. Multiple markets add great clarity here. If the campaign succeeds in multiple markets, then there is a higher likelihood that it will succeed nationally. However, if your efforts fail in one location but succeed in another, there is cause for concern. More research is needed to determine what caused the discrepancy. Perhaps the differences were due to a fluke, but perhaps they also were due to previously unrecognized differences among the target markets.

Market Isolation

To the greatest extent possible, test markets should be selected such that your communication efforts will be relatively self-contained in the markets you choose. This is the digital era, and there is no such thing as complete containment. Your 30-second commercial in Wichita, Kansas, could be showing on YouTube just a few minutes after it first airs. However, that is unlikely with most communication efforts.

If your public relations efforts reach out to media professionals in Dallas, then you had better ensure that your control markets do not receive delivery of the *Dallas Morning News*. Likewise, if a media market receives media from two different markets, then it is likely a poor choice for a test market because you do not know which consumers will ever know of your communications efforts. If your news releases are retransmitted on public relations networks, test marketing efforts can fail. To the greatest extent possible, one needs to ensure that the test market receives only communications targeted to that market, and that messages targeted to that market are not widely disseminated to other markets.

DURATION OF TEST

When looking at traditional test market efforts—such as the introduction of a new line of sandwiches at a fast-food chain—the duration of test marketing is easier to predict. Due to the great variability in communications efforts, however, it is less clear with advertising and public relations. If there is seasonal variation involved with the product or service, then the test marketing should reflect this. It would be foolish to test market a lawnmower advertising campaign in the fall for a spring launch. In these cases, the test marketing would likely occur over the full product cycle a year in advance of a possible national launch. As this illustrates, test marketing can be slow to develop.

In general, test marketing of communications efforts is tied to the purchase cycle. Most people eat fast food at least a couple of times per month. Therefore one can expect that effects due to advertising and public relations efforts will manifest themselves rather quickly. Conversely, people purchase automobiles every three to five years at best. Thus, it is impossible for a test market effort to capture a repeat purchase cycle. However, the efforts should be mindful of the increase in sales at the beginning of a new model year and the discounts associated with the end of the model year. Failure to account for these types of fluctuations could dramatically bias results.

WHEN TO IMPLEMENT TEST MARKETING

Test marketing is advised when it is economically realistic, when management has committed to well-defined goals, and overall strategy is not likely to be compromised by the competition being aware of your communication efforts. Test markets are economical when small local media buys can inform far larger national ones. Conversely, however, much of the expense in public relations is involved in the time of public relations professionals. In these instances, a national launch might make more sense than a test market effort that would cost nearly as much. If goals are not clearly delineated in advance, then there is no way to determine its effectiveness. Was the campaign designed to increase top-of-mind awareness for an established brand, or was it designed solely to move product? Some campaigns merely seek to increase favorable public opinion about an entity. In this case, posttest attitudes can be measures. However, increasing favorability will be insufficient if management were to decide that sales were most important halfway through the test market.

EVALUATION

Test market evaluation is directly linked to the goals of the campaign. If sales are most crucial, then cooperation is needed from retailers. Store audits and scanner data will establish how much of the product was sold. The corporation usually is limited to distribution data, which can be misleading if extra product made it to the shelf but never sold. Just because it left your warehouse doesn't guarantee that it made it to the customer's pantry. Perhaps your public relations efforts were persuasive only to store managers, who increased your shelf space in anticipation of customers who never appeared.

If favorable attitudes or brand awareness were the goal, then surveys and focus groups can be used to assess effectiveness. Here one might pair a panel study with a test market to examine changes in attitudes over time. Once again, clearly established goals are necessary. If a series of event sponsorships in the market were designed to improve top-of-mind awareness from 33 percent to 50 percent, that needs to be outlined. Only then will you know whether 43 percent awareness is a success or failure.

Evaluation efforts should also be mindful of competitors. Although you will be unable to obtain their sales data in most cases, you should be able to observe any counter-maneuvers. Corporations have been known to flood a market with coupons to ensure that consumers stock up on their brand—even if the coupons cause a loss on the sales—in order to prevent them from buying from a competitor clearly engaging in a test market. Although underhanded, such tactics are not illegal. Failing to notice them could compromise test market evaluation.

Finally, large corporations must guard against cannibalization. When you have two brands of detergent on the market, it does not suffice to know only that you increase sales of one brand. If this increase in sales came exclusively at the expense of your other brand, then the communications effort cannot be considered a success. Advertising and public relations are costly, and these expenses are ill-advised if they lead to no net change in corporate sales.

SUMMARY

There are several common ways that advertising and public relations professionals use field experiments to inform their efforts. Panel studies are longitudinal studies that assess the same group of people over time. The effects of communications efforts can be assessed by examining attitudes and behavior before and after the communication. Split runs are simple experiments that show different versions of messages to different audiences. When combined with some type of response, the relative effectiveness of different messages can be assessed almost instantly. Test markets can be used to pretest advertising and public relations efforts on a small scale before launching them nationally and regionally.

DISCUSSION QUESTIONS

1. What are some reasons why panel studies are quasi-experiments and not true experiments?
2. Is it possible to use split run tests effectively without a direct consumer response?
3. When is test marketing advisable for advertising and public relations research?
4. Why are clearly defined goals important for test marketing?

EXERCISES

1. A public relations firm has been hired to increase public support for alternative energy adoption, specifically wind power. Suggest a panel study design to help the firm gauge the success of their efforts.
2. A sports drink company has hired a retired major league pitcher to endorse a new knee brace that is being sold via mail order. They have also paid the licensing rights to allow the pitcher to be shown in his actual uniform. However, the contract for the licensing rights is short-term. Design a study to determine whether sales improve when the pitcher is shown in his actual uniform compared to a generic uniform that does not require licensing rights.
3. A manufacturer of snow blowers is planning a large regional advertising campaign for their newest model. Outline the major challenges this manufacturer would face if executives were to request a test market of the advertisements.

ADDITIONAL READING

Segal, M.N., and J.S. Johar. 1992. On improving the effectiveness of test marketing decisions. *European Journal of Marketing,* 26(4), 21–33.

Shah, D.V., J. Cho, S. Nah, M.R. Gotlieb, H. Hwang, N-J. Lee, R.M. Scholl, and D.M. McLeod. 2007. Campaign ads, online messaging, and participation: extending the communication mediation model. *Journal of Communication,* 57, 676–703.

Waldman, E. 1956. Selection of newspapers for split-run tests. *Journal of Marketing,* 20(3), 271–74.

22 Quasi-Experimental Research

LEARNING OBJECTIVES

This chapter is intended to help you:

- Understand the difference between a genuine experimental design and a quasi-experimental design;
- Recognize situations where quasi-experimental designs may be appropriate;
- Learn how to interpret results from nonequivalent group, posttest only design;
- Understand how the addition of a pretest improves a nonequivalent group, post-test only design;
- Interpret an interrupted time series design;
- Understand how the addition of a control group improves a time series design.

WHEN AN EXPERIMENT IS NOT QUITE AN EXPERIMENT

What does it take to be a full-fledged experiment? How exactly does a quasi-experiment get demoted to being only somewhat like an experiment? The primary difference between an experiment and a quasi-experiment is that quasi-experiments lack true random assignment. Although it may sound nitpicky to belabor the necessity of random assignment, the entire foundation of logical inference upon which experiments are built depends upon true random assignment. Each experimental participant must have an equal chance of being assigned to the experimental group or the control group.

Although random assignment is ideal, often there are situations in advertising and public relations research that do not allow for true experimental designs. In these cases, it is better to collect some data rather than no data. Quasi-experiments can provide meaningful insight if conducted correctly. However, interpretation of data must always be in light of the lack of true randomization. Quasi-experiments can hint at causation, but they cannot assure it. One must be careful not to draw rigid conclusions based upon quasi-experiments.

NONEQUIVALENT GROUP, POSTTEST ONLY

This design represents the weakest, least helpful quasi-experimental design. Here there are two groups, but participants are not randomly assigned to a group. Consider an

Exhibit 22.1

Nonequivalent Group, Posttest Only

Experimental Treatment	Posttest
X	O_1
	O_2

online merchant tracking future purchases of customers who did and did not register complaints with the company's customer service department. It does not take much imagination to assume that complaint-filing customers likely will buy less merchandise in the future. However, can you infer that the event that led to the complaint *caused* the decrease in purchases? The two events seem related, but perhaps only certain types of people file complaints. Perhaps every customer receives the same poor customer service (hopefully not), but only really uptight people become mad enough to file a complaint. And since they have worked themselves up so much, they remember the bad experience and let it influence their behavior the next time they buy. Here it looks as if the decrease in purchasing is due to a complaint when in reality it was probably due to a personality trait of certain customers. Exhibit 22.1 shows that there is no random assignment.

Another way that communications professionals use nonequivalent groups with only posttests is to follow up after the broadcast of television commercials. Using telephone calling similar to a survey, researchers can try to determine whether a television advertisement had an effect on top-of-mind awareness, or the likelihood that the respondent mentions the target business when asked to name a business in that product category. Consumers might be asked to name an automotive dealership that comes to mind. After those questions are answered, respondents can be asked to recall the television programs that they watched the night before. Here television viewing can be considered the experimental treatment. When combining the viewing data with the awareness data, researchers can separate participants into two groups: those who likely saw the ads and those who likely did not. If the target dealership is named more often by viewers, then there is evidence that the ad may have been effective. However, because participants were not randomly assigned, any differences observed may have been due to some other variable, such as the type of people who watch programs on that television network. Perhaps the television program appeals to affluent viewers, who may be more likely to name the luxury car client regardless of whether they saw the advertisement. In this case, the variables of income and television viewing (and hence exposure to the advertisement) are confounded. Either variable could have increased top-of-mind awareness, and quasi-experimental designs do not provide any way to distinguish between the rival explanations.

Due to the fact that participants are not randomly assigned to the groups, there is no reason to assume that the individuals are equivalent in other respects. Recall that the use of random assignment and groups larger than thirty tends to even out individual differences. With large samples, experimental and control groups tend to have the same number of women, extroverts, and people born in January, for ex-

Exhibit 22.2

Nonequivalent Group, Pretest-Posttest

Pretest	Experimental Treatment	Posttest
O_1	X	O_2
O_3		O_4

ample. Without random assignment, these equivalencies cannot be assumed and are often not the case. To err on the side of caution, we must assume that the groups are nonequivalent. Although we can hope that results obtained are due to the variables of interest, we can never completely rule out alternative explanations without random assignment. Demographic data can be recorded during the posttest, and comparisons can be made between those variables. If ages, incomes, and education levels are equivalent, researchers can have some confidence that the groups might be equivalent. However, this is not a certainty. No one can think of every possible difference, and even if every relevant difference could be queried, participants would never tolerate this many questions.

NONEQUIVALENT GROUP, PRETEST-POSTTEST

The inclusion of pretests allows researchers to feel more confident about results obtained. Both groups are measured before some treatment or stimulus, and both groups are again measured after stimulus presentation. Once again, however, there is no random assignment. Participants self select the group to which they will belong—either knowingly or unknowingly. And whatever caused participants to wind up in the experimental group was not random and may have been the ultimate cause of changes observed in the posttest rather than the experimental treatment. Exhibit 22.2 illustrates the addition of a pretest.

As an example of this technique: a major agricultural company's public relations department could put together a series of training modules for reporters who write about agriculture. The modules would be designed to keep reporters up-to-speed on the importance of agriculture for society, best practices, new technologies, and food safety issues. The online modules could be offered to reporters across the nation, but voluntary participation would fall far short of 100 percent. In order to examine the effectiveness of these modules, the public relations department could collect articles written before (pretest) and after the introduction of the modules (posttest). Through online registration, the research team could identify reporters who viewed the modules and those who did not. Those who saw the modules are the experimental group, and those who did not view the modules are the control group.

Then the team could perform a detailed content analysis of all the news stories written by these reporters. The content analysis could examine the language used by the reporters to look for bias toward or against agriculture. If the modules were successful, then the articles written after the experimental group viewed the training modules would contain less bias against agriculture, and perhaps they would paint the agricultural community in a favorable light. The inclusion of a pretest—in this case a content analysis of news stories written before the modules—allows for the public relations team to feel more confident that the changes observed were due to the modules. Furthermore, if both groups showed equivalent bias before the modules, and only the module-group showed a decline in bias, then there is additional evidence of effectiveness. Looking at Exhibit 22.2, one would hope to see no change between O_3 and O_4 but a significant change between O_1 and O_2. However, the lack of random assignments precludes ruling out alternative explanations. Perhaps some reporters had a change of heart about agriculture, and that change of heart led them to seek out the modules. Thus, the changes in coverage observed were simply due to attitudinal changes that occurred independently from the modules. Although this is unlikely, it cannot be ruled out.

INTERRUPTED TIME SERIES DESIGN

Time represents one of the most important—and most often overlooked—aspects in all areas of research. Nothing happens in a moment; everything happens over time. Imagine a photograph of an automobile on a roadway. This is a snapshot in time, and it tells us almost nothing. Is the car moving quickly or slowly? Accelerating or decelerating? Where did it come from? Where is it going? Snapshots such as this miss most of the interesting questions. Therefore most researchers agree on the importance of longitudinal studies. And when they agree, most researchers mean that everyone else should do the time-consuming longitudinal studies. Most research projects in advertising and public relations do not have sufficient time, money, or inclination to include longitudinal designs.

The interrupted time series design allows for researchers to examine some key variable over time. This variable is measured at several instances before and after the experimental treatment, when the advertising or public relations professional introduces some new communication into the marketplace. Consumer reactions are studied at multiple points before and after the communication. At the most basic level, the interrupted time series design is an experimental-group only quasi-experiment with multiple pretests and multiple posttests. (See Exhibit 22.3.) The benefit to the multiple measurements is that they allow for researchers to see trends that might have been occurring independently from the experimental manipulation. This ability to capture patterns is both an asset and a limitation. The interrupted time series design lacks control over other events in the world that occur. Given that other, uncontrolled variables may co-occur with the experimental treatment, true causation cannot be demonstrated. In addition, the interrupted time series design lacks a nonequivalent control group—let alone a genuine control group. Hence it is truly a quasi-experimental design.

Executives in charge of a regional chain of hospitals may worry that the rising cost of health care has tarnished their brand. They want to launch a public relations campaign to boost public opinion. The external corporate communications team hires a survey research firm to conduct 500 surveys a month for the four months before and after the campaign launch. By measuring opinions over time, the team hopes to capture ongoing trends and the duration of effects of the campaign. If the campaign

Exhibit 22.3

Interrupted Time Series Design

Experimental Treatment								
O_1	O_2	O_3	O_4	X	O_5	O_6	O_7	O_8

Exhibit 22.4   **Percentage of Respondents with a Favorable Opinion of Hospital Chain over an Eight-Month Period**

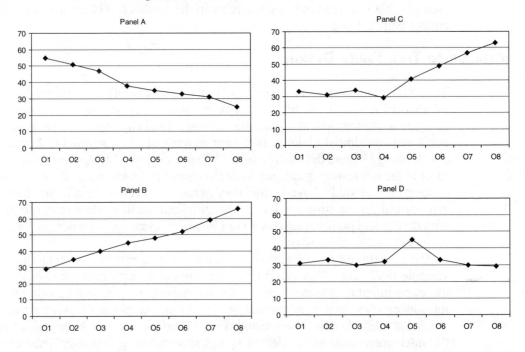

produces only a short-term bump in favorability, then it can hardly be considered a success. Even worse, the campaign may have no effect at all.

Consider the four possible outcomes illustrated in Exhibit 22.4. In each case, a public relations campaign was launched between Month 4 and Month 5. Which of these outcomes suggests that the campaign was effective? Panel A is the worst possible outcome. Public opinion was declining and continued to decline despite the campaign. Because the study is a quasi-experimental design, we cannot know whether the campaign prevented an even greater decrease or caused a decrease when public opinion otherwise would have leveled off. Panel B appears to be the opposite case. Public opinion was on the rise, and it continued to improve after the campaign. Once again there is no way to know whether the campaign played a role. Panel C represents the best possible outcome. There were small fluctuations in opinion before the campaign (likely due to sampling error), and then opinion began to improve—and continued to improve—after the campaign. The effects appear to be both successful

Exhibit 22.5

Multiple Time Series Design

				Experimental Treatment				
O_1	O_3	O_5	O_7	X	O_9	O_{11}	O_{13}	O_{15}
O_2	O_4	O_6	O_8		O_{10}	O_{12}	O_{14}	O_{16}

and long lasting, although this, too, is subject to alternative explanations. Panel D illustrates the benefit of the interrupted time series design. Here there is an immediate increase in favorable ratings following the campaign, but the increase is short-lived. Although the campaign demonstrated improvement immediately after the campaign, the improvement was short-lived and appeared to have very little effect with long-term public relations. This fleeting nature of improvement would have been missed with a simple pretest-posttest design. This illustrates the importance of longitudinal studies despite the increased time and expense. Even two snapshots in time can miss longer-term patterns.

MULTIPLE TIME SERIES DESIGN

This design is a simple extension of the interrupted time series design. In this case, there is an attempt to add a control group to the design. Thus, two different groups are measured over time. One group receives the experimental treatment while the other does not. As with the designs discussed above, there is no random assignment to groups. Some people were exposed to the experimental treatment and some did not receive the treatment. Therefore, inferences about the experimental treatment causing differences between the groups should be made with caution. Differences between the groups *before* the experimental treatment suggest that the groups are indeed nonequivalent on some relevant dimension.

SUMMARY

Genuine experimental designs are always preferable to quasi-experimental designs; however, time pressures and financial limitations in the professional world often make true experimental designs impossible. Quasi-experiments allow researchers to collect data when full experimental designs are not possible. Nonequivalent group, posttest only designs allow researchers to compare outcomes between a group that received some stimulus and a control group that did not. However, participants are not randomly assigned, so any posttest differences may be due to extraneous third variables. This design is improved upon with the addition of a pretest. Changes before and after the experimental treatment can be assessed, and pretest differences between the experimental and control groups can be uncovered. Changes over time before and after a communications effort can be assessed using an interrupted time series design. Additional rigor can be added to this design with the inclusion of a control group in a multiple time series design.

DISCUSSION QUESTIONS

1. Why can researchers not be assured that an experimental treatment caused differences between the experimental and control in a nonequivalent group, posttest only?
2. How does the addition of a pretest improve upon the nonequivalent group, posttest only design?
3. To what does the "interrupt" refer in an interrupted time series design?
4. Why would researchers want to add a control group to an interrupted time series design?

EXERCISES

1. Your ad agency is about to launch a campaign promoting a new type of bread at a regional sub sandwich chain. The bread will be introduced in four of the eight media markets in which the chain has restaurants. Design a quasi-experiment to determine whether the advertisements increase awareness of the new bread.
2. Looking at Exhibit 22.5, consider which observations should be different and which should be the same between the control group and experimental group if the groups are roughly equivalent and the manipulation had an effect.

ADDITIONAL READING

Campbell, D.T., and J.C. Stanley. 1963. *Experimental and quasi-experimental designs for research.* Boston, MA: Houghton Mifflin.

Caporaso, J.A., and L.L. Roos Jr. 1973. *Quasi-experimental approaches: Testing theory and evaluation policy.* Evanston, IL: Northwestern University Press.

Cook. T.D., and D.T. Campbell. 1979. *Quasi-experimentation: Design & analysis issues for field settings.* Boston, MA: Houghton Mifflin.

23 Experimental Applications in Advertising and Public Relations

LEARNING OBJECTIVES

This chapter is intended to help you:

- Understand the benefits and limitations of experiments involving psychophysiology and eye tracking;
- Interpret studies measuring skin conductance;
- Comprehend the use of heart rate as a measure of attention and arousal;
- Understand the use of facial electromyography (EMG) as a measure of emotional response.

TELLING STORIES

The majority of the research described in this textbook places a great burden upon respondents if the research is to have any value. They are asked to answer questions from their own perceived experiences—in scientific terms, their *self-report*, or the participant's subjective assessment of their own cognitive or emotional state. This requires that participants engage in conscious introspection to report their attitudes, opinions, beliefs, and preferences. Unfortunately for researchers, people do not seem to be especially good at conscious introspection. Ask almost anyone a question about her attitude or why she drinks that particular brand of coffee, and an answer will almost always be forthcoming. Too often, however, those answers have little to do with reality.

Too often people have what author Malcolm Gladwell calls a storytelling problem. "We're a bit too quick to come up with explanations for things we don't really have an explanation for" (Gladwell 2005, 69). Ask someone why they chose Pepsi, and she'll tell you it's because it tastes better. Ask someone why they buy Clorox bleach, and he'll tell you that it gets clothes cleaner. Ask someone why they buy clothes at Hollister, and she'll tell you the blue jeans fit better. But if you strip away the brand labels, consumers are not nearly as good at picking their allegedly better tasting, better cleaning, better fitting favorites. Few people want to believe that they pay premium prices for brand name products simply because they've fallen for the brands. Not only do they not want to tell researchers, they often do not believe it themselves. But the data say otherwise. Gladwell's storytelling problem is a major impediment to research in advertising and public relations.

In recent years, researchers have turned to behavioral and psychophysiological methods that circumvent this need for self-report. Rather than showing a participant a television commercial and asking what he or she thinks, psychophsyiologists simply want to note how the body responds while the consumer is watching the commercial or thinking about the brand. It should not come as a surprise that many of these technologies are rooted in lie detection. In advertising and public relations, however, we're not interested in catching participants in a lie. Instead, we're interested in preventing them from lying in the first place.

THE MIND AND THE BODY

Take a moment to look around you. What do you notice? Look for something you like. Think about why you like it. We interpret this conscious awareness as part of what makes us human. When we "think" about something, it seems as if this is what happens in the brain. But the truth is that these thoughts—these pictures in our heads— are just a narrow band of brain activity. Many functions of the mind simply are not available to conscious introspection. Much of the hardware charged with keeping us alive is invisible to conscious self-report. Right now parts of your brain are charged with regulating your blood pressure and monitoring your breathing rate. It's easy to understand that these mental functions are hidden from thought, but the truth is that so much more is going on below the surface of perception.

The human mind is in the prediction business. While you're trying to figure out what to do right now, your mind is trying to figure out what is going to come next. Hopefully, fight-or-flight responses are exceedingly rare for the average person. Life would not be much fun if you were constantly fighting for your survival. Even though fight-or-flight is rare, your brain had better be efficient at shifting you into escape mode if the need arises. If a mugger pounces on you, there is no time for conscious consideration of the circumstances. You need to run. NOW!

Of course it would be possible for you to remain hyper vigilant at all times. The human mind and body could be perpetually prepared for vigorous action. You could be like a hummingbird. But this takes lots of energy—calories. To be perpetually prepared for flight would cause a constant need for nourishment. You'd have to eat all the time in order to keep your heart beating above 100 beats per minutes, supplying every muscle with an abundance of fuel. So you would be on a constant quest for food. And you'd often be too busy eating to notice if a predator were to sneak up on you, which would defeat the entire purpose of hyper vigilance.

The maximal preparedness strategy simply is too inefficient to be effective. So your mind is always trying to predict what action is likely to be required in the immediate future. If you're in a calm, safe place meditating, not much energy is likely to be required. So your heart slows greatly, and the muscles of your body relax. You are at peace. Someone walks up behind you and places a hand on your shoulder, startling you. The peace is shattered. Your heart rate skyrockets as your body prepares to fight or escape this possible danger.

This type of knee-jerk reaction is not the only way that the body prepares. Sometimes danger feels as if it is imminent. For most people, watching a horror movie elicits this type of response. Of course, you *know* you're not in any real danger while watching a scary movie. If I ask you, you'll tell me that you're not ready to flee the movie theater. But your body will tell a different story. Your heart rate increases, even pounding in your chest at moments of intense action. Your palms begin to sweat below the skin's surface, preparing you to get a better grip if needed. More than likely, the facial muscles you use to frown are tightly constricted, and you'd look unhappy to anyone casting a glance your way.

In this situation, your self-report and your physiology are at odds. You readily admit that you are in no danger, but your body acts as if it is in a state of sheer terror. Your conscious control is voluntarily keeping you seated in that movie theater even as every muscle in your body proceeds to exit that movie theater as fast as possible. Why the contradiction? You know the villain is likely around the corner, and you know that even when he jumps out, you are in no danger. But you don't know when. So there's suspense. You're waiting for something unknown to happen. In order to keep you alive, your brain assumes that the something unknown might be bad. This is a good, protective reflex. We probably wouldn't last long if we could simply disarm this reflex. So we get scared watching scary movies, and real tears come to our eyes when a child dies in a fictional television program. Your conscious self-report knows better, but the subconscious parts of the brain charged with keeping you alive never stop predicting. And the safest prediction is: if it feels as if it is going to be bad, it probably will be.

Your body is much more attuned to these predictions than your conscious awareness. You've got things to think about, and it would not be very efficient for a thought to pop into your head every time your heart speeds up or slows down. Even when you are aware of these types of physiological changes, the self-report part of the brain—the storyteller—may simply explain the way. Instead, it's possible to bypass the self-report altogether. Place some sensors in places of interest and record the signal. The body is pretty reliable: It tends to prepare to approach things that you like and avoid things that you dislike. Attach the sensors and see what happens. This is why lie detection is generally effective: Psychophysiological responses are largely automatic and immune to the influence of conscious modification. Here the advertising and public relations research can learn much about what is happening below the surface.

SKIN CONDUCTANCE

Measuring skin conductance is one of the oldest uses of psychophysiology to study persuasive communication. Conductance is a measure of how easily electrical current can flow between two paths. Water increases conductivity, which is why it's so dangerous to have hair dryers near a bathtub. In general, the wetter a surface, the more easily electricity can flow across it. Within the field of psychophysiology, skin conductance is used to measure the activity of sweat glands in the palm of the hand. Both the palms of the hand and the soles of the feet contain a special kind of sweat gland, known as *eccrine* sweat glands. These sweat glands are controlled by

Exhibit 23.1

Placement of Electrodes to Measure Skin Conductance

Physiological sensors placed on the palm of the hand to record skin conductance, an index of physiological arousal.

the sympathetic nervous system, which is associated with physiological arousal. As the body prepares for action, arousal increases, and the eccrine sweat glands begin to activate.

Most of the time, the sweat released by these glands never reaches the surface of the palms. It would be annoying indeed if every time you began to take action your palms dripped with sweat. However, the presence of increased moisture below the surface of the skin makes it easier for electricity to flow across the palm. Psychophysiologists attach two sensors to the surface of the palm of the hand and send a small current between the two electrodes. This current is typically one half of a volt—or one third of the power of an AA battery—and cannot be felt by the participant, nor does it pose any danger. As the sweat glands become more active, the conductivity of the palm increases, and the current flows more easily between the two sensors. See Exhibit 23.1 for an illustration of where electrodes can be placed on the palm to measure skin conductance. This is a reliable measure of physiological arousal. If you show someone an episode of the Discovery Channel's *Dirty Jobs,* you're likely to elicit greater skin conductance that if you show them an episode of C-SPAN's *BookTV.* However, both of these are likely to be trumped by any horror movie. And it would be bad advice to tell advertisers to turn all of their ads into horror movies.

The interpretation of skin conductance results is not straightforward. As the horror movies example shows, you cannot simply have participants read two press releases and pick the most arousing one. Arousal can be good *and* bad. Your body can be preparing to approach something good or avoid something bad. In this sense, skin conductance data are not directional. Researchers must use other criteria to judge whether elicited arousal is good or bad.

One of the reasons that arousal has been a popular measure is that physiological arousal is known to correlate with memory. This relationship is not linear however. Arousal affects memory in a ∩-shaped function, known as Duffy's curve. At extremely low levels of arousal, such as extreme fatigue, memory for events is quite poor. As arousal increases, memory increases. At extreme levels of arousal, such as running for your life, memory tends to be poor as all cognitive resources are directed away from memory and toward survival. Professionals in advertising and public relations generally want their campaigns to be memorable, and recent research suggests that more arousing ads are indeed better remembered (Bolls, Lang, Potter 2001).

HEART RATE

Heart rate is an often used but difficult to interpret psychophysiological measure. There are two ways to measure heart rate, over time and in response to a very specific event. Measuring heart rate over time is called *tonic* heart rate, and this applies to longer periods, such as during an entire television commercial or televised speech. When a celebrity comes on screen, however, the response to their presence can be measured in the few seconds that follow their appearance. This is known as *phasic* heart rate, and it is typically measured in the six seconds following an event.

Whereas the eccrine sweat glands of the palm are controlled solely by the sympathetic nervous system, the heart serves two masters. The sympathetic nervous system attempts to speed up the heart, and the parasympathetic nervous system attempts to slow down the heart. Measuring heart rate alone, there is no way to tell which branch of the autonomic nervous system is winning. If your heart slows down, it may be due to greater activity in the parasympathetic nervous system or lesser activity in the sympathetic nervous system. There is no way to differentiate when looking at tonic heart rates.

In general, faster heart rates are associated with physiological arousal. For this reason, heart rate often is used as a measure of arousal by people who do not have access to equipment to measure skin conductance. However, this is ill advised when studying media messages. As people pay more attention to an external stimulus (something out in the world) while they are in a safe controlled environment, their heart slows down due to increased parasympathetic activity. When watching a television advertisement or a corporate spokesperson on the news, attention and arousal are battling to control the speed of the heart. It is quite possible for an attention getting, mildly arousing television message to increase skin conductance but slow heart rate. Many media research studies have observed exactly this pattern.

When examining the two measures together, the researcher can make some logical inferences. If skin conductance is high during a message, then that must be a result of increased physiological arousal (itself caused by sympathetic nervous system activity). If at the same time heart rate decreases, one can infer that the deceleration must be due to activity in the parasympathetic nervous system, since one knows that sympathetic nervous system activity is increasing rather than decreasing. This is admittedly complicated, and recent research has shown that this logical inference is not necessarily guaranteed. A more pure measure of heart rate and attention can be derived by incorporating information about breathing rate—called *respiratory sinus arrhythmia*—but this is too complicated for most industry researchers.

Due to the complexity of heart rate analysis, it is not feasible for many industry researchers. However it is included here because it is commonly used, and researchers in advertising and public relations need to be aware of limitations in interpretation when they run across heart rate data. Simply showing an increase in heart rate is insufficient to demonstrate that a message has led to an increase in physiological arousal.

Bolls and colleagues (2001) were able to demonstrate that participants showed slower heart rates during negative radio ads compared to positive radio ads. However, skin conductance was greater during the positive ads. Thus, the faster heart rates during the positive advertisements could be due to either increased arousal, decreased attention, or both.

FACIAL ELECTROMYOGRAPHY

Most theories of persuasion include the rather straightforward notion that you're more likely to be persuaded by messages that cause you to have positive thoughts. Conversely, it's probably a bad idea to engender negative thoughts among those you're attempting to persuade. But what's the best way to measure those thoughts? By this point in the chapter, you have likely surmised that the answer is not going to be: "ask them." But you *can* ask people. If they hated a commercial they should know it, and they can tell you. Likewise if they loved the commercial. However, you run into the story-telling problem when you ask people *why* they did or did not like a commercial. People will give you answers. But the very process of trying to answer the commercials causes them to think more about the commercial than they otherwise would have. So the thoughts generated during this rumination are not likely to match the low involvement thoughts that would have occurred in the few seconds before the next commercial drew their interest away.

To get a better idea of real-time emotion that occurs while a participant watches television, reads a newspaper, or even plays a video game, researchers measure the activity of facial muscles involved with smiling and frowning. Research has demonstrated that even very low levels of positive and negative emotions activate these muscle groups. The activation can be so small that it does not move the skin, and participants are not even aware of it. Thus, sensors placed directly over the muscles can measure electrical activity (action potentials) in the muscles that cannot be detected by videotaping participants and later coding their facial expressions.

Hazlett and Hazlett (1999) compared electromyography (EMG) data with self-report during television commercial viewing and found that EMG was a more sensitive measure of viewer response. Using measures from the three muscle groups described here—*corrugator supercilli, zygomaticus major,* and *orbicularis oculi*—the researchers found moment-to-moment differences within the commercials, allowing them not only to identify which commercials in general elicited positive and negative emotion, but to look within each message to identify which parts of the messages were liked and disliked. Furthermore, emotional response as measured

Exhibit 23.2

Sensor Placement over Facial Muscles

Physiological sensors placed over the *corrugator supercilli* (brow), *orbicularis oculi* (eye), and *zygomaticus major* (cheek) muscle groups to measure activity associated with frowning (brow) and smiling (eye and cheek).

by EMG was a better predictor of recall than was self-report. See Exhibit 23.2 for an illustration of sensor placement over these three muscle groups.

Corrugator supercilli

The muscle group just above your eyes (on the inside by your nose) draws the brow down toward the nose, characteristic of a frown. These muscles, known as *corrugator supercilli,* are activated as you experience negative emotion. Two sensors placed above this muscle group can be used to measure this experienced unpleasantness. This muscle group appears to be sensitive to both positive and negative emotions. As negativity increases, activity increases. However, positive emotion actually decreases muscle activity compared to a neutral state. Thus *corrugator supercilli* may be the most sensitive measure of facial EMG.

Zygomaticus major

The *zygomaticus major* muscle group is located in the cheeks, and it draws up the corners of the mouth during a smile. You can locate these muscles by drawing a line straight down from the outside corner of the eye and straight out from the corner of the mouth. Sensors placed over this muscle group record smiling activity associated with positive emotion. However, these muscles are under voluntary control, and facial EMG cannot distinguish genuine activity in this muscle group from social smiling.

Orbicularis oculi

Unlike the muscles in the cheek, the muscles that draw up the corners of the eye during a genuine smile are not under voluntary control. Thus EMG activity over the *orbicularis oculi* muscle group can be used to differentiate genuine smiles—known as Duchenne smiles—from faked smiles. To illustrate this difference, look in the mirror and force yourself to smile. Then, while still looking in the mirror, think of something especially happy or funny. Notice how this real smile curves up the outside corners of the eyes. This muscle activity can be measured by placing two sensors just under the eye. The first sensor goes immediately below the pupil on the skin of the cheek (not the lower eyelid). The second sensor goes just outside of that. In most studies in advertising and public relations, the *orbicularis oculi* sensors are not necessary. Participants usually are unaware that you're attempting to measure emotion, so they will not try to present fake smiles.

Facial EMG Data

After an experiment is conducted, facial EMG data can be plotted over time. During the course of a viewing session, moment-by-moment changes in positive and negative emotion can be identified. In addition, overtime trends can be used to identify messages that tend to generally be more positive or more negative. Rather than post-viewing introspection, these measures reflect real-time emotion experienced as the message is being viewed.

FUNCTIONAL MAGNETIC RESONANCE IMAGING

Perhaps the newest research tool to appear in advertising, marketing, and public relations circles is the functional MRI (fMRI). These brain-scanning devices cost millions of dollars, so few are within the range of communications researchers. The output is visually impressive, showing colorful patches of blood flow activity on anatomically correct brain slices. Increased blood flow correlates with increased activity in a brain region. However, translating this blood flow to meaningful data in advertising and public relations research is quite a bit of a stretch. At the present time, the dazzling images are far more style than substance when it comes to the complicated types of messages produced by advertising and public relations research. Although the pictures may impress a client, we are still likely years away from regularly producing meaningful fMRI research in advertising and public relations research.

EYE TRACKING

Conventional wisdom suggests that the eyes are the windows to the soul. It is true that the eyes can tell us a great deal about what is happening in the mind. At the very least, eye tracking tells us where the eyes are pointing. As most daydreaming students know, however, we can point our eyes toward the front of the classroom while our minds are altogether somewhere different. Eye-tracking devices allow the computer to record moment-by-moment movement across a screen or a page. Looking at printer materials, eye tracking is not especially helpful. Speakers of most Western languages read from left-to-right and top-to-bottom. Thus, we all tend to proceed through a page in Z-like fashion—much the way you probably read this page. We tend to pause on headlines, figures, and photographs. This is rather predictable, and it's somewhat silly to go to the trouble of conducting an eye-tracking study to find out what we already know.

For television messages and Web sites, however, eye-tracking can shed light on the patterns of visual search—and how long the eyes remain fixated in a given location. This can give valuable clues to effectiveness during the design phases. Which parts of the Web page capture attention, and which areas are so cluttered that the eyes skip right past? The computer software that comes with eye-tracking hardware can produce plots that overlay a Web page or television screen that show patterns of fixation and the duration of fixations that are common across users. This information gives a good idea of what is capturing and holding a user's attention. For example, Google recently published eye-tracking results on the blog for the search result "how to tie a tie." Not surprisingly, most of the visual attention is devoted to the first search result. However, looking at the video of the fixations, one can see attention shift from the title of the search result to the green URL (Web page address) under the search. This kind of usability testing is especially valuable as advertising dollars increasingly shift online.

SUMMARY

Psychophysiological measures and eye-tracking studies can provide us with valuable information that is not available to conscious introspection and self-report. Skin conductance is an index of physiological arousal, which is associated with increased memory. Heart rate can be used to measure attention over time, however, the fact that attention and arousal both affect heart rate make it difficult to interpret. Facial electromyography can be used to measure emotion. Activity over *corrugator supercilli* indexes negative emotion while activity over *zygomaticus major* and *orbicularis oculi* index positive emotion. Studies using fMRI brain imaging technologies are becoming increasingly popular in marketing communications; however, the data being produced in these studies is more style than substance. Finally, eye-tracking studies can be used to track patterns of visual fixation and record the time that participants spend looking at computer monitors and television screens.

DISCUSSION QUESTIONS

1. All of the technologies mentioned in this chapter cost more than simple pen and paper surveys. What is their benefit over self-report?
2. What can you learn by using *orbicularis oculi* facial EMG data compared to *zygomaticus major* data?
3. Why are eye-tracking studies less helpful for studies involving print media?

EXERCISES

1. Look for a news story talking about consumers' emotional attachments to a product or service. Try to determine how psychophysiology or eye-tracking could shed more light on the subject.
2. If you have written a television commercial, identify three things that you would want to know from a psychophysiological study of that commercial.

ADDITIONAL READING

Stern, R.M., W.J. Ray, and K.W. Quigley. 2001. *Psychophysiological recording.* 2d ed. Oxford: Oxford University Press.

REFERENCES

Bolls, P.D., A. Lang, and R.F. Potter. 2001. The effects of message valence and listener arousal on attention, memory, and facial muscular responses to radio advertisements. *Communication Research,* 28, 627–51.

Gladwell, M. 2005. *Blink: The power of thinking without thinking.* New York: Little, Brown.

Hazlett, R.L., and S.Y. Hazlett. 1999. Emotional response to television commercials: Facial EMG vs. self-report. *Journal of Advertising Research,* 39(2), 7–23.

PART V

PRIMARY RESEARCH IN ADVERTISING AND PUBLIC RELATIONS: OTHER RESEARCH METHODS

24 Historical and Legal Research and Critical Analysis

LEARNING OBJECTIVES

This chapter is intended to help you:

- Understand that there are additional research approaches of use in public relations and advertising;
- Learn about historical research;
- See how legal research works;
- Comprehend the basic steps in critical analysis.

There are some additional research approaches that can be applied to advertising and public relations situations. Because these approaches are not usually quantitative in nature, they can be referred to as qualitative research methods. However, these additional approaches do not fit well under the umbrella of qualitative research, so we shall examine them separately.

HISTORICAL RESEARCH

Qualitative research methods fit most closely to the methods of historical research. Many of the research techniques utilized in other qualitative research can be applied to historical research. The research methods that we have covered so far are mostly designed for use in the preparation of campaigns and materials, whereas historical research is unlikely to help with that task but may be useful in evaluating the work after it appears. Keep in mind, too, the saying that "Those who ignore history are doomed to repeat it."

Conducting historical research is closely related to the production of standard college research papers that you have probably been researching and writing for years. The initial stages start with a search of the existing literature, usually in a library, then progress into other research approaches that are fitted more precisely to historical research. Hypotheses may or may not be needed with historical research but research questions are certainly appropriate, if not absolutely necessary.

Before we go further, it will be useful to understand the differences between the terms "historic" and "historical." Historic resources are those that actually experienced

---

Exhibit 24.1

Guidelines for Using the Internet for Research

Using the Internet for research is handy and quick. Huge amounts of information are available; however not all of it is reliable.

So how can you be certain whether the information you find is reliable? You can't be, at least, not absolutely, but you can use care and caution to make your search findings more trustworthy and reliable. Keep in mind that before a book or journal is published, it is usually vetted or scrutinized by editors and subject experts who have checked the claims and facts; that is not the case with Internet information.

Be careful of sources that can be edited by anyone. For example, although information from "wiki" sites such as Wikipedia may generally be reliable, you should know that such sites allow visitors to add, remove, and otherwise edit or change some of the content. Consequently, the same ease of interaction and operation that makes a wiki an effective tool also means that anyone may have posted a belief or opinion that may or may not be true.

So you may need to conduct your own research. Who is the author of the information and what credentials does that person hold?

What type of site is it? Is an .edu or .gov site more likely to contain reliable information than, say, a .com or .biz site?

What is the purpose of the site? Are there reasons to suspect bias on the part of those who write for or control the site? Did an original reliable site switch you to another site that may not have the same level of credibility?

How recently was the site updated? Can you find other sites that corroborate the information that you have found? Even if a particular site or page may not seem credible, you still may be able to use it to help generate some ideas of your own or to lead you to other, more reliable sites.

Watch for page protections, such as copyright protection. If there is a copyright symbol (©), it may mean that the author or site owner wants to protect the accuracy of the information found there. It may also mean, however, that you cannot legally use the information without permission, such as a signed release.

To be safe, you can always check your findings against references in a good research library.

---

the history being studied, such as original documents and persons who actually lived through the occasion, era, or event being studied. Historical items, on the other hand, include those written about the time or occasion under study but that did not actually experience that history.

HISTORICAL DOCUMENTS

Books about historical events, magazine articles, Internet sites, and similar resources that talk about the history that interests you are the place to begin historical research. Many of these items can be found in a good research library or online. Sometimes, specific books and articles will be found only at specialized libraries or research centers, although traveling to those locations may not be necessary; borrowing through inter-library loans or acquiring photocopies of the items will suffice for most historical studies.

Except for the most general type of historical study, historical items that contain specific quotations, sections of diaries, period statistics, and first-hand accounts will likely be most useful. Then books and other documents that summarize events may be useful. These materials often contain extensive bibliographies that can be used to find additional information.

Searching for these materials is similar to police work. You must use your powers of thinking and deduction along with your intuition, and you must stay "on the case" until you have found not just adequate sources but the very best sources for your study.

ORIGINAL SOURCES

Original sources, which are often referred to as "primary sources" by historians, are the historic (as opposed to historical) items that actually record what happened at the time it occurred. Examples are eyewitness accounts of events, personal diaries, and official records, such as those maintained by governments, the military, or similar organizations.

Even though these items are original, it is still possible that the author may have had a particular point of view. For example, a writer recalling an advertising campaign on which he or she worked may want to "spin" the story to make the campaign look good, or even to make himself or herself look good. You also need to consider the fact that there may have been interpretations imposed on earlier sources; consider each item in the environment in which it was created. Do not attempt to impose your own modern viewpoint on period items and materials.

ORAL HISTORIES AND OTHER INTERVIEWS

Another type of primary source often used by historians is an oral history. Talking with persons who actually experienced the historic event or era may provide special knowledge and insights about the era or event you are studying. These interviews are usually recorded and perhaps transcribed into print, so the actual words and expressions can be recalled and studied.

Oral histories are like other open-ended interviews, in that probing may be necessary. There may be questions established in advance, but to gain the maximum amount of information, it is necessary to be flexible and let the interview take you wherever it will—often to new ideas or toward knowledge that did not exist before. So these interviews are much like those outlined in the earlier discussions of qualitative research.

Keep in mind that, even though a person was present or involved in some historic event, the person may still be biased toward or against some particular point of view, or may be trying to make the event look better or worse than others might have seen it. An oral history is also based on the observations of only one person, who may have had limited contact with the actual event. Then, too, memories can be faulty, so an oral history reflects only what that one person recalls about what may be a small part of the total occurrence.

Other in-depth interviews may be conducted with persons who are knowledgeable about the era or events under study, even though those persons were not there. A historian who has written articles and books about public relations history or about the development of advertising may have knowledge that will be useful, even though it is not in the same category as an oral history.

RESEARCH INTO THE FUTURE

Trying to predict the future is tricky and often faulty. Even though research into the future is operating in exactly the opposite direction from historical research, the research methods and techniques used are identical. Research into the future uses secondary sources, then primary sources and, often, personal interviews with persons who are likely to have special knowledge. So, ironic as it may be, future research utilizes the same methods as historical research.

PROBLEMS WITH HISTORICAL RESEARCH

As we have just seen, relying on information from the past often involves biased information. Who wrote these items? What was their background? What point of view did they have? Were they instructed what and how to write, or did they have complete freedom of expression?

It is always a good idea to try to find corroborating information from another independent source, if possible. If other sources cannot be found, then the possibility of bias or perspective should be pointed out in the research report. If there are inconsistencies in the information you find, try to verify the facts, if possible.

Gathering historical evidence should not be done from only one point of view. Using multiple sources, or trying to piece together varying facts and materials and then trying to derive one's own conclusions, can help to overcome the problems with historical research.

You may also have your own prejudices, as well as the biases that you may discover in the sources you use for your research. Maintain your balance and impartiality.

LEGAL RESEARCH

In most of the United States, the practice of law is based on the British system of referring to precedents and past actions and decisions. Thus, trying to find other similar situations from the past that can be cited as precedents is a vital part of legal research. In some ways, legal research is like library research, trying to find what is already established information about the situation under study.

Legal research is somewhat specialized and preferably should be undertaken by researchers who have some background and experience in the law and who know where to look for past cases, court decisions, and precedents.

Although legal research may not be among the most-often-used method of research in advertising and public relations, it is necessary to prevent problems and forestall lawsuits or other legal entanglements.

Primary sources include statutes (the laws themselves, as passed by legislative bodies and enacted by government authorities) as well as case law (legal precedents from court decisions). Secondary sources include law books, legal reports, law journals, legal digests, and encyclopedias. You will need to know under what jurisdiction a law or legal decision was made. It will also be helpful to be familiar with the abbreviations and citations that are used in the legal profession. When you keep encountering

Exhibit 24.2

Some Places to Conduct Legal Research

- Law libraries.
- Depositories of government materials, such as archives.
- Government reports.
- Internet.
- Legal reference books.
- Legal journals and articles.
- Law codebooks.
- Court rules and rulings.
- Court reports and opinions.
- Legal digests.
- "Looseleaf" services that collect material on certain legal topics.
- *Westlaw* legal research service.
- *LexisNexis* research service.

the same laws, legal decisions or legal rules, you can usually assume that you have exhausted most of the obvious sources.

CRITICAL ANALYSIS

Although not strictly a method of conducting research, critical analysis is often used in the development of campaigns and especially in the post-analysis of a campaign's success or failure. Critical analysis is often utilized in the assessment of creative activities such as books, motion pictures, television programs, the visual and performing arts, and similar creative ventures.

The key to critical analysis is to maintain standards and to try to keep one's own biases and viewpoints out of the analysis, at least until the final report is created to summarize the critique. The categories to be examined should be established in advance, along with a clear understanding of what constitutes good or bad performance on these factors.

Then the creative result is measured against those standards and in those categories. Try to find patterns or themes that help explain the creative work. Describe the intended audience and explain how the material is organized. Once the evaluation is complete, the final judgment can be rendered. At this point, personal observations and sometimes personal opinions can be included, but that occurs best only after a clear and representative assessment of the qualities and character of the creative effort has been evaluated against the established standards. Maintain the focus on the creative work rather than on yourself.

In a critical analysis, try to summarize the original work in a paragraph and try to state the theme of the work in a sentence. If you want to quote from the work, short passages are usually allowed for the purposes of reviews, but it always pays to make sure what copyright protection the works may have.

SUMMARY

Historical and legal research have specialized applications to advertising and public relations, as does critical analysis. The methods used here have similarities to other

Exhibit 24.3

Categories and Criteria in Using Critical Analysis

Suppose you want to evaluate a magazine advertisement using critical analysis. Before you begin, you need to establish the categories that comprise a magazine advertisement and the special character-istics that make for a good magazine promotion. Here are some categories and criteria that might be used in evaluating magazine advertising.

Layout
- Layout is cohesive and unified.
- Text, illustrations, headlines, and logotype all fit together well.

Type
- Type size is readable and typeface is clear.
- Type font is appropriate for this product or service and for this appeal.

Illustration
- Illustrations are easy to see and understand.
- Illustrations add to the message and complement the copy.

Copy
- Copy is clear, easy to read, and easy to understand.
- Copy is relevant to the message and the product or service.
- Copy tells a clear story leading to a firm conclusion.
- Desired action is suggested in the copy.

Eye gaze
- Reader's eye is led through the advertisement and ends on the logo.
- Eye gaze is not interrupted by insignificant or non-essential elements.

Advertiser
- Brand name is clearly presented and identified.
- Reader comes away with understanding of brand name and characteristics

Appeal
- Appeal is unique to this product or service.
- Appeal is meaningful and attractive to the reader.

qualitative research but also include special approaches that are somewhat unique to these particular applications. These three types of research require certain experience and expertise and may best be left to researchers who have this background and ability.

DISCUSSION QUESTIONS

1. Why is it necessary to differentiate between "historical" and "historic," and what differences in applications are there?
2. When and why might legal research be used in public relations? In advertising?
3. Is critical analysis really research, or simply an essay exercise?
4. How can critical analysis be used in advertising? In public relations?
5. How do these three methods compare with the other research methods discussed earlier in this book?

EXERCISES

1. Outline a history of media education at your university.
2. Using the Internet, find legal research in your area of interest: either advertising or public relations.
3. Select an advertisement, a television program, a corporate annual report, or a motion picture, and write a critical analysis of it.

ADDITIONAL READING

Danto, E. 2008. *Historical research.* New York: Oxford University Press.
Sloan, A. 2009. *Basic legal research: Tools and strategies.* 4th ed. New York: Aspen Law and Business.
Orlik, P. 2008. *Electronic media criticism: Applied perspectives.* New York: Routledge/Taylor and Francis.
Naskrent, J. 2007. *Marketing activities: A critical analysis from an ethical point of view.* Saarbrücken, Germany: VDM Verlag.

PART VI

ADVERTISING AND PUBLIC RELATIONS RESEARCH DATA ANALYSIS

25 Handling Data

LEARNING OBJECTIVES

This chapter is intended to help you:

- Understand the importance of proper data handling;
- Know the importance of note taking;
- Recognize when taking notes during observation is appropriate;
- Understand the data handling process for focus groups;
- Understand the function of open, axial, and selective coding.

Data handling may sound like nothing more than bureaucratic bookkeeping, but almost every method used by researchers in advertising and public relations is likely to generate a great deal of data. These data must be organized, interpreted, summarized, and preserved by the researcher. The process of summarizing—or distilling—the data may be the most important step in the process. Academic researchers can write lengthy journal articles or even entire books about their research, but professional researchers are under constant pressure to convey as much information as quickly as possible. Rather than dozens of pages, researchers in advertising and public relations may have to convey their findings on a three-page executive summary or a handful of PowerPoint slides. Getting the right data in this limited space is clearly crucial, and the process begins the moment the data are collected.

Data can take many forms in advertising and public relations. Quantitative data are relatively straightforward. See Chapter 18. Responses in a survey, behavior during an experiment, and coding decisions in a content analysis are relatively easily tabulated and presented. Qualitative data, however, require special consideration as handling of these data is not as clear-cut.

FIELD NOTES

Much of qualitative research relies upon interviewing and observation. From the in-depth interview to participant observation and ethnography, the qualitative researchers must take notes about the research environment and interpret these notes later. Even if a picture is not quite worth 1,000 words, not everything can be recorded in a note-

---

Exhibit 25.1

Organizing and Coding Data Points

Both quantitative and qualitative researchers are likely to have thousands—or tens of thousands—of data points. For the quantitative researcher, however, these are often easily organized in a spreadsheet.

Most qualitative researchers like to actually handle their data, however. Software programs exist to help researchers identify and relate concepts and themes. It's difficult to see the data all at once in a computer. Therefore, coding of qualitative data tends to be a very space-intensive process.

It's not uncommon to see thousands of index cards spread across a table for the qualitative researcher to sort and resort as themes emerge, broader themes are divided into sub-themes, and narrow themes are collapsed together.

The index card is far from the only notation device, however. Transcripts printed on regular 8.5″ × 11″ paper can be cut with scissors and tacked to the wall or a bulletin board. Perhaps nothing is better suited to the continuous process of recoding than the Post-it note. These self-adhesive sticky notes come in a variety of sizes and colors and can be reorganized as new themes develop.

Thus, rather than a metaphor, the handling of qualitative data involves quite literally handling. With an array of index cards spread across the table or pinned to a bulletin board, the researcher can step back and look at the overall picture. By examining clusters of themes in this sense, the researcher can get a better feel for the data, which is helpful in the inductive reasoning process.

---

pad, and decisions about what to include or exclude will forever color the research results. Thus data handling is a perpetual series of decisions about what to include and what to exclude.

TAKING NOTES

During in-depth interviews and even focus groups, participants will expect the researcher to be taking notes, so this will not be especially disruptive. However, studies in which the researcher is more of a covert participant preclude note taking. For instance, it is helpful to understand how consumers shop in natural environments. A recent study in *Advertising Age* found that 39.4 percent of grocery store purchase decisions were made as participants stood at the shelf. Clearly these types of naturalistic data are beneficial. Despite the benefit of observing consumers in the marketplace, it would be foolish to expect realistic behavior to arise when shoppers are being stalked with researchers carrying clipboards and scribbling furiously as the shoppers select a package of macaroni from the grocery shelf.

Thus, the general rule of thumb is to take the most detailed notes possible as quickly as possible after the observation takes place. If you're observing the behavior of customers stopping by an informational booth at a sponsored event, make the most detailed mental notes possible. Perhaps the researcher may step away from the booth periodically to take notes about previous interactions. However, this might not be possible if you're conducting research for a major beer manufacturer, and you're conducting field research about alcohol choices in a sports bar. Here, the researcher may have to wait until returning to the office or a hotel room in order to take notes. Whatever the time interval between observation and note taking, it should be kept to a minimum. The researcher then must attempt to record as much detail as possible, often using a simple word processing program.

COMPUTERS

The challenge in note taking in qualitative research is that it is not typically clear what the major themes will be in advance. This makes note taking especially difficult, because the researcher can never be sure when the key details are being recorded and when they are being overlooked. For this reason, computers are almost a requirement in note taking. Researchers can record as much information as possible, and this information can later easily be rearranged as necessary through cut-and-paste. Handwritten notes taken in the field also can be quickly transcribed using word processing. Once again, time is of the essence. An observation in bad handwriting might be recovered while it is still fresh in the mind; however, it may be lost altogether if the researcher attempts to decipher that same bad handwriting a week later.

Transcriptions do not necessarily solve problems. Jeffrey E. Durgee (2006) tells the story of equipping fifty consumers in the Columbus, Ohio, area with voice recording devices to spontaneously record their thoughts about snacks and beverages throughout the day. The consumers readily complied, and the voice recordings were later transcribed into *thousands* of pages of notes. Despite the sheer volume of data, however, there were almost no useful insights, Durgee said. Without a skilled interviewer to probe for further insights, participants largely recorded superficial minutia. All the computing power in the world cannot save a researcher from bad data.

FOCUS GROUPS

Focus groups are typically video recorded or tape recorded and then transcribed later. It is a bad idea for the moderator to attempt to take notes on the fly, as this will inhibit the ability to direct the focus group and recognize developing themes in order to probe for more information. With some researchers recommending that moderators ask up to 240 questions in a one-hour-and-45-minutes focus group, it is not feasible for the moderator to be the primary data recorder. However, this does not mean that the focus group moderator is absolved of data responsibilities. The focus group moderator should be debriefed by a researcher immediately after each focus group session. If it is a small data collection team, then the moderator can do a self-debriefing by taking detailed notes on a computer.

The debriefing should include the moderator's thoughts about major themes that emerged during the session and the moderator's attempts to direct the group. Notes taken at this stage should include what was learned during the session and how the session differed from previous sessions. If there was a participant or event that made the session unique, it should be noted during the debriefing. The moderator can include questions to be included in future sessions and notes about group dynamics. Any insight or observation is fair game for the debriefing, as details that later prove to be irrelevant can easily be put aside later. However, key insights discarded early can never be regained. Typically the debriefing notes will later be compared and reconciled with the transcripts and even the actual recordings. At no time, however, should the debriefing notes take the place of detailed transcripts. Far too much information would be lost doing so.

Even transcripts and debriefing notes together may miss some very important information conveyed through nonverbal channels. Sometimes with research in advertising and public relations—such as attitudinal data—how something is said is as important as what is said. Video recordings are preferable to audio recordings, and the original video record should be preserved for the later coding process. Therefore, any ambiguities or uncertainties can be resolved later by looking at gestures, facial expressions, or other nonverbal communication that may have occurred during the focus groups.

CODING

Perhaps the data coding process best exemplifies the basic philosophical differences between qualitative and quantitative research. Although these generalities are not 100 percent uniform, they highlight fundamental differences typically seen between the two approaches. Most quantitative research begins with a general idea of the research problems. Specific variables are often measures due to a researcher's belief that one variable reliably influences another. Attitude toward a company might be measured along with purchases from that company because many researchers believe those two variables to be related. This is often not the case with qualitative research, where major themes are not necessarily identified in advance. Instead, the researchers seek to understand some behavior as it occurs in the world, and they want their preconceived notions to affect the outcome as little as possible. Qualitative researchers tend to be more accepting of the fact that they do not have a complete grasp on the research situation before data collection begins. This does not mean that all qualitative data analysis should be considered to be exploratory, however. Qualitative researchers simply tend to believe that themes are more likely to emerge from those under study than from the researchers themselves.

OPEN CODING

Perhaps the best example of allowing themes to arise from the data is open coding, sometimes also referred to as conceptual or thematic coding. In this process, the researcher begins reading through notes and transcripts, identifying possible themes as they arise. Themes can be separated onto note cards, transcripts can literally be cut apart with various themes piled together, or computers can be used to highlight key concepts and themes as they arise.

An important aspect of open coding is that themes are not static and inflexible. As the researcher continues reading through notes and transcripts, she might realize that one previously identified theme really should be two separate themes. Likewise, themes that occur too infrequently can later be combined. The data form the road map, and the researcher simply is trying to identify important themes already present in the data. Open coding is often associated with Grounded Theory, which is an inductive approach to data analysis. Rather than attempting to deduce hypotheses from theories, this approach to qualitative data analysis focuses on eliciting themes from the data. Multiple iterations through the data may be required to distill the key concepts in open coding.

Researchers DeVries and Fitzpatrick (2006) used open coding to examine public relations materials and subsequent news coverage during a crisis at Washington, D.C.'s National Zoo from 2002–2004. Published texts were coded in an attempt to uncover themes and concepts related to the crisis, which was touched off by the death of a giraffe and the zoo's handling of that death. This open coding revealed themes related to the animals, the zoo's infrastructure, and the zoo's staff. Once these themes were identified, the researchers were able to examine whether they were treated differently in news and public relations materials.

AXIAL CODING

After concepts or themes have been identified, the next step is to search for the natural relationship between concepts and which concepts are central to the research. Water, steam, and heat are all important concepts, but one cannot understand the broader picture until the relationship between these concepts is understood. The same is true with concepts in qualitative data analysis. In this process, phenomena are identified, and the researcher attempts to identify causal situations and the contexts in which a phenomenon might occur. If another situation might moderate a causal relationship, this might be identified, too.

Frosch and colleagues (2007) used open and axial coding to identify major themes in television advertisements for prescription drugs, also known as direct-to-consumer advertising because these marketing efforts bypass the physician. This inductive analysis resulted in the identification of seven themes in the ads regarding how the medicine was portrayed in the characters' lives. While some ads focused on consequences of disease, such as the loss of control caused by a medical condition, other ads took a more positive approach, focusing on overcoming disease by regaining control over the condition. By identifying themes inductively, these researchers may have gained more insight than if they had simply searched for themes that they expected to find before the study began. Open and axial coding provide a framework to build up from the data.

SELECTIVE CODING

Once the central concepts and their interrelationships have been identified, researchers may want to increase their understanding by searching for the one key concept around which all other concepts are organized. This is the organizing idea or storyline around which all other concepts are arranged. Data can then be selectively coded around the key concept, letting other less relevant concepts drop from the analysis.

Selective coding can be thought of as the theory-building phase of analysis. By looking for central concepts and causal relationships, the researcher is now looking to explain the situation rather than simply describe it. Sallot and colleagues (2004) used selective coding to identify key themes after a series of focus groups on public relations practitioners' Web use and how it relates to their status and power. This study found, for example, that practitioners are using the Internet to directly target opinion leaders, where once they would have had to go through mass media "gatekeepers."

SUMMARY

Data are the essence of research, and even projects modest in scope can produce an overwhelming amount of data. For qualitative research studies, much of the data will take the form of notes. Notes can be taken in the field, written after the fact, and transcribed from recordings of actual conversations. Focus group moderators typically take brief notes during the session, but they conduct debriefings after each session as well as transcribe comments made by participants. These notes and transcripts are later coded for major themes and concepts. Often coding is inductive. That is, the researcher searches the notes for codes that emerged during the research rather than looking for evidence of codes that were suspected before the research began. Open coding involves the search for codes within the data. Axial coding searches for initial relationships between concepts identified during open coding. Finally, selective coding attempts to distill the data in order to find the key concepts that link all the others and best explain the phenomena.

DISCUSSION QUESTIONS

1. Why should you not take notes during covert observation research?
2. If you are precluded from taking notes in the field, when should you record notes?
3. Why are open, axial, and selective coding referred to as inductive reasoning?

EXERCISES

1. Go to any retail store and casually watch people shop. You should make sure to make casual observation and not make shoppers feel uncomfortable or have security called on you. When you get home, write down everything that you can remember. Compare how much you are able to remember with how much you thought that you would be able to remember.
2. Use your preferred search engine to look for a "focus group transcript." Print and read the transcript for themes, and then use scissors to cut out individual comments. Arrange comments on the same theme together. Do your definitions of themes change over time as you learn more about your topic?
3. Go to the Web site for three different national newspapers (such as the *New York Times*). Look for each newspaper's story about the top business story of the day. (If you use smaller papers, they will all likely use the same wire story). Read each story, looking for the common themes that arise about the story.

ADDITIONAL READING

Durgee, J.F. 2005. *Creative insight: The researcher's art.* Chicago, IL: The Copy Workshop.

REFERENCES

DeVries, D.S., and K.R. Fitzpatrick. 2006. Defining the characteristics of a lingering crisis: Lessons from the National Zoo. *Public Relations Review,* 32, 160–67.

Frosch, D.L., P.M. Krueger, R.C. Hornik, P.F. Cronholm, and F.K. Bard. 2007. Creating demand for prescription drugs: A content analysis of television direct-to-consumer advertising. *Annals of Family Medicine,* 5, 6–13.

Sallot, L. M., L. V. Porter, and C. Acosta-Alzuru. 2004. Practitioners' web use and perceptions of their own roles and power: a qualitative study. *Public Relations Review,* 30 (3) (September), 269–78.

26 Scaling Techniques

LEARNING OBJECTIVES

This chapter is intended to help you:

- Understand the utility of multiple-item scales;
- Learn about Likert-type scales that measure agreement;
- Understand bipolar semantic differential scales;
- Comprehend the rank ordering of ordinal scales;
- Learn about fixed sum scales;
- Understand applications of nonverbal pictorial scales.

The general purpose of most scales is to examine some variable across some range of possible values. Rather than seeking to determine whether or not someone has an attitude about a particular phenomenon, scales often are designed to capture the intensity of an attitude or feeling. Scales involve multiple questions, or items, designed to measure the same underlying concept or construct. Much of this analysis of scales involves attempting to capture this entire range of intensity.

To analyze the type of data gathered in response to scale items, the data typically are converted to numerical form. Often times this is for convenience, and the researcher must take care not to assume that these assigned numbers automatically correspond to real numbers. It is quite possible to assign numeric values to nominal level data. However, assigning a "1" to females and a "2" to males, for example, does not mean that females are any "more" or "less" of some variable than males. Consider how absurd it sounds to say that you conducted a survey and the average gender was 1.62.

SCALE RELIABILITY

An important issue to consider is whether you really have a scale at all. Although this runs the risk of being exceedingly nit-picky, the first step in scale assessment is to see whether a scale exists at all. Just because a set of questions has formed a scale many times in the past does not mean that that same set will form a scale in the future. The world changes. Perhaps the terms in your scale have become outdated; perhaps your instructions mislead participants; perhaps your group of participants read something

Exhibit 26.1

Analyzing Results from Scaling Techniques

When looking at the results from scaling techniques, it is often helpful to go beyond merely calculating and analyzing averages. Measures of central tendency—including averages—can be very misleading at times.

Consider a five-option scale where the points on the scale are equidistant, and we agree to treat the scale as a ratio scale so that we can perform an average. So, if someone were to tell you that the average response was Choice 3, what would you know?

We hope you recognized that you would not know anything. All of your participants may have chosen Choice 3, or none of them may have chosen Choice 3. You simply cannot tell by the average. How is this possible, you ask? Let's look at the possibilities.

First, if every single participant answered Choice 3, then Choice 3 is clearly the average. There is nothing tricky about that. However, what if exactly 20 percent of respondents chose each of the five options? That is, what if an equal number selected every option? Without boring you with the math, it turns out that the middle option will be the average—even though just as many people selected Choice 1 as Choice 3. However, let's look at a more extreme case. What if 50 percent of respondents chose Choice 1 and 50 percent chose Choice 5? The average is still 3! Although this seems absurd given that no one actually chose that option, it is the average nonetheless.

This is where a frequency table can help. If the data are perfectly normally distributed (that is, they look like they are in a bell shape), then the average will make a lot of sense. If however, the data are distributed non-normally, a frequency table can help the researcher spot patterns that are not clear in the raw data.

into the questions that previous groups did not see. Thus it is an empirical question rather than a certainty that you have any scale at all. This question is most easily and most directly addressed using a test of scale reliability called Cronbach's α (alpha). This statistic measures whether the individual items in a multi-item scale appear to be measuring the same thing, that is, have internal consistency. Typically values for α range from 0 to 1, although negative numbers technically are possible. In practice, one should never observe negative numbers unless the multi-item scale were so poorly designed that the items had virtually no relationship to one another whatsoever. If your multiple items are indeed measuring the same underlying construct, then the scale reliability should be high. A typical and widely cited benchmark for Cronbach's α is .70. Numbers greater than that are ideal. Once an acceptable level of scale reliability has been observed, then you are ready for formal data analyses.

To illustrate the concept of scale reliability, let's turn to some actual data collected by advertising agency DDB Needham. These data are part of an annual survey known as the Life Style Study, and they are used to keep the agency apprised of changes in social trends rather than researching specific goods and services. The data were made famous by sociologist Robert Putnam in his book *Bowling Alone* where he analyzed changing trends in American society. Although the data used by Putnam are a bit dated now, they still nicely illustrate some of the concepts we are discussing in this chapter.

Suppose you work at a public relations firm, and you have been hired by a large energy company that is interested in increasing public support for government financing of alternative fuel efforts. In order to change public opinion, you need to understand public opinion. Perhaps you have a gut feeling that political orientation may affect attitudes toward government funding of alternative energy sources. You suspect that liberals might have a different attitude than conservatives. But what does it mean to be liberal or conservative? Those words have become politically charged, and the labels that people chose for themselves might not reflect their actual views. Indeed there are likely many dimensions to the concepts of liberalism and conservatism. One way to measure this continuum would be to ask people to assess their agreement with a series of statements that you suspect might show a difference between liberals and conservatives. Let's look at the DDB Needham data to see whether we can find such statements.

Consider the following list:

- "Couples should live together before getting married;"
- "The use of marijuana should be legalized;"
- "I am in favor of legalizing same sex marriages;"
- "I think the women's liberation movement is a good thing;" and
- "I am in favor of legalizing doctor-assisted suicide."

It's probably not much of a stretch for you to imagine that liberals and conservatives might answer those questions differently. Any given individual might have very wide-ranging opinions on these matters; however, across society a pattern should develop if agreement with these statements is tapping into a more general concept of political liberalism. DDB Needham used a 6-point Likert scale to assess agreement with these statements (definitely disagree; generally disagree; moderately disagree; moderately agree; generally agree; and definitely agree). In order to examine whether a single underlying concept might be driving responses to these Likert items, we can examine the scale reliability. In this case, these five statements exhibit moderate scale reliability with Cronbach's $\alpha = .72$. This gives us some confidence that these items are assessing a single underlying concept, and we could be comfortable including them in the questionnaire we are designing about alternative energy sources. In short, the relatively high reliability suggests that we have a genuine scale and not merely a set of unrelated measures.

LIKERT SCALES

The analysis of Likert scales is not without controversy. It is common practice to treat Likert scale responses as interval data and assign numbers to the responses. In the case of a five-point Likert scale,

- "Strongly disagree" is typically coded as a 1;
- "Disagree" is coded as a 2;
- "Neutral" is coded as a 3;
- "Agree" is coded as a 4; and
- "Strongly agree" is coded as a 5.

This type of coding scheme is extremely convenient because it allows for easy comparisons and the use of inferential statistics. When multiple Likert items are used to form a true scale, these scales can be averaged, and comparisons can easily be made.

Let's return to the DDB Needham data and our constructed liberalism scale to examine this. In the original dataset, the data were coded from 1 to 6 with 1 equaling "definitely disagree" and 6 equaling "definitely agree." Thus as the numbers go up, agreement goes up. For each person who answered the survey, we can average the response for each of the five questions. This will give us a single number for each participant that ranges from 1 to 6. We can say that this score represents their liberalism. We would expect that Democrats would score higher than Republicans on this scale of liberalism. Indeed, this is the case, although the difference is not as large as you might expect. Of the 3,938 Democrats who answered these five questions between 1975 and 1998, the average score was 3.17, which is below the midpoint of the scale (which is 3.5 on a 1 to 6 scale). So these Democrats do not appear to be very liberal. The 3,422 Republicans were a bit less liberal, averaging 2.67, which is exactly 0.5 less than the Democrats. As an aside, this test also suggests that our scale has construct validity (recall Chapter 14) in that our scale relates to another variable in the manner that we would expect.

This type of analysis shows the convenience of treating Likert scale data as interval data. In this case since both groups' averages are below the theoretical midpoint of the scale, we can say that, on average, both groups showed mild disagreement with these statements. We can also say that Republicans tended to disagree a bit more. However, we are making a rather large assumption when we treat Likert data as interval data. We are assuming that for these participants, they treated the difference between "definitely disagree" and "generally disagree" (that is, the interval) to be exactly equal to the difference between "moderately disagree" and "moderately agree." It seems unlikely that most participants would be able to keep such exact differences in mind when making these types of decisions.

Instead we might want to play it safe and treat the data as ordinal data. Here, assigning 1s and 6s and taking averages are meaningless. Since we have a large dataset for the current example, we can look at the percentage of respondents who chose each option. That is, we would expect a greater percentage of Democrats to choose the "agree" options and a greater percentage of Republicans to choose the "disagree" options.

To see what this would look like, look at Exhibit 26.2. Here you can see the percentages of each political group that chose each Likert option for two of the questions, living together before marriage and marijuana legalization. The data look much like one would expect. Democrats are more likely—although not totally likely—to agree that couples should live together before marriage and that marijuana should be legalized. Republicans, conversely, are more likely to have disagreed with these statements. Since the DDB Needham dataset is so large, comparisons such as the one in Exhibit 26.2 are possible. Furthermore, this large dataset allows statistics such as χ^2 to be run in order to assess whether the differences observed might be due to chance. However, for small samples that are more typical of the kinds of studies often conducted in advertising agencies and public relations firms, it might be possible to have no one choose one of the options in a Likert scale. When there are empty "cells" in the data, statistics such as χ^2 cannot be run.

Exhibit 26.2

Treating Data as Ordinal Data: Example (in percent)

	Live together before marriage		Marijuana use should be legalized	
	D	R	D	R
Definitely agree	9.0	7.1	10.4	7.0
Generally agree	11.0	8.4	7.7	5.2
Moderately agree	21.3	16.0	12.6	9.6
Moderately disagree	12.8	12.5	9.4	7.4
Generally disagree	12.3	13.0	10.2	11.9
Definitely disagree	33.6	43.0	49.8	59.0

In the case of small sample studies, it is often best simply to report the percentages selecting the more extreme options. In this case, we might report the percentage of each group that selected either the "definitely" or "generally" agree or disagree options. In this case, 20 percent of Democrats but just 15.5 percent of Republicans at least generally agree that couples should live together before marriage. In turn, just 35.9 percent of Democrats but 56 percent of Republicans generally disagreed that couples should live together before getting married. This type of brief snapshot is generally well understood and is commonly seen in executive summaries, formal presentations, and annual reports. Although it is true that inferential statistics do provide more information, they also often clutter the page and confuse many audiences. Almost anyone can understand that more than half of Republicans—but just more than a third of Democrats—generally or definitely disagree that couples should live together before getting married.

ORDINAL SCALES

As the name implies, ordinal scales capture the order of some variable. You might be asked to rank your favorite hamburger joints or to assess the relative corporate responsibility of several Fortune 500 competitors. As with all ordinal level data, we can infer that the order is correct, but we can assume nothing about the distances between choices. Consider two hypothetical fast food diners. Bill, a seventeen-year-old high school junior loves Burger King. He doesn't care for either McDonald's or Wendy's. Filling out your questionnaire, he must choose. After some thought, Bill decides that if he had to choose, he'd place Wendy's second and McDonald's last. Contrast Bill with Tim. Tim is a twenty-six-year-old account planner who lives in Columbus, Ohio. Of all the burger places, Tim slightly prefers Burger King's flame-broiled taste. But he works just a couple of miles from Wendy's corporate headquarters, and he must admit that he likes their burgers, too. And Tim's not opposed to the occasional Big Mac. So Tim ranks them Burger King, Wendy's, and McDonald's. Just like Bill. But their attitudes toward these three restaurants bear little similarity toward one another.

Looking at any two individuals, the researcher cannot say much. In the aggregate, however, any company would rather be picked first than last—even it means winning by a nose. And in these patterns, we can learn something. Assume that we ask 500 people in our target market to fill out these ordinal scales, and we find that 45 percent of people rank McDonald's first, 25 percent of people rank Wendy's first, 21 percent of people rank Burger King first, and the remaining 9 percent chose some other option. In this case, we can conclude that it's pretty good to be McDonald's and that Wendy's and Burger King have some work to do. Again, for any given individual, we do not know anything about the intensity of his or her choices. But in the aggregate, patterns emerge even among ordinal scales. And if our sample sizes are large enough, we can perform statistical tests to determine whether these differences are due to more than sampling error. However, with ordinal scales, the data tabulation typically is confined to percentages, such as those shown with the hamburger chains above.

SEMANTIC DIFFERENTIAL

Recall that the semantic differential calls for pairs of opposing adjectives separated by several points, typically nine. As with Likert scales, semantic differentials are measured at least at the ordinal level of measurement. How you analyze these data again comes down to an assumption you must make: are they ordinal or are they interval? Most people, however, treat semantic differential data as interval level data. And given that participants typically choose a point from among several points that are equally spaced on the page, the interval argument holds more weight. That is, if you took a ruler and actually measured the intervals between the points, those measurements would be equal. It is still an assumption, however, that participants treat those points as equidistant.

If one makes the assumption that the data are interval, then numbers can meaningfully be assigned, and more statistical options are available. Consider a mainstay of advertising research, the attitude toward the advertisement (usually called A_{ad}). You could simply ask consumers what they thought of an ad, but that type of question is loaded with many problems discussed in previous chapters. You could also ask a single-item question, but single-item measures risk missing some of the dimensions of attitudes. For instance, you might admit that an advertisement is good but still not like it. In an attempt to capture these multiple dimensions of attitudes, A_{ad} measures often employ multiple semantic differentials. Here one would typically assign the lowest option a "1" and the highest option a "7." The theoretical midpoint is a 4. Scores above 4 are generally positive, and scores below 4 are generally negative.

For instance, you might use semantic differentials with the following pairs: good-bad, pleasant-unpleasant, annoying-pleasing, inferior-superior, positive-negative. By using a well-designed five-item measure to capture A_{ad}, you are more likely to capture multiple facets of the attitude construct. Note here that the positive attitude adjective is on the right three times and on the left three times. This is called reversing the scale, and as you might imagine has both proponents and opponents. Many people think (and empirical data support) that people get careless, lazy, and fatigued as they proceed through a questionnaire. If your participants learn that all of the "good" adjectives are on the left—and they like an ad—they may be tempted to simply choose all the rightmost points. In order to counteract this, some items are reversed in an attempt to force participants to pay attention. There is risk inherent in this practice, because your participants may be so careless, lazy, or fatigued that they fail to notice your reversal and select all the rightmost points anyway (assuming the first item had their choice on the right). Then instead of having overly consistent data, you have meaningless data. And there is no perfect way to discern after the fact whether a participant was careless or just fickle.

There is another complication with scale reversal that causes a need to be especially vigilant in data entry. Using a 7-point semantic differential, you want to pick a coding method and stick with it. If "good" is a 7, and "bad" is a 1, then "pleasant" and "favorable" had better be 7's, also. If all the positive adjectives are on the same side, this is simple. Scale reversal makes this much more complicated. There are two general schemes to coding reversed data. The first requires you to note the reversal and enter the numbers correctly into the computer during data entry. Although simple, this is fraught with opportunity for human error. The preferable way is to enter everything in a consistent manner. The left is always your minimum score (for example, a "1"), and the right is always your maximum score (for example, a "7"). Then once all of the data are in the computer, you determine which items are reversed. You can "unreverse" them by simply subtracting each person's score from the maximum score plus one. Since our maximum here is a 7, you would subtract everything from 8. This flips the scores perfectly. Eight minus seven is one, and eight minus one is seven. The items are perfectly flipped. The computer provides the added bonus that it will not make mistakes during reversal, while such human error is difficult to prevent altogether.

A rather old-fashioned but helpful way to present semantic differential data is shown in Exhibit 26.3. These data reflect average ratings of Coca-Cola and Pepsi by a group of college students (Bradley, Maxian, Laubacher, and Baker 2007). In many ways, the two brands appear to have a similar semantic structure. However, market leader Coca-Cola fares slightly better than Pepsi for positive emotion adjectives "good," "happy," "loved," and "pleasant." The executives in Atlanta likely are happy to see this. At the same time, Pepsi's ongoing campaign theme of youth and a "new generation" appears to have taken hold, too. Pepsi is more "energetic," "modern," and "young" than its counterpart. For most of the other adjective pairs, these brands are quite comparable. This type of visual presentation provides a quick differentiation between a small number of alternatives, and this layout is easy for clients and executives to interpret.

FIXED SUM SCALES

Consider that a telephone pollster were to call you and ask, "Should the government spend more money on early childhood education?" What would you say? Most people would say "yes." It's easy to recommend money for one program when you don't have to take it away from another. Likewise, it's easy to be generous with scale items when saying good things about BMW, for instance, when doing so does not prevent you from saying good things about Lexus, too. This task becomes much more difficult when affinity toward one choice necessitates a poor rating for another choice. Fixed sum scales attempt to capture just such a phenomenon.

Most people reading this chapter will be in college, and many of the others will

Exhibit 26.3   **Semantic Differential Example: Average Ratings of Coca-Cola and Pepsi by College Students**

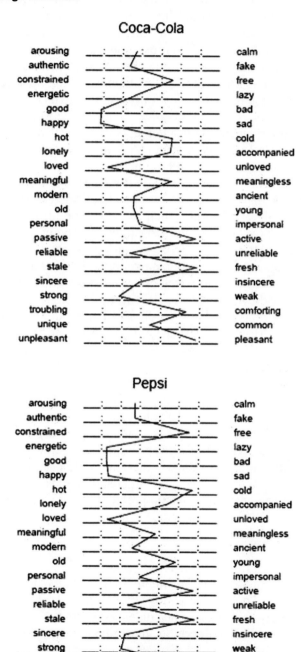

Source: Bradley, Maxian, Laubacher, and Baker 2007.

have once been a college student. Why did you choose the college that you chose? Was it a difficult decision? Or was it easy. Imagine a student who has been admitted to Harvard, Yale, and State University. Both Harvard and Yale have Ivy League prestige; however, choosing one of those two options would mean a great deal of student loan debt. State U is far less prestigious, but our student has been offered a full-ride scholarship. If she chooses to stay home, she'll graduate college debt free. Plus she'll be able to come home more often. Complicating the decision is that her grandfather went to Yale, so there's some family pressure to head to New Haven. The point is that all of the choices are good choices. Thus, if we were to ask our prospective student to rate her agreement with statements such as "It would be a wise decision to attend Yale" using a Likert-type scale, then all of the contenders might merit a "Strongly Agree." We have solved nothing here.

Imagine that we give our student a fixed sum of points to distribute. Sometimes we express this sum with a simple number, such as 100, and sometimes we attach a currency value to the sum, such as $100. The idea is the same: distribute the $100 among the three universities. More money (or points) assigned to an option means that it is a relatively better option. This task presents a much more difficult challenge. If the decision were simple, one university might get all $100, and the other two might get $0. No problem. However, assigning these values forces difficult decisions. How much value do you place on a debt-free education? How much value do you place on family traditions? Perhaps the choices come out $34, $33, $33. Then there really is a dead heat. However, perhaps introspection leads to a slight separation: Yale merits $40, and both Harvard and State U receive $30. In this case, fixed sum scales created some separation.

Analysis of these data is straightforward compared to the other scales mentioned thus far. Fixed sum scales truly are ratio level data because you can assign 0 points (or dollars). Furthermore, 10 points should be exactly double 20 points. Thus the full range of inferential statistics is available for analysis. Mean values are meaningful, and a table displaying those means is informative. Although inferential statistics would not help this student decide whether her single $40 to $30 advantage were significant, one can use such statistics with larger samples. Thus we might find out that a sample of her classmates indeed would prefer Harvard to Yale or State University.

NONVERBAL SCALES

You'll pardon the cliché here that a picture is worth a thousand words, and perhaps you'll remember from freshman English that words have both connotations and denotations. Those connotations can be trouble. Courses on research methods can be especially tricky for some students despite the best efforts of instructors (and especially textbook writers). So, unfortunately, some students fail exams. What does it mean to use a verbal scale in order to understand the attitudes of those failing students? Imagine a semantic differential separated by "good" and "bad." *Of course* the students feel bad. It would be an odd occasion for the student to feel good. However, the range of bad feelings can vary. Imagine the scholarship football player who has to keep a certain GPA in order to continue playing. An "F" on an exam could quite

Exhibit 26.4   **Nonverbal Scale Example: Specifying Degree of Discomfort in a Physician's Office**

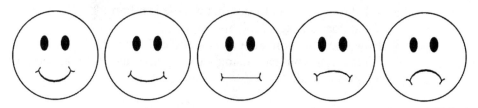

literally keep this player off of the field (and from the view of NFL scouts). So this student feels really, really, bad. Meanwhile, consider another student who is taking the course as an elective (preposterous as it seems, it does happen) and has chosen to take the course pass/fail. This student had a 95 percent average going into the final exam and needed only a 10 percent on the final in order to pass the class. Although he is probably not overjoyed by the 50 percent, it was well above what was necessary and accomplishes the task at hand.

Nonverbal scales represent an attempt to get away from potentially loaded words, such as "good" and "bad." Imagine instead that we ask participants to choose an option along the nonverbal continuum, such as the one portrayed in Exhibit 26.4. Some researchers believe that it is easier to identify with pictorial scales, such as this one. And research on the relative merits of verbal and nonverbal scales seems to support the notion (Bradley and Lang 1994). In fact, most physicians' offices now have a pictorial scale similar to Exhibit 26.4 on the wall in order to allow patients to indicate their degree of discomfort.

However, these scales clearly are vulnerable to all of the same claims as Likert scales. Few would argue with an ordinal level of measurement. Once again, the ordinal level greatly restricts the analytical tools available. Despite that the faces in Exhibit 26.4 are placed at equal intervals, it requires an assumption to treat these scales at the interval level of measurement. Once the interval or ordinal decision is made, the analysis proceeds in the same fashion as for Likert scale data.

SUMMARY

Scales are generally used to investigate a phenomenon across a range rather than to simply look for simple features, such as presence or absence. Scales typically involve multiple questions designed to elicit the intensity of response to the same general phenomenon. In order to ensure that the multiple questions reference the same topic, we can measure their reliability statistically. Most people are familiar with Likert-type scales, which present a statement and then ask respondents to rate their agreement with ratings such as "Strongly agree." Semantic differentials use two opposite adjectives and a series of unlabeled points between them. Ordinal scales ask participants to rank order choices, such as most favorite, second favorite, and so on. Fixed sum scales ask participants to divide a fixed sum (such as pretend money) among several different options. And pictorial scales use images as rating points rather than words.

DISCUSSION QUESTIONS

1. What does it mean to say that a scale is reliable?
2. What does a Likert scale measure?
3. How does one construct a semantic differential?
4. What might you learn using a fixed sum scale that you could not learn using an ordinal scale?

EXERCISES

1. Develop four Likert-type items to measure a person's attitude toward iPods.
2. Develop three semantic differential items to measure the credibility of a company's chief executive officer.
3. Develop a fixed sum scale for fast-food restaurants.

ADDITIONAL READING

Dawes, J. 2008. Do data characteristics change according to the number of scale points used? An experiment using 5-point, 7-point and 10-point scales. *International Journal of Market Research,* 50 (1), 61–77.

Likert, R. 1932. A technique for the measurement of attitudes. *Archives of Psychology,* 140: 1–55.

Osgood, C., G. Suci, and P. Tannenbaum. 1957. *The measurement of meaning.* Urbana: University of Illinois Press.

REFERENCES

Bradley, M.M., and P.J. Lang. 1994. Measuring emotion: The self-assessment Manikin and the semantic differential. *Journal of Behavior Therapy and Experimental Psychiatry,* 25, 49–59.

Bradley, S.D., W. Maxian, T.C. Laubacher, and M. Baker. 2007. In search of Lovemarks: The semantic structure of brands. In *Proceedings of the American Academy of Advertising,* ed. K.B. Sheehan, 42–9. Eugene, OR: American Academy of Advertising.

27 | Mapping Techniques

LEARNING OBJECTIVES

This chapter is intended to help you:

- Understand how mapping helps in presenting research results;
- See the differences between cognitive mapping and perceptual mapping;
- Learn how cognitive mapping works;
- Learn how perceptual mapping works.

Presenting the findings from research is a critical stage in the overall research process. As previous chapters have demonstrated, there are numerous approaches to presenting research data. In advertising and public relations, many of the final users of the research information may not be highly skilled in conducting research and may not understand all the statistical and other qualifications that are applied to research findings.

For these reasons, we often present the research findings in easy-to-understand formats. In addition to scaling and tables, we often use graphs. Pie charts, line graphs, and bar charts are commonly used in research presentations and reports. Another approach, very similar to graphs, is the use of mapping. Because mapping is somewhat different from most research presentation formats, it will be treated separately in this brief chapter.

COGNITIVE MAPPING

Cognitive maps help process and record the mental paths that people follow when they think about some idea or other phenomenon, especially when they are storing information to be recalled at some later time. It is a process of coding and later decoding information. Cognitive maps are often used in marketing and management to keep track of processes. Because research respondents use these mental processes when they are asked questions in a study, cognitive maps can help represent the resulting information.

With mapping, information is recorded as a visual representation, which helps in gaining information, in coding it, and in storing and recalling it. Information from research respondents is stored in this pictorial view, recording how the respondent's responses and ideas are developed and how they are related. Using cognitive maps, interviewers can rapidly take visual "notes" and then record the interview transcripts so that the findings can easily be analyzed and comprehended. Cognitive maps can also be used to record historical and other qualitative responses.

Suppose that a respondent answers two or more questions with much the same response. That answer is obviously in the forefront of the respondent's mind. These repeated responses can be recorded as a single issue, a key point of information that is very useful when trying to summarize the responses.

First, the response is divided into short phrases that summarize the response. If they are connected, lines can be drawn to show the relationships, with arrows, if necessary, to indicate direction or chronology. It would require a long narrative explanation to record this information in writing, but it is quick and simple using graphic maps. Next, the similar responses are joined into a single overriding idea or concept, which contrasts against other responses or groupings of responses; these contrasts help understand the differences in the responses and also contribute to a deeper understanding of both (or all) of the phrases used in the responses. Finally, similar phrases are linked (again, using visual lines, arrows, or other diagram elements) to show how the concepts and ideas relate to one another and how they differ, all while indicating the relative importance of each. Afterwards, the cognitive maps may be shared with the respondents to determine whether they agree with the interviewer's interpretations.

Suppose your research with a business executive indicates that the respondent is interested in expanding his or her company's sales territories into new areas. As you can see in Exhibit 27.1, Panel A, expansion into Eastern markets may be high in this person's mind.

Using probing questions, it is possible to determine in greater depth what this respondent thinks are possible benefits to be derived from this market expansion. Exhibit 27.1, Panel B shows that there are multiple results that the respondent believes might be gained; the arrows in the exhibit show the subsequent outcomes so the arrows lead from the original expansion idea to the eventual results, in chronological order of where they occur in the marketing channel rather than when they arose in the research process.

The next stage involves additional probing questions to uncover possible steps leading to the expansion plans. In Exhibit 27.1, Panel C, these lead-ins are shown with arrows leading to the original expansion idea because they exist in the supply channel; even though these contributing ideas were discovered last, they come first in the market process so the arrows lead in chronological order from the possible problem areas to the expansion idea.

So you can see that mapping techniques help elicit and record key concepts and relationships between the findings and thus help to construct a map for patterns, relationships, and chronology in the findings. Differences and difficulties are uncovered and the relationships and order are more easily understood.

Mapping helps reveal ideas that are important to the respondents, rather than simply recording all responses as equal to one another. As with so much of research, there are expanded explanations and tutorials of mapping techniques available, in books and on the Internet.

Exhibit 27.1 **Example of Cognitive Mapping**

Panel A

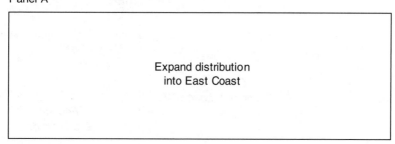

Panel B

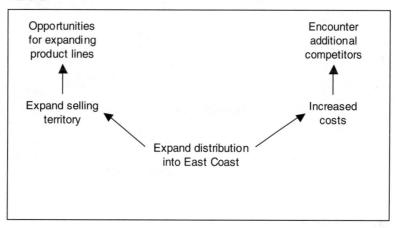

Panel C

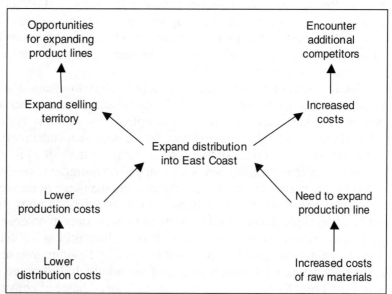

Exhibit 27.2 **Perceptual Mapping of Local Financial Institutions**

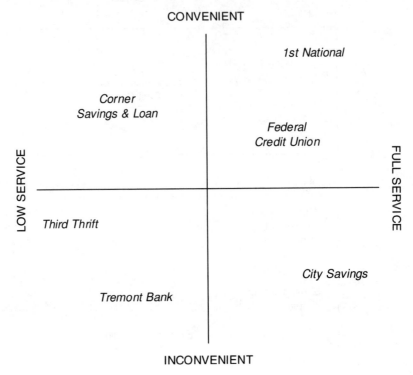

PERCEPTUAL MAPPING

Similar to cognitive mapping, perceptual maps use visual presentations to show the ideas of respondents and, in keeping with the name of the technique, of the perceptions on the part of customers. As with product or service positioning, perceptual mapping presents the positions of various brands, products, or firms as they relate to one another in consumers' minds.

Usually, perceptual maps are used in public relations and marketing to show the relative merits, in respondents' minds, of various products, services, ideas, brands, or firms and their competitors. For example, if you were to work on a campaign for a local bank, you might want to know how convenient consumers perceive that bank to be and how the services of that bank compare with those of its competitors. As you can see in Exhibit 27.2, the banks are mapped on a simple two-dimensional grid, with convenience portrayed on the vertical axis and the range of services portrayed on the horizontal axis. First National Bank is ranked highest in both convenience and full range of services. Tremont Bank is ranked lowest in convenience and Third Thrift is ranked lowest in the range of services. If your client is First National, you are working from a position of strengths. If your client is City Savings, you may want to improve convenience while taking advantage of the relatively full range of services. If your client is Corner Savings and Loan, you can take advance of convenience while trying

Exhibit 27.3

Practical Applications of Mapping Techniques

Cognitive mapping (also referred to as mind mapping)
- Allows consumers to visualize their view of the brand.
- Starts them off with key items from which to map.
- Sensory items: taste, smell, sight, hearing.
- Memories.
- Brand associations.
- Explore what the brand might do at a party, what they would wear, etc.

Perceptual mapping
- Attribute map: e.g., candy: chocolate versus non-chocolate with creamy vs. chewy.
- Benefit map: e.g., household cleaner: gentle/strong-acting with convenient/time-consuming.
- Value map: e.g., wristwatch: traditional/modern with popular/high status.
- Combination map: mix it up on the axis. Go wild.

to improve the degree of service. And if your client happens to be either Third Thrift or Tremont Bank, you need to work on both areas.

So both cognitive mapping and perceptual mapping help present information in an easy-to-use visual format that shows relationships, comparative evaluations, and relative attributes.

SUMMARY

Mapping helps present research findings in easy-to-understand and easy-to-use visual forms. Conceptual mapping portrays how the mind works. Perceptual mapping shows the relative strengths and weaknesses of companies, products, or brands using two (or sometimes more) elements.

DISCUSSION QUESTIONS

1. What do you see as the primary drawbacks of using mapping techniques to present research findings?
2. Which is more limited in scope, perceptual mapping or cognitive mapping?
3. Which is more useful for public relations and advertising, perceptual mapping or cognitive mapping?
4. What limitations on research questions might be posed if you intended to use mapping techniques to portray your research findings?

EXERCISES

1. In Exhibit 27.2, what would you do to enhance the position of Tremont Bank?
2. In Exhibit 27.2, what would you do to enhance the position of Third Thrift?
3. Prepare your own chart of banks in your community, using your own perceptions and opinions of their relative merits.

ADDITIONAL READING

Davis, J. 1997. *Advertising research: Theory and practice.* Upper Saddle River, NJ: Prentice-Hall.

Ackermann, F., C. Eden, and S. Cropper. 2004. *Getting started with cognitive mapping.* http://www.banxia.com/dexplore/pdf/GettingStartedWithCogMapping.pdf.

Schuster, P.M. 2007. *Concept mapping: A critical-thinking approach to care planning.* 2d ed. Philadelphia: F.A. Davis.

Lilien, G., and A. Rangaswamy. 2002. *Marketing strategy module.* Upper Saddle River, NJ: Pearson Education.

28 Statistics

LEARNING OBJECTIVES

This chapter is intended to help you:

- See how statistics are intended to simplify quantitative data;
- Learn how to calculate simple statistical measures;
- Understand why we use certain statistical applications;
- Observe how statistics can help determine whether your research is meaningful.

WHY WE HAVE STATISTICS

At first, statistics may seem complicated, even complex. But that is not the case. In fact, statistics exist to make things easier: easier to understand and easier to apply. Statistics take large sets of numbers and break them down into just one or a few figures, which helps us better understand the numbers. Think of it this way. There are three tools that help us see things that cannot be seen with the naked eye: microscopes, telescopes, and statistics. Statistics clarify patterns that cannot be seen amid a sea of data.

Imagine that you have tracked the number of visitors to your store over the course of the past year. If the store was open most days of the year, you have more than three hundred attendance figures, which—one-by-one—are difficult to understand and utilize. But if you calculate the average number of customers per day, you have a single number that represents those hundreds of individual attendance figures, and that average number is easier to understand that all those individual data were—and you can use that average figure to calculate other useful statistics, such as the range of the number of customers above and below average, how this year's average compared with previous years, projecting customer visits for the coming year, and scheduling staffing, merchandise orders, cash flow expectations, and many other figures.

Keep in mind that there are entire courses and entire books about statistics, so what is covered in this chapter can be only be a very basic introduction to the field.

MEASURES OF CENTRAL TENDENCY

One way that statistics makes large amounts of data easier to comprehend is through measures of central tendency, or averages. What most people consider the average is more specifically called the mean, which is the number that represents the middle of the weights of a set of numbers. The most common type of mean is the arithmetic mean (or simply the mean) of a list of numbers, which is the sum of all of the list divided by the number of items in the list. If the data represent the entire population being studied, the mean of that population is called a population mean. If the research used a sample, the mean of the sample is a sample mean. Again, the mean is determined by adding all the figures and then dividing by the number of items. See Exhibit 28.1 for examples.

Another type of average is the median, which is the middle score. To determine the median, it is first necessary to arrange the figures in either ascending or descending numerical order. The median is simply the score that is in the middle. The median may actually be more representative than the mean in some cases, where there are extreme skewed figures. For example, very high incomes can skew the average (mean) household income figures for a city, so the median may be more representative of the average household.

A third type of average is the mode, which is the most common figure, the one that appears most often. If one score or figure comes up much of the time, it may be important to recognize that frequency.

HYPOTHESES

You will recall from Chapter 3 that we often state a hypothesis, our expected or anticipated outcome of our research. Because the hypothesis is what is expected, we often measure against the null hypothesis, what is not expected, because it is easier to recognize something that is unusual or unexpected than it is the expected, the norm.

In empirical research we cannot really prove our hypotheses, because all we are doing is examining the hypothesis, often using a sample instead of the entire population base. Thus, in empirical research, we can support or reject our hypotheses. Of course, there are times when we err, and we accept a hypothesis that should have been rejected (because it was untrue), or on the flip side, we reject a hypothesis that should have been supported (because it was true). Because we rarely have access to the "truth," we can never know for sure when we are errantly rejecting or supporting a hypothesis. Instead, we must infer the likelihood that we are making a mistake based upon probabilities.

TOLERATED ERROR

When using a sample for a study, we will encounter sampling error. Because you are not studying everyone in the population, the sample results may be a bit "off," not exactly the same as might have been gained by studying the entire population. Wise researchers want to determine in advance the degree of error that they will accept, which is called the tolerated error.

Commonly in public relations and advertising, the tolerated error may be set at 3 or 4 percent, although there are certainly studies where the tolerated error is 10 percent or higher. Keep in mind that the tolerated error is plus or minus, that is, a 3 percent

Exhibit 28.1

Mean, Median, and Mode

Your public relations department conducts an employee question-and-answer session every four weeks (thirteen times a year). To determine whether these sessions are effective, you have tracked employee attendance for the past year.

Session Number	Attendance
1	22
2	14
3	19
4	52
5	19
6	91
7	36
8	42
9	19
10	57
11	73
12	70
13	49

To calculate the mean (average) number of attendees, you simply add the total attendance and divide by the number of meeting sessions.

$$\text{Mean} = \frac{\text{Sum}}{\text{Number}} = \frac{\Sigma}{n} = \frac{563}{13} = 43.3$$

To determine the mode, you find the most popular score, that is, the score that comes up most often. The figure of 19 attendees occurred three times during the thirteen sessions, so that is the mode: Mode = 19.

To determine the median, you must rearrange the scores in either ascending or descending order, and then select the middle score. In ascending order, the attendance numbers looks like this:

14
19
19
19
22
36
42
49
52
57
70
73
91

The middle score here is 42, so that is the median: Median = 42. Finding the median is simpler when there is an odd number of items, because the middle score is obvious. If you have an even number of items, take the average (mean) of the two middle scores to determine the median.

So, summarizing this set of attendance numbers:

The mean   = 43.3,
The median = 42, and
The mode   = 19.

tolerated error could be off by 3 percent, either higher or lower than the "true" figure for the entire population.

There is a difference between an error of a certain percent and an error of a certain number of percentage points. If the average age of the participants in your sample turned out to be 34 years, an error of 4 percentage points would mean that the actual average age is likely to be somewhere between 30 and 38 years (34 plus or minus 4 percentage points). But if the error is 4 percent (instead of 4 percentage points), then the actual average age is likely to be somewhere between 32.98 and 35.02 years (4 percent of 34 is 1.02 percentage points, so the range would be 34 plus or minus 1.02 percentage points).

CONFIDENCE LEVELS

It makes sense that we want to be confident that our research results are accurate. Yet the degree of confidence can vary.

Commonly in advertising and public relations research, we want to be confident that our results are right, maybe, 90 percent of the time (which we reverse and call the 0.10 level of confidence, meaning that there is a 10 percent chance that our results are not accurate and a 90 percent chance that they are accurate). If we wanted to be more confident, we might aim at being confident 95 percent of the time (0.05 level of confidence that our results are not accurate and a 95 percent chance that the results are accurate). Rarely in commercial research, we may want even more confidence, perhaps at the 0.01 level of confidence (99 percent confident that our results are accurate and only 1 percent chance that the results are not accurate).

It would likely be unwise to have less confidence than 90 percent (0.10 level of confidence).

The level of confidence is applied back onto the tolerated or sampling error. As we saw above, if we think the average age of our sample respondents was 34 years, plus or minus 4 years, then we project the age range as likely to be between 30 and 38 years. But the level of confidence tells us how likely it is that the actual average age is outside those ranges. At the 0.10 level of confidence, there is a 10 percent chance that the actual average age is younger than 30 or older than 38, and a 90 percent chance that the true average or mean age is within our range of 30 to 38. Similarly, at the 0.05 level of confidence, there is a 5 percent chance that the actual average age is outside the stated range and a 95 percent chance that the true average is within that range. In fact, if you run a hundred studies at the 0.05 level of confidence, then five of those studies will have ranges beyond those shown and at the 0.01 level of confidence, one of every hundred studies will fall outside the expected range.

STANDARD DEVIATION

Imagine that you are conducting research into the average height of two men. One of the men is 69 inches tall and the other is 71 inches tall, so their average height is 70 inches. Now imagine that you are studying two other men, one of whom is 60 inches tall and the other is 80 inches tall, so again the average height is 70 inches.

Does it make sense that the 70-inch average height better represents the first pair of men than it does the second pair of men? For the first pair, the average was only one inch away from each subject's height, whereas in the second pair, the average was 10 inches away from each subject's height.

So we need to know not only the mean but also how well the mean represents that set of data or figures. We use the standard deviation to tell us how far away, on the average, are the figures from the mean, and a smaller standard deviation is more desirable than a larger standard deviation.

Another way of thinking about the standard deviation is that it tells how well the mean represents a set of data or figures. If the members of a population are fairly similar to one another in age, occupation, income, and other measures, the standard deviation will be relatively small because the population is fairly homogeneous. On the other hand, if the members of a population are very different, the standard deviation will be larger because of the heterogeneous population.

Exhibit 28.2 shows the formula for calculating a standard deviation.

STANDARD ERROR OF THE MEAN

In research, we hope that our sample statistics represent the population fairly well. We hope that our sample mean is close to the real or true mean of the entire population. The standard error of the mean tells us exactly that: how well does the sample mean represent the true mean, or how far away from the true mean is the sample mean likely to be. Again, as with standard deviation, a smaller standard error is preferable to a larger standard error. A formula for calculating the standard error is shown in Exhibit 28.3.

RELATION TO SAMPLE SIZE

A larger sample does not necessarily provide more accuracy than does a small sample. In fact, a sample of, say, 1,500 subjects may be just as representative of an entire state as it is for a single city within that state. Population size does not directly affect sample size. More important is the diversity of the population. The more homogeneous the population, the more similar are the subjects and thus a smaller sample can suffice, whereas a heterogeneous population has more diversity in the population and thus may require a larger sample.

What is important, then, is the standard deviation, because the standard deviation will be smaller for a homogeneous population and larger for a heterogeneous population. Exhibit 28.4 shows how the standard deviation may impact the sample size.

CORRELATION

As the term implies, correlation means that two or more sets of variables are related to one another: co-related. In empirical research, we cannot prove that one set of variable causes the other set of variables to change; we can only demonstrate that they change together. Positive correlation means that two (or more) sets of variables

Exhibit 28.2

Standard Deviation

A traditional formula for determining the standard deviation is:

$$ s = \sqrt{\text{var}} = \sqrt{\frac{\sum (X - \overline{X})^2}{N - 1}} $$

In this formula, s is the standard deviation of a sample. The symbol Σ means that you add what follows the symbol. N is the sample size.

To apply this formula, find the difference between each score or figure and the mean, square them,* then add them. Then divide that product by $N-1$, and then take the square root of the result.

Go back to Exhibit 28.1. There, the mean was 43.3. If you subtract each score from the mean, you will get these results:

[Mean minus each score		equals the disparity,		which is then squared]
43.3 – 22	=	21.3	=	453.69
43.3 – 14	=	29.3	=	858.49
43.3 – 19	=	24.3	=	590.49
43.3 – 52	=	–8.7	=	75.69
43.3 – 19	=	24.3	=	590.49
43.3 – 91	=	–47.7	=	2,275.29
43.3 – 36	=	7.3	=	53.29
43.3 – 42	=	1.3	=	1.69
43.3 – 19	=	24.3	=	590.49
43.3 – 57	=	–13.7	=	186.69
43.3 – 73	=	–29.7	=	882.09
43.3 – 70	=	–26.7	=	712.89
43.3 – 49	=	–5.7	=	32.49
				$\Sigma = 7{,}303.77$

So if we go back to our formula,

$$ \frac{7{,}303.77}{13 - 1} = \frac{7{,}303.77}{12} = 608.6 $$

And the square root of 608.6 = 24.7, which is our standard deviation. That figure means that the average score was almost 25 points away from the mean, so the mean is not a very strong representative of this data set. Remember, a smaller standard deviation is preferable to a larger one.

Note that if we are seeking the standard deviation of an entire population, we would divide by N, but when we want to find the standard deviation of a sample, we divide by $N-1$, which will give us a slightly larger result for the standard deviation. In our example, N is 13, so $N-1$ is 12. Why did we divide by $N-1$ for the sample? Because the results from a sample are not likely to be quite as accurate as from the entire population, we use $N-1$ to compensate for this sampling error; this practice reflects what are known as *degrees of freedom* in statistics, but somewhat more complicated than we need to be at this time.

Depending on your particular situation, there are many other formulas for standard deviation that you might use. You can also look on the Internet for Web sites that allow you to enter your figures and that will calculate the standard deviation for you.

---

*You will remember that squaring a number is multiplying it by itself. Thus, $3^2 = 3 \times 3 = 9$. The reason we square the results is to compensate for negative numbers. If we simply take the difference between each score and the mean, the negative and positive scores will cancel each other out. So we square each difference (or disparity) to get positive results for each number (after all, a negative number multiplied by a negative number results in a positive number), and then we take the square root of the sum to reduce the squared scores down to their real values.

Exhibit 28.3

Standard Error of the Mean

A common formula for determining the standard error of the mean is:

$$SE_{\bar{x}} = \frac{s}{\sqrt{n}}$$

In the formula, s is the standard deviation from your sample and n is the size of the sample (such as the number of subjects or respondents).

Using the data from Exhibit 28.2, our standard deviation was 24.7 and n was 13 (the number of cases). The square root of 13 is 3.6.

So now we are solving for 24.7/3.6, and that answer is 6.86, which means that the sample means is likely to be within 6.86 points of the true mean—at the 0.05 level of confidence, so there is a 5 percent chance that the sample mean is farther away from the true mean than 6.86 points. Remember, if you run a hundred studies at the 0.05 level of confidence, then five of those studies will have ranges beyond the standard deviation and beyond the standard error, or one of every 20 studies.

Of course, there are other formulas that you can use, depending on your data and your application needs.

Remember that a smaller standard error is preferable to a larger one. On the Internet, you can find many Web sites where you can simply enter your figures and the standard error of the mean will be calculated for you.

---

gain in value together, not necessarily at the same rate, but that as one set increases in value, so does the other set. Negative correlation means that one set of variables increases while the other set (or sets) decreases. See Exhibit 28.5 for examples.

Again, we cannot show cause—that one set forces the other to react—only that the two sets react together. For example, our advertising budget has increased and the subsequent sales also increased, and so we believe that these two sets of value or figures are positively correlated. However, we cannot prove that the increased advertising caused the sales to rise; perhaps a growing economy allowed us to increase the size of the advertising budget and also permitted consumers to buy more of our products. We cannot prove causality with empirical research.

REGRESSION

Perhaps the most common method of determining correlation is regression analysis. The charts in Exhibit 28.5 are regression lines, with each figure showing the relationship between two variables. That is the simplest kind of regression: two variables for which the relationship can be shown by a single line, or linear regression (the term "linear" simply means that it is represented by a line). Linear regression is a type of regression analysis in which the relationship between the independent variable and the dependent variable can be demonstrated through a linear regression equation. This subject can become much more complicated than our elementary treatment here and can result in various kinds of statistical analyses. See Exhibit 28.6 for a simple regression formula.

There can also be more complicated kinds of regression, such as multiple regressions with more than two sets of variables.

Exhibit 28.4

Sample Size

The size of a research sample is related to the standard deviation. Perhaps surprisingly, the sample size is not affected very much by the population size, except that a larger population is likely to be more diverse and heterogeneous, which would require a larger sample because the standard deviation is likely to be larger. Similarly, a smaller population may be more homogeneous and thus have a smaller standard deviation, requiring a smaller sample size.

A simple formula for sample size is:

$$n = \frac{K^2 C^2}{r^2}$$

In this case, the sample size is represented by n, which is the solution to the formula. K is either 2 or 3, depending on whether the confidence level is 0.05 (then $K = 2$) or the confidence level is 0.01 (then $K = 3$).* C is the standard deviation, relative to the mean in percent; because the percentage could not be larger than 100 percent, it would be safe to insert 100 for C. The figure r is the tolerated error in percent.

So let's say we want to determine the size of a research sample at the 0.05 level of confidence ($K = 2$), with a 10 percent tolerated error ($r = 10$), and we are not sure what the standard deviation will be but we are certain that it will not be larger than 100 percent ($C = 100$). Then the formula would look like this:

$$n = \frac{K^2 C^2}{r^2} = \frac{2^2 \times 100^2}{10^2} = \frac{4 \times 10,000}{100} = \frac{40,000}{100} = 400 \quad \text{(size of sample)}$$

In fact, research samples are often set at a size of 400 because, at the 0.05 level of confidence, the tolerated error will be no larger than 10 percent, and probably smaller, depending on the standard deviation.

Of course, there are other formulas to determine sample size; the example here is one of the simpler approaches. If you look on the Internet, there are Web sites that will calculate sample size for you.

---

*The value of K is determined by statistics that are more advanced than we are using here. K is based on what is known as the z value, and the z value that occurs 5 percent of the time is 1.96, which can be rounded to 2, so we insert 2 for the value of K when we want a confidence level of 0.05; similarly, the z value that occurs 1 percent of the time is 2.58, which can be rounded to 3, so we insert 3 for the value of K when we want a confidence level of 0.01.

OTHER METHODS FOR DETERMINING CORRELATION

In addition to simple linear correlations, there are many other approaches to determining correlation. Which one to use depends on the nature of the data, the purposes to which the statistics may be applied, and the degree of detail necessary for the findings. Some additional correlation methods are more advanced types of regression while others are more novel approaches. Although they are beyond the scope of this book, you may wish to be familiar with some of the names of correlations tests, which include one-tailed and two-tailed tests, t tests, rank-order correlation, ANOVA, and many others.

SIGNIFICANCE

In much research, we want to be able to determine what were our most important findings, that is, what results of our study were most meaningful. Be careful, how-

Exhibit 28.5   **Positive and Negative Correlation**

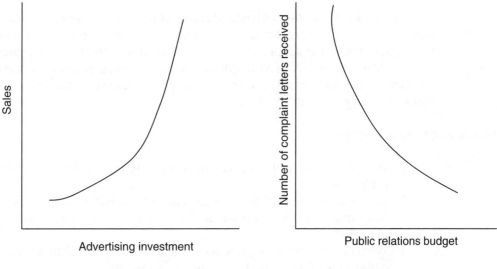

POSITIVE CORRELATION   NEGATIVE CORRELATION

Exhibit 28.6

Regression Formula

The simplest kind of regression is a simple graph showing how two variables relate to one another. The two variables can be graphed, with the two corresponding variables matched and the points plotted, as was done in Exhibit 28.5.

The two sets of variables can also be entered into a formula. Here is a simple regression formula.

$$r = \frac{n\sum(xy) - \sum x \sum y}{\sqrt{\left[n\sum(x^2) - (\sum x)^2\right] - \left[n\sum(y^2) - (\sum y)^2\right]}}$$

The letter *r* represents regression, and then it is possible to consult tables of statistical data to determine whether that value of *r* is significant at the 0.05 or even the 0.01 level of confidence. If it is significant, it means that the two sets are unlikely to occur together by chance—that is, that the two sets of variables are likely linked to one another. Significance does not mean that one of the variables necessarily causes the other; that might be the case, but it is also possible that some outside factor is causing both variables to react together.

ever, not to say that the findings were the most significant, because significance has a special meaning in research and statistics.

Significance means that we believe the variables are related to each other and that the differences or changes in the variables did not occur by chance. The term statistical significance means that we have used statistics to determine that the variables are really related to each other, although there is still a chance that is not true (a 5 percent chance at the 0.05 level of significance and a 10 percent chance at the 0.10 level of significance).

Summary

Statistics make it easier to understand reams of research finding data. There are three major measures of central tendency. Standard deviation indicates how well the mean represents a particular set of data, and standard error of the mean indicates how well the sample mean is likely to represent the population mean. Regression and correlation are used to determine whether the relationship between sets of variables is significant, that is, unlikely to occur by chance.

Discussion Questions

1. Why do we have three types of measuring central tendency? When might each be used?
2. In simple terms, why do we need standard deviation? What does it indicate?
3. In simple terms, why do we need standard error of the mean? What does it indicate?
4. What does the term "significance" mean in statistics? Why would using other definitions of that term be confusing in research?
5. What is correlation? For what is it used?
6. What is regression? For what is it used?

Exercises

1. Ask seven of your friends their height, and convert the values into inches. What is the mean, median, and mode?
2. After completing the exercise, add the data for an eighth, hypothetical friend who is 6-feet, 8 inches tall. How do the three measures of central tendency change?
3. For a standard deviation of 5 and 36 participants, what is the standard error of the mean?
4. Calculate the standard deviation for these 4 test scores: 72, 88, 75, 85.

Additional Reading

Agresti, A., and B. Finlay. 2009. *Statistical methods for the social sciences*. 4th ed. Boston: Pearson.

Hayes, A.F. 2005. *Statistical methods for communication science*. Mahwah, NJ: Erlbaum.

Rowntree, D. 2004. *Statistics without tears: A primer for non-mathematicians*. 2d ed. Boston: Pearson.

29 Statistical Analytic Tools

LEARNING OBJECTIVES

This chapter is intended to help you:

- Calculate descriptive statistics in SPSS;
- Calculate bivariate correlations in SPSS;
- Calculate simple linear regression in SPSS;
- Interpret the output for descriptives, frequencies, explore, correlation, and regression in SPSS;
- Calculate descriptive statistics in Microsoft Excel;
- Calculate correlations in Excel.

GETTING STARTED CALCULATING STATISTICS

Even the simplest statistics are laborious to compute by hand. For this reason, researchers in advertising and public relations almost exclusively rely upon computer software to calculate statistics. Although many statistics can be performed in Microsoft Excel, many researchers turn to SPSS, short for Statistical Package for the Social Sciences.

SPSS is relatively easy to use and can be quickly learned. However, there are two major considerations to keep in mind before diving into SPSS. First, it is an incredibly broad and diverse statistical package. The majority of users will use only a fraction of the tools offered by SPSS, but each researcher needs a unique subset of those tools. Therefore SPSS must offer hundreds of possible functions. This variety can be intimidating to those new at statistics who want to use only a few functions. The second major consideration of SPSS is that the program has no idea what you actually did. SPSS sees only numbers, and it will readily calculate meaningless statistics and tests that are inappropriate for your given data. Due to the fact that SPSS does not know where the data came from, it will offer no warnings that you may have made a mistake. Only the user can prevent these types of errors. It is more important to learn which functions are appropriate for which types of data than how to use the pull-down menus.

Exhibit 29.1   **SPSS: Type in Data**

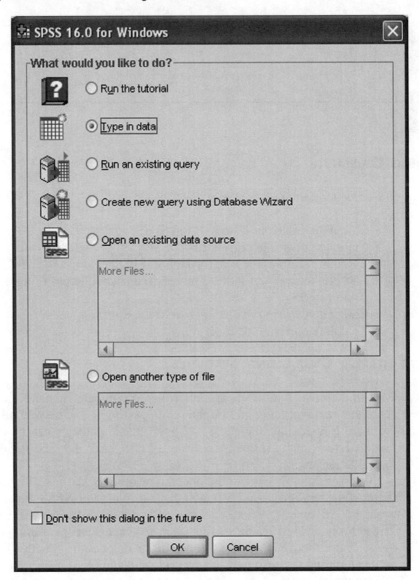

ENTERING DATA WITH SPSS

When launching SPSS, the user has several choices. Most commonly, readers of this book will either "Type in data" or "Open an existing data source." See Exhibit 29.1. If you have recently been working with a file, it will appear in the window under "Open an existing data source." If you want to browse for a data file, select "More data files . . ." and click "OK." Note that SPSS makes a distinction between file types

Exhibit 29.2 **SPSS Data View**

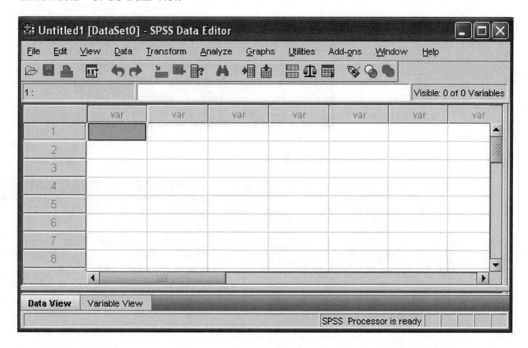

in opening. If you want to open an output file, for example, you must select "Open another type file." This is also true of the main program, where you must select which type of file you intend to open.

If you opt to type in data, you will see a blank window like the one shown in Exhibit 29.2. The default view is the "Data View." If you look at the bottom left corner of Exhibit 29.2, you will see that the Data View is highlighted. This is where actual data are entered. No variables exist in this data set yet, and each column header is the generic "var" for variable. If you begin simply typing data in, SPSS will automatically name the variables sequentially. The first variable will be "VAR00001," and so on. Although you can change the variable names later, it is difficult to remember what "VAR00009" stands for, so it is advisable to name the variables before you type in data.

In order to specify the variable names—and set many additional properties of variables, click on "Variable View" in the bottom left corner of the screen. See Exhibit 29.3. In the variable view, the user has several options, many of which are conveniences and not necessary for actual data analysis. A hypothetical data set is shown in Exhibit 29.4. Each participant is given a unique subject number, which is represented by the variable "subject." These data represent the results from a phone survey where participants were asked their age, whether they were male or female, and two advertising-related questions. We wanted to know whether there was a relationship between watching shows in which Coca-Cola is advertised and the average number of Cokes they drink each day. First, participants were asked which television shows they watched regularly. For each participant, we added up all of those programs

Exhibit 29.3   **SPSS: Specifying Variable Names**

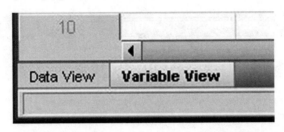

Exhibit 29.4   **SPSS: Variable View**

	Name	Type	Width	Decimals	Label	Values	Missing	Columns	Align	Measure
1	subject	Numeric	8	0		None	None	8	Right	Ordinal
2	age	Numeric	8	0		None	None	8	Right	Scale
3	gender	String	8	0		{1, female}...	None	8	Left	Nominal
4	n_shows	Numeric	8	2		None	None	8	Right	Scale
5	n_cokes	Numeric	8	2		None	None	8	Right	Scale
6										
7										
8										

sampleData.sav [DataSet0] - SPSS Data Editor

File   Edit   View   Data   Transform   Analyze   Graphs   Utilities   Add-ons   Window   Help

Data View   Variable View

SPSS Processor is ready

in which Coca-Cola advertises. We called this variable "n_shows," where "n" stands for "number." Second, participants were asked how many Coca-Cola soft drinks they drink on an average day. This variable was called "n_cokes."

Looking at Exhibit 29.4, you can see that several variable properties have been set. For instance, "gender" has been classified as a "string," meaning that it contains letters. Gender also is classified as "Nominal" in the far left column. SPSS offers three levels of classification, nominal, ordinal, and scale. See Exhibit 29.5. Both interval and ratio data are classified as scale data by SPSS. Scale is the default data type, and any numerical data entered by hand will remain classified as scale data unless the user manually changes the Measure column in Variable View. Most users never change the data from scale because it is not necessary. Switching the type of measure disables certain statistics that are appropriate for scale data. Thus, by properly classifying ordinal data as ordinal, SPSS prevents the user from calculating meaningless scale-level statistics. In this sense, you are saving you from yourself by changing the Measure type to "nominal" or "ordinal." In addition, certain types of graphs also will be unavailable for nominal or ordinal data.

It also is possible to have SPSS display data labels rather than the actual values. For instance, in this data set the gender of participants was not entered as "female"

Exhibit 29.5 **SPSS: Levels of Classification**

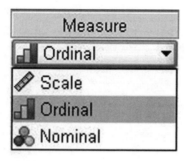

Exhibit 29.6 **SPSS Value Labels**

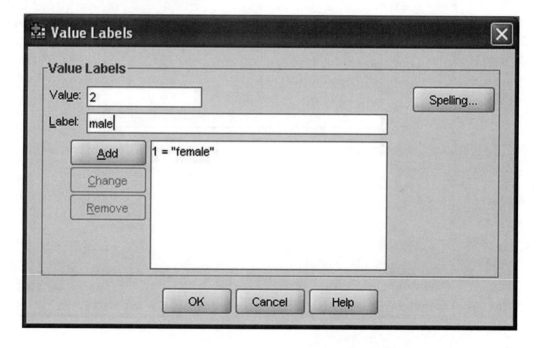

and "male." Instead, females were coded as 1, and males were coded as 2. There is no problem simply leaving the data as 1s and 2s; however, it can be confusing later. Looking at a data report several days later, it can be quite difficult to remember whether "1" meant male or female. To circumvent this type of confusion, labels can be entered in the "Label" column. After Value Labels were added to this data set, the words male and female will be displayed on all output. See Exhibit 29.6. However, the actual raw data will remain 1s and 2s. In order to set a Value Label, simple enter the raw Value (in this case "2") and the Label that you would like displayed (in this case "male"). Then click "Add" and "OK," and the Value Label will be added.

Exhibit 29.7   **SPSS: Descriptives Screen Shot**

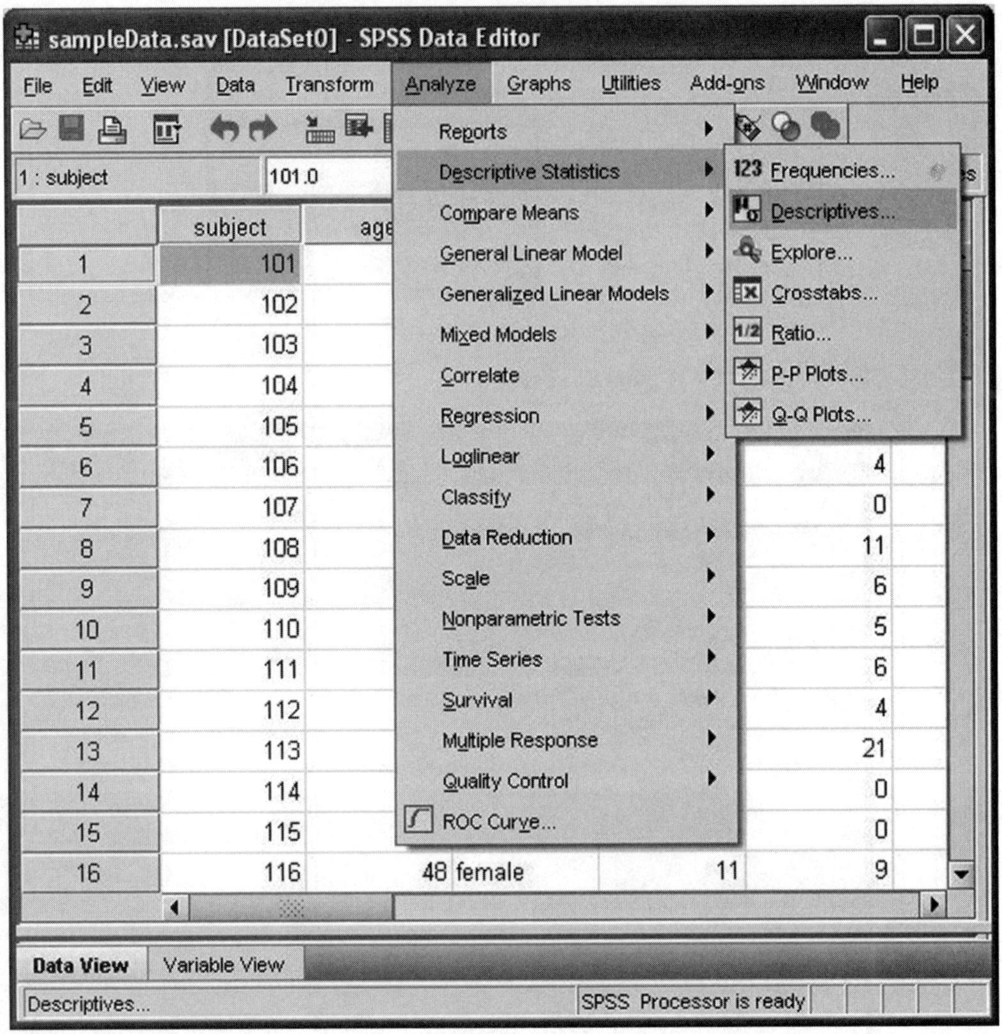

LEARNING ABOUT YOUR DATA

As you learned in Chapter 28, statistics can tell us much about our data that we cannot see with the naked eye. Measures of central tendency and dispersion describe the data. For this reason, such measures are commonly referred to as descriptive statistics. SPSS offers a wide range of descriptive statistics. These statistics are accessed from the "Analyze" pull-down menu in SPSS. See Exhibit 29.7. Under Analyze, move the mouse pointer to "Descriptive Statistics." Hovering the mouse over Descriptive Statistics will offer several choices. Although each successive version of SPSS tends to offer more options, "Frequencies" and "Descriptives" are most commonly used.

If you click on "Descriptives," you will see a window like the one shown in Exhibit

Exhibit 29.8   **SPSS: Descriptives Variable Panel**

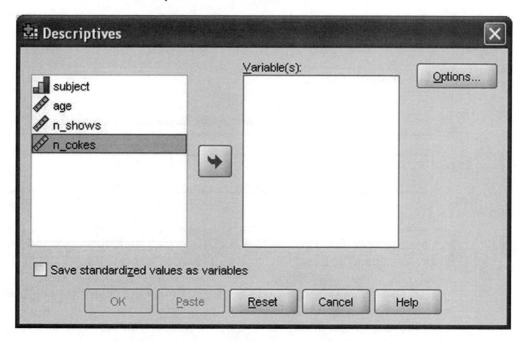

29.8. Here you highlight each variable of interest and click on the center arrow to move to the "Variable(s)" panel. This allows you to obtain descriptive statistics for multiple variables at one time. Multiple variables can be moved to the "Variable(s)" panel by holding down the "Shift" key and clicking each variable. If you accidentally move the wrong variables to the right, you can move them back or click "Reset." Variables that are categorized as "String" in the variable view will not appear in the Descriptives window. However, SPSS *will* calculate descriptive for data categorized as "Nominal." If the data are truly nominal, then the resulting descriptive are meaningless. If you had 67 women (coded as 1) and 33 men in a study (coded as 2), the mean gender would be 1.67, which is nonsensical.

The standard Descriptives function reports mean, standard deviation, minimum value, and maximum value. If you wish to see additional descriptive, such as range and standard error of the mean, you can select these by clicking the Options button. You can also choose other options beyond the scope of this book. Once at least one variable is moved to the "Variable(s)" panel, the "OK" button becomes active.

Clicking "OK" will produce a new output window with output similar to that shown in Exhibit 29.9. This shows the basic data provided by the Descriptives function. The "N" shows the number of participants who gave a response for this variable (the average number of Cokes consumed weekly), which in this case was 50. There may have been more than 50 participants in this study, but there are valid "n_cokes" data for only 50. The next two columns show the minimum and maximum values, respectively. Among these respondents, at least one person drinks zero Coca-Colas in an average week. At the other end, at least one person drinks 21 Cokes in an aver-

Exhibit 29.9 **SPSS: Output Using the Descriptives Data Function**

➡ Descriptives

[DataSet0] C:

Descriptive Statistics

	N	Minimum	Maximum	Mean	Std. Deviation
n_cokes	50	0	21	7.64	4.738
Valid N (listwise)	50				

age week, or about three a day. On average, this sample drinks 7.64 Cokes per week, or about one per day. The standard deviation is 4.738, indicating that there is some dispersion among respondents. The final piece of information, "Valid N (listwise)," is not quite as easy to understand. For each variable in the dataset, there may be missing data from some participants. They may not have answered the question, or they may have provided an invalid answer, such as "old" for age. Data might also have been illegible or lost during the data-entry process. Furthermore, some respondents may have skipped one question while others skipped different questions. The "Valid N (listwise)" represents the number of respondents who have valid data for every variable in the list selected for Descriptive Statistics. In this case there was only one variable selected, so the number is 50 for N and Valid N.

Even if you are not explicitly interested in descriptive statistics, you should always examine these data. This is one of the quickest ways to find errors made during the data-entry process. For instance, research in advertising and public relations often uses Likert-type scales. A seven-point scale ranging from "Strongly Disagree" to "Strongly Agree" is often coded from 1 to 7. By looking at the descriptive statistics, one could quickly discern whether a "9" had accidentally been entered, as it would show up under maximum values. In addition, appropriate age ranges also can be checked here.

If you refer back to Chapter 28, you will see more statistics covered than shown in Exhibit 29.9. Given the versatility of SPSS, there are multiple ways to examine your data. After looking at the "Descriptives" output, return to the "Analyze" menu and select "Descriptive statistics" and then "Frequencies." This will show how often each answer was given. See Exhibit 29.10. At the top of the Frequencies output, SPSS shows that 50 respondents had valid data, and that in this instance zero cases had missing data. In the second table, the frequency of each response is given, from the minimum of "0" to the maximum of "21." Inspecting this table is one way to determine the mode, or most common response. In this case, the most common response was "6" Cokes per week. Eight people gave this response.

SPSS also provides the percent of people who give each response. In this case, 16 percent of respondents report drinking an average of six Cokes per week. SPSS also

Exhibit 29.10   **SPSS: Frequencies Screen Shot**

➡ **Frequencies**

Statistics

n_cokes

N	Valid	50
	Missing	0

n_cokes

		Frequency	Percent	Valid Percent	Cumulative Percent
Valid	0	3	6.0	6.0	6.0
	1	1	2.0	2.0	8.0
	2	2	4.0	4.0	12.0
	3	3	6.0	6.0	18.0
	4	3	6.0	6.0	24.0
	5	5	10.0	10.0	34.0
	6	8	16.0	16.0	50.0
	7	2	4.0	4.0	54.0
	8	4	8.0	8.0	62.0
	9	4	8.0	8.0	70.0
	10	2	4.0	4.0	74.0
	11	4	8.0	8.0	82.0
	12	2	4.0	4.0	86.0
	13	1	2.0	2.0	88.0
	14	2	4.0	4.0	92.0
	15	1	2.0	2.0	94.0
	17	1	2.0	2.0	96.0
	19	1	2.0	2.0	98.0
	21	1	2.0	2.0	100.0
	Total	50	100.0	100.0	

provides the Valid Percent. This is useful when there is missing data. In these cases, Percent tells the percentage of all respondents with a given response. The Valid Percent is the percentage of those respondents with a valid response who provided a given response. When all participants have a valid response—as is the case here—Percent and Valid Percent will be the same. Finally, SPSS provides the Cumulative Percent. This is helpful in providing summary reports in advertising and public relations. For instance, a quick glance shows that 50 percent of respondents drink six or fewer Coca-Colas per week. We can also quickly tell that 74 percent of respondents drink 10 or fewer Cokes each week. However, there are some descriptive statistics that are still difficult to determine here.

To learn more about our data, we return to the "Analyze" pull-down menu, select "Descriptive Statistics," and then "Explore." Although there are many options that can be selected, the basic output is shown in Exhibit 29.11. Here in one compact table

Exhibit 29.11 **SPSS: Output Using the Explore Command**

➔ Explore

Case Processing Summary

	Cases					
	Valid		Missing		Total	
	N	Percent	N	Percent	N	Percent
n_cokes	50	100.0%	0	.0%	50	100.0%

Descriptives

			Statistic	Std. Error
n_cokes	Mean		7.64	.672
	95% Confidence Interval for Mean	Lower Bound	6.29	
		Upper Bound	8.99	
	5% Trimmed Mean		7.41	
	Median		6.50	
	Variance		22.562	
	Std. Deviation		4.750	
	Minimum		0	
	Maximum		21	
	Range		21	
	Interquartile Range		6	
	Skewness		.700	.337
	Kurtosis		.475	.662

are most of the descriptive statistics of interest. Explore shows the mean, median, standard deviation, variance, standard error, and range. Unfortunately, the Explore command does not provide the mode, or most common response. That is more easily determined using Frequencies, as described above. As you learn more about statistics, the Explore command can also provide additional descriptive statistics and graphical representations of data that are beyond the scope of this text.

CORRELATIONS

One of the most basic statistics described in Chapter 28 is the correlation, referred to as a Bivariate Correlation in SPSS. Recall that this is basically a measure of how two variables co-occur. Correlations can help you determine whether an increase in one variable in associated with another variable increasing, decreasing, or showing no relationship. Because correlational data are collected at one time, we cannot make claims to causation. That is, we cannot know which variable caused the other.

Exhibit 29.12 **SPSS: Bivariate Correlations**

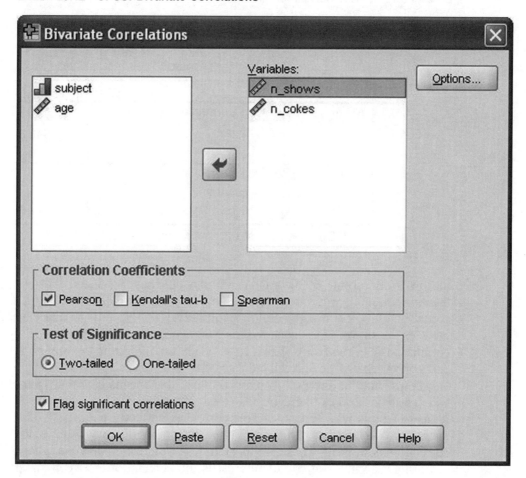

Returning to our simplified example for this chapter, we wanted to know whether viewing television programs in which Coca-Cola advertises is associated with drinking more Coca-Cola. We can take an initial examination of this relationship between these two variables using correlations. Under the "Analyze" pull-down menu in SPSS, select "Correlate." This will bring up multiple options, and you want to select "Bivariate," which is the same statistic outlined in Chapter 28. Selecting "Bivariate" will pull up the window shown in Exhibit 29.12.

Here both "n_shows" and "n_cokes" have been moved over to the right panel using the center arrow. Every other option is the default option. There will rarely be a need to change these options. Should you accidentally select the wrong variable, it can be moved back using the center arrow. You may enter as many scale variables as you would like here, and SPSS will compute the correlation between each pair of variables (hence the name bivariate correlation: two at a time). Clicking "OK" leads to a correlation matrix such as the one shown in Exhibit 29.13.

Each variable is shown as a row down the left-hand column and as a column across

Exhibit 29.13 **SPSS: Correlation Matrix**

➡ Correlations

Correlations

		n_shows	n_cokes
n_shows	Pearson Correlation	1.000	.283*
	Sig. (2-tailed)		.046
	N	50	50
n_cokes	Pearson Correlation	.283*	1.000
	Sig. (2-tailed)	.046	
	N	50	50

*. Correlation is significant at the 0.05 level (2-tailed).

the top. If we had entered 10 variables, SPSS would have produced a correlation matrix that is 10 columns wide by 10 rows high. A correlation matrix can be tricky to interpret at first. Look at the first cell in Exhibit 29.13. SPSS tells us that the correlation between "n_shows" and "n_shows" is 1.000. What does this even mean? Recall that correlations can run from −1 to +1, with 0 in the middle indicating no relationship between variables. The first cell indicates there is a perfect positive correlation between "n_shows" and "n_shows." In plain English, that means if you answered that you watch 5 shows a week, then you answered that you watch 5 shows a week. Of course it has to be this way. Every variable correlates perfectly with itself. This is simply an artifact of a correlation matrix, and the diagonal will always show each variable's correlation with itself. These are meaningless data, which you can ignore.

In this case, the statistic of interest is the correlation between "n_shows" and "n_cokes." You can see in two places that this correlation is .283. Why does SPSS show this value twice? Once again this is an artifact of the correlation matrix. One side of the diagonal will always be the mirror of the opposite. Most people simply ignore the numbers above the diagonal as they are a repeat of the numbers below. SPSS displays .283 twice simply because the correlation between "n_cokes" and "n_shows" is identical to the correlation between "n_shows" and "n_cokes." This is a relatively modest correlation between the two variables, and it suggests that there is some relationship between watching the programs that have ads and Coca-Cola consumption. Once again it must be emphasized that the data are merely correlational. We do not know whether the ads cause you to consume Coca-Cola, or whether the advertising agency has done a really good job in placing the ads in programs that Coke drinkers watch. It is always a mistake to infer causation from correlation.

The second number of interest here is .046. This is known as the statistical significance, or p value. This tells us the probability of finding a correlation as large as .283 (or larger) given that there is no genuine correlation between the variables. Recall that in sampling, we are always trying to estimate values of the population. There is always sampling error present, and we can never be sure what that sampling error is. In this case, there is less than a 5 percent chance (the conventional threshold for statistical significance in the social sciences) that we would have observed this large of a correlation due to sampling error alone. Thus, we know that there is only a 1:20 chance that this correlation does not exist in the population. The final number, 50, is once again the number of individuals in the sample.

REGRESSION

The correlation tells us that there is a relationship between the two variables, but it does not give us much predictive power. Regression is a more complicated inferential statistic that allows us to make predictions about one variable based upon the value on another. For instance, if I watch 8 shows a week that regularly contain Coca-Cola ads, how many Cokes would you predict that I drink? The correlation is no help here. Since the correlation is positive, you can infer that I am likely to drink more than someone who watches 6 such shows. How much more is unclear looking solely at the correlation between the two variables.

Regression uses the basic formula for a line—which most readers will have learned (and likely forgotten) in junior high or high school algebra. This formula allows us to make predictions about one variable based upon another. Once again, the data remain correlational (they have not changed), but the researcher can select one variable to predict the other. In this case, we want to predict carbonated soft drink consumption from television viewing.

There is more than one way to compute regression in SPSS. The most straight-forward is obtained under the "Analyze" pull-down menu, then "Regression," then "Linear." You may notice 10 or more options for Regression depending upon your version of SPSS. It is an incredibly powerful statistic, and it is possible to take multiple graduate school courses simply on regression. However, simple linear regression will suffice for our purposes. In Exhibit 29.14, you can see that there is a place for both an Independent Variable and a Dependent Variable. When the data are correlational, this is a bit of a misnomer by SPSS. The term "Independent Variable" implies that this variable is doing the causing, which is not the case for correlational data. However, this terminology helps us to remember that the dependent variable is the one that we are trying to predict.

In Exhibit 29.14, "n_shows" has been entered as the independent variable, and "n_cokes" has been entered as the dependent variable. For the simplest case of linear regression, this is all that is needed. Enter the two variables in the correct panels using the large arrow and click "OK." Even the simplest regression output is fairly complicated—far more complicated than the correlation. For the purposes of this textbook, let's overlook the top table (titled ANOVA) in Exhibit 29.15 altogether. With a simple linear regression, this tells us very little additional information. The bottom table is titled "Coefficients," and this is an information-dense table.

In order to predict the "dependent" variable, we need the "Unstandardized Coefficients," which are labeled as "B." There are two. One is for "(constant)," and the

Exhibit 29.14 **SPSS: Linear Regression Example**

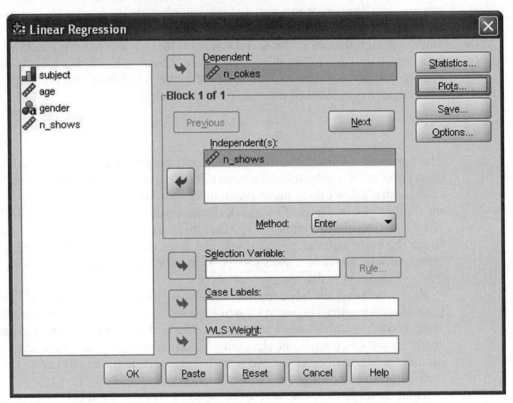

other is for our "independent" variable, n_shows. The unstandardized coefficient for (constant) is called the "Y intercept" in linear algebra. This is the number of Cokes we would expect someone to drink if she watched zero programs with Coca-Cola ads. In this case, that would be 5.16 drinks. So if I know nothing about a customer except that she does not watch any television, I would predict that she drinks about 5 Cokes a week. The prediction is not deterministic, and any given consumer may drink no soft drinks whatsoever or may drink a case a week. But the "(constant)" is our best guess. The unstandardized coefficient for our variable, n_shows, is known as the slope in linear algebra. For each additional show you watch, we expect you to drink .210 additional Coca-Colas. This is not much. You'd have to watch 5 shows for us to expect you to average one extra Coke a week. Putting these two numbers together, we get the prediction formula:

Number of Cokes = 5.16 + (.210 × Number of Shows).

Although this prediction will not necessarily be accurate for any given individual, our sample suggests that it will tend to be generally accurate for the population. At the far right of that table is a column with the header "Sig." This is the same as the

Exhibit 29.15 **SPSS: Regression Output**

➡ Regression

ANOVA[b]

Model		Sum of Squares	df	Mean Square	F	Sig.
1	Regression	88.618	1	88.618	4.183	.046[a]
	Residual	1016.902	48	21.185		
	Total	1105.520	49			

a. Predictors: (Constant), n_shows

b. Dependent Variable: n_cokes

Coefficients[a]

Model		Unstandardized Coefficients		Standardized Coefficients	t	Sig.
		B	Std. Error	Beta		
1	(Constant)	5.162	1.375		3.754	.000
	n_shows	.210	.102	.283	2.045	.046

a. Dependent Variable: n_cokes

statistical significance in the correlation. Once again, there is a .046 probability that the relationship between n_shows and n_cokes shown here would have been observed if there were no real relationship within the population. It is not a coincidence that this is the same probability as the correlation, but an explanation is quite complicated. Although the correlation statistic showed that there is a relationship among the variables, the regression allowed a better examination of the relationship: it takes 5 shows to average an additional Coke consumed.

WORKING IN MICROSOFT EXCEL

Many of these same functions can be computed easily with Microsoft Excel. This is advantageous since far more people have access to Excel than SPSS. However, many of the user interfaces are not as straightforward. There is, for example, no dialog box to click for descriptive statistics. In order to find the arithmetic mean for a set of data, for example, the cursor must be placed in a blank cell. In Exhibit 29.16, the cursor has been placed in the empty cell F2. Here, clicking the f_x function button (directly above column C) pulls up the dialogue window. From here, the user can search any number of functions. In this case, the search for the word "average" brings up the function "AVERAGE." This is the function we want, so we click "OK."

This brings up the window shown in Exhibit 29.17. Here the user must manually select the data to be averaged. This is done by clicking the arrow to the right of the

Exhibit 29.16   **Microsoft Excel: Insert Function Window**

Microsoft® Excel® screen shot reprinted with permission from Microsoft Corporation.

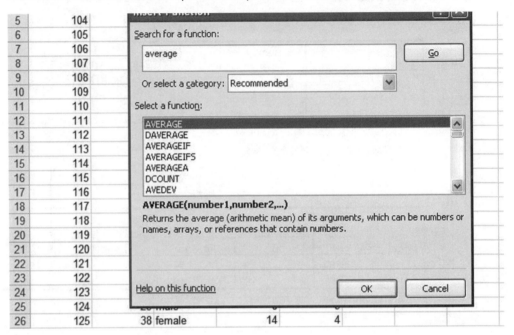

"Number 1" entry field. This allows the user to click on the topmost value (in this case, cell E2) and drag to the bottommost value (in this case, cell E51). The value, 7.64, is shown in the bottom of Exhibit 29.17 as "Formula result = 7.64." However, this result will disappear unless the user clicks "OK." Clicking OK will insert the formula into the spreadsheet at cell F2, where the cursor was. This exact procedure can be replicated for median and standard deviation.

Correlations also can be obtained in roughly the same fashion. Place the cursor in a blank cell and click the f_x function button. Searching for the function "CORREL" and clicking "OK" brings up the window shown in Exhibit 29.18. Since correlations are between two sets of data, the user must click the arrow button to the right of "Array 1" and "Array 2." In this instance, all of the data for n_shows are selected for Array 1, and all of the data for n_cokes are selected for Array 2. Clicking "OK" after selecting both arrays will place the formula result in the previously selected blank cell. In Exhibit 29.18, the formula result of 0.283 is shown in the lower left portion of the window. That is the same result obtained in SPSS.

Microsoft Excel is an incredibly powerful spreadsheet program. All of the formulas from Chapter 28 can be entered into Excel, so it can calculate virtually any statistic if the user has enough experience with spreadsheets and formulas. However, this is seldom the case for students taking their first course in research. Therefore, SPSS is often the preferred statistical package, even though it is not widely available off of college campuses.

Exhibit 29.17 **Microsoft Excel: Function Arguments Window**

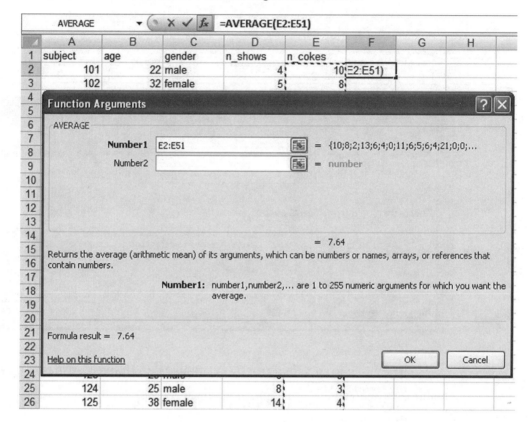

SUMMARY

Although Microsoft Excel is more widely available, SPSS is a more powerful statistical package for the advertising and public relations researcher. SPSS allows you to quickly compute descriptive statistics, bivariate correlations, and simple linear regression. Useful descriptive statistics include measures of central tendency and dispersion, frequency tables, and the explore function of SPSS. You can quickly calculate correlations and measures of central tendency with Excel, the other functions often require more sophisticated equations that are beyond the comfort level of beginning users.

DISCUSSION QUESTIONS

1. What are some characteristics of data where it may be necessary to inspect both the descriptive statistics and the frequencies?
2. If there were a gross error in your data—such as a human age of 1,000—would

Exhibit 29.18 **Microsoft Excel: Correlation Result**

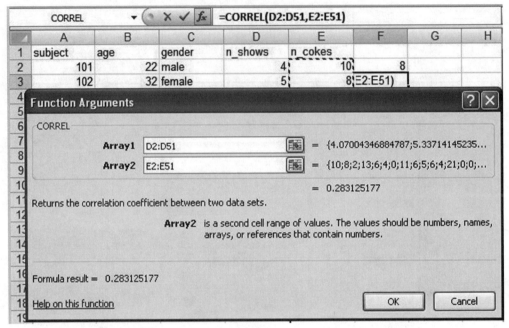

it be easier to spot this error by examining descriptive statistics or by examining frequencies?
3. Why should researchers always examine all measures of central tendency in their computer output?

EXERCISES

1. Collect height, foot length, and GPA data from fifteen of your friends. Calculate the mean, median, and mode for each variable.
2. Is there a correlation between height and foot length? Is there a correlation between height and GPA?
3. Calculate a regression in SPSS to predict height from foot length.

ADDITIONAL READING

Cronk, B.C. 2006. *How to use SPSS: A step-by-step guide to analysis and interpretation.* 4th ed. Glendale, CA: Pyrczak.

Sweet, S.A., and K. Grace-Martin. 2008. *Data analysis with SPSS: A first course in applied statistics.* 3d ed. Boston, MA: Pearson.

PART VII

PRACTICAL ASPECTS OF
ADVERTISING AND PUBLIC RELATIONS RESEARCH

30 Who Should Conduct the Research?

LEARNING OBJECTIVES

This chapter is intended to help you:

- Learn when to use internal versus external research;
- Understand how to select a research partner;
- Learn who should summarize research results and provide action items as a result of research.

Every day there are thousands of research issues and projects being conducted by advertising and public relations agencies and their clients. In fact, there is an entire research industry that has been spawned to conduct research and answer these questions.

While there are many outside research suppliers to the advertising and public relations industry, a good deal of research is done in-house by either staff research professionals, account planners, or others who have had some amount of research training.

There are many reasons, pro and con, for doing research in-house or engaging an outside firm; these reasons include credibility and budget, or may depend on other factors, such as the types of research required.

ISSUE OF BIAS AND CREDIBILITY

The key reason why you would select an outside research firm to conduct a research study is to maintain objectivity and have results that are credible. It is all about eliminating bias. If you created an ad and then tested it, would you have as much credibility as a third party who would test it? The answer obviously is no.

Advertising and public relations are creative fields that involve changing public perception. Both creative people and the consumers whom they are trying to persuade can be a fickle bunch. Even with the best of intentions, an agency may be too close to the situation to be objective. It can be like asking a class who deserves an A the most. Wouldn't most of the students raise their hands? You wouldn't get an objective viewpoint of the situation. The bottom line is that people tend to be skeptical about the objectivity of research that is created and analyzed by someone who has a vested interest in the results.

Eliminating bias is an important consideration in the decision to do research in-house or to hire an outside firm. The other side to eliminating bias is the issue of credibility. It is much more credible for a third party to say that your creative is liked by consumers rather than the agency saying it. A third party or research company may be needed if the research in question is being used to support the allocation of advertising or public relations funds.

A CEO of a publicly traded company isn't going to tell his shareholders and Wall Street analysts that he needs to spend more on advertising and public relations just because the agency told him so. He needs another viewpoint that would corroborate what the agency is counseling him to do. It is only prudent that big decisions are made with some form of research as support.

The key filter then to decide if you would conduct research inside or hire an outside research firm comes down to the issue of being able to provide an objective viewpoint (elimination of bias) and being credible in that viewpoint. Therefore as a general rule of thumb, primary research is conducted by an outside research firm.

INTERNAL RESEARCH STUDIES

When you think of all the secondary and syndicated research that is available to an advertising agency or public relations firm, there is little doubt that the majority of research is done internally.

Much of that research focuses on analyzing secondary or syndicated research. Within syndicated research your analysis might take the form of constructing a cross tabulation of information to shed a new insight. For example, you have a client who markets pet food to dog owners. You review syndicated data for the brand's target profile but you want to understand what other products these people purchase. With the syndicated data available, you construct a cross tabulation of data where you cross your brand's target profile with other brands that they purchase. This insight could lead to you co-marketing with another brand or to have messages in areas outside the normal channels.

Analyzing secondary and syndicated information meets that key filter of being un-biased and having credibility. You didn't conduct the research from a primary research standpoint. You are merely interpreting that research. This is not only acceptable in business but a way that you can add value to your client's business.

Another form of analysis that falls into this same camp is content analysis. This is a process in which you review existing content and then interpret its meaning. For example, you may review all the competitive advertising for a category in which your brand competes. You develop a report that details what you found and the implications for the creative development for the brand you work on. Or you may do a review of the blog world for a client to better understand what consumers are saying about the brand. From this content analysis, you may recommend that your client begin to message in a certain way to counteract what is being said about the brand.

Secondary and syndicated research plus content analysis form the basis for the

Exhibit 30.1

Internal vs. External Research

Internal	External
Secondary/syndicated	Primary
Observational	Qualitative
Content analysis	Quantitative

day-to-day research that goes on in the advertising and public relations world. In each case, the data exists, so there is no question about the bias or credibility of the information. Your role is not to just report the information to the client but to interpret it in a meaningful manner that will result in some form of decision for the brand.

There is one place where primary research is conducted by the advertising agency or public relations firm. That is in the area called observational research. Observational research is a fancy name for "observing consumers in their nature setting." While there are research companies that specialize in observational or ethnographic research, any advertising agency or public relations professional should be an observational researcher.

In advertising agencies, the account-planning group is responsible for developing the consumer insights that help to fashion a creative brief. Many of these insights come from observational research. For example, an observational truth may be that no one likes a big oil company. Or that moms feel guilty about not having enough time to make a traditional meal for their families. Or it might be that students believe that getting drunk is a rite of passage. Any of these observations could suggest a problem or opportunity for advertising to solve.

So, observational research can become a key component to developing a creative strategy. While many times, these insights can come from a variety of qualitative research, they can come equally from general observations about consumers and how they interact with the brand.

EXTERNAL RESEARCH STUDIES

Every client wants to know how their advertising or public relations campaign is performing in the marketplace. That is one of many roles for using an external research company. In fact, tracking campaign effectiveness, testing advertising copy and/or creative, and developing customer segmentation studies are the most often commissioned primary research studies in the advertising industry.

Nearly every research study that involves a quantitative methodology requires the use of an outside research company. Other than the lack of bias and added credibility that a research company offers, there are more practical reasons for using an outside research partner. First and foremost is that this is their profession, what they do for a living. Just as you may turn to an expert in advertising or public relations to solve a communications problem, you should turn to an expert in market/advertising research to solve a research problem. Not only will a quality research

Exhibit 30.2

Most Often Commissioned Research

Type
- Customer/target segmentation study
- Campaign tracking study (AAU)
- Advertising copy testing/Message testing/Creative testing

company have great experience but they will have the necessary infrastructure to conduct the research.

If you are conducting a quantitative study, that could mean doing a telephone survey, mail survey, panel study, or a Web site survey. All of these methodologies require people to design the study, program the study for ease of data collection, field the study, and provide a report of the findings. Research companies that conduct telephone surveys can have hundreds of trained interviewers prepared to call on your client's behalf. There is no credible or practical way that an advertising agency could hire, train, and supervise a large-scale survey for just a few clients. It requires a constant volume of work so a company can invest in the proper infrastructure and training to do a quality job of quantitative research.

One of the largest specialty areas within the advertising industry is composed of companies that test messages and ranges of creative expressions of those messages. Using what is usually referred to as "copy testing" research, these companies provide diagnostics on creative from print, to broadcast, to online. Many of these companies develop "normative data" that clients rely on to help them understand how their creative stacks up to others in their industry or in general. To generate a "norm," a research company may aggregate all their tests into an average score either overall or by product category (for example, food products). These "norms" become benchmarks for the creative team to beat with their specific execution. Within the package goods industry, there are copy testing research companies and methods that move beyond just providing "norms" to providing market validation of their methods. This means that they can predict with some degree of certainty that if a commercial meets a certain benchmark, it will perform at a certain level within the marketplace. Obviously, this type of information is extremely valuable to a brand manager or advertising director who is investing tens of millions of dollars on an advertising campaign. Although it must be said that "norms" and even market validation can be a controversial topic within the advertising agency community, they are regularly used as guidelines for creative development.

Qualitative research can differ markedly from quantitative research. Many qualitative researchers are sole practitioners who then contract with research facilities to recruit and host their specific qualitative sessions. So, in these cases, you may be working with a qualitative researcher as well as a research company.

When most people think of qualitative research, they think of focus groups. Focus groups are a common occurrence in the marketing and advertising fields. However, qualitative research runs the gamut from focus groups to one-on-ones to ethnography, to Zmet style research. The reason to conduct qualitative research is to gain deeper emotional insights or identify reactions of consumers that can't be recognized through quantitative research. Therefore, there are a myriad of techniques of qualitative research in today's marketplace.

Also, the move to online qualitative research is a current trend in the market. With iChat and other communication tools, it is now possible to hold intimate conversations with consumers online that were previously possible only in person. Working with an online panel can be a real time saver compared with traveling from market to market conducting focus groups.

Qualitative insights are as good or as poor as the interaction of the researcher and the respondent. A quality researcher can make a respondent feel comfortable and work to gain insights on a deep level. The respondent must be willing to give, not just be relevant to the brand. So, there can be a lot of nuance to qualitative research. One size does not fit all.

With the application of technology to the research arena, there are constantly new innovations either in methodology or in ways of doing an existing methodology. All of this makes the job of hiring an external research partner a complex and critical one.

SELECTING A RESEARCH PARTNER

You know what you want to learn. Now you have to find a trusted research partner to conduct the study. The question becomes, who do you turn to? There are literally thousands of research companies that do some form of quantitative or qualitative research for advertising agencies and public relations firms.

The key reference source for finding a research firm is called *The Green Book. The Green Book* or the *International Directory of Marketing Research Companies and Services* is published annually by the New York Chapter of the American Marketing Association. This reference source categorizes research companies by type of study, industry specialties, and consumer specialty areas. So, if your client was in the healthcare category and had a project to better understand the Hispanic audience, you could find research companies that specialize in healthcare and ones who do work in the Hispanic marketplace. Those research companies that are listed in *The Green Book* typically have good track records and are reputable.

Selecting a research firm is a lot like selecting a surgeon. If you need knee surgery, you wouldn't want someone who works only on hands. So, you would look for someone with a good track record in that specialty area. The same is true in research. You want a company or individual that has a good track record. However, if there was a new surgery procedure or technique that is better than the standard method, you would likely consider the merits of it. The same is true in research. While you may have an idea of the methodology you think best suits the task, you should be open to new and better ways of getting at the insights you desire.

Unless you have a specific person or company in mind, most agencies develop and send an RFP (request for proposal) to a variety of research firms to solicit bids on the project. Usually, you would send an RFP to no more than five companies and typically you would send it to only three. Since RFP's do take time and cost the research company money, it is important to spell out what you are looking for. This would include the goal of the research, any timing, a budget, and the expectation

Exhibit 30.3

Primary Research Vendor Checklist

Quantitative

- Methodology
- Sampling: Phone, mail, online, panel
- Data collection
- Data analysis
- Timetable
- Cost (cost per complete)
- In-market validation (if appropriate)
- Normative values (if appropriate)

Qualitative

- Methodology
- Respondent qualifications/recruitment
- Facility
- Filming/viewing
- Cataloging: words, nonverbal, emotional filters
- Analysis/observations
- Timetable
- Cost
- Client background

---

of the deliverables. The latter could be just a report or a report plus one or several presentations and interpretations of the results.

Once you have sent out the RFP, you will need to develop criteria for selecting the best partner. Exhibit 30.3 shows a primary research vendor checklist of key items. Beyond the track record of the company, you will want to understand the methodology that they recommend and why they recommend it.

Once the methodology has been established, you will want to understand their sampling strategy for quantitative studies and their respondent or recruitment strategy if it is a qualitative study. You will need to know how large the sample is and what the composition of the sample will be. For example, if you are trying to understand the perceptions of a fast food brand, do you sample fast food eaters who go that restaurant and ones who don't? Or do you sample those who don't go to fast food restaurants at all? And how many of each of these groups do you need? You will need to weigh those alternatives along with your client to make the best decision.

Data collection and analysis becomes a crucial aspect of the consideration. In a quantitative study, you may want to know what type of statistical analysis the research company recommends to get the most out of the information. You will also want to know if there are normative data available to put your information in some form of context. Finally, you may want to know if there is any in-market validation of the research. So that once you get a research result, you can forecast what impact that might have in the real marketplace.

For qualitative research, you will want to understand how the research will be cataloged. Will it be filmed? Will there be both video and audio accounts of the research? And if there is, will there be a cataloging or analysis of key words, nonverbal reactions, or emotional filters. All of this can be crucial to both the researcher's as well as your understanding of the meaning of the research.

You will want to understand the timetable for the research as well as the costs. One way that costs are sometimes analyzed is to establish the cost to conduct an interview or cost per completed interview. For example, if a study cost $50,000 and surveyed 250 respondents, the cost per complete would be $200 ($50,000/250 = 200) This form of analysis is very common in quantitative studies where sample sizes can be over 1,000 respondents and subsequently, the costs are significant. While this type of analysis should not be the deciding factor in determining the research partner, it is one benchmark you can use.

The final factor in selecting a research partner is chemistry and trust. You obviously want someone who is competent, has a good track record, and can add value to the project. But, you also want someone whom you can discuss issues with and whom you trust to give good counsel. In research, there are no absolutes. Even a rigorous quantitative study has a margin of error. That means that you will need to make a judgment. Having a good research partner that you trust can aid in making a sound judgment.

INTERPRETING RESULTS

You've done your primary research, now comes the moment of truth: the interpretation of the results. Do you let the research company do it or do you take the research company results and do it yourself? That is a question that faces advertising and public relations professionals quite often.

In this case, we are not talking about presenting the results of the research. Clearly that is the purview of the research company. Since they designed the study, collected the data, and provided a report, they should present the results of the study. The real question becomes how you use the information.

Most agency professionals want to provide the action plan or interpretation of what the results mean to the client. In this way, the agency adds value to the client's business. The agency should have considerably more knowledge of the client's business than the research company. So, it makes the most sense for the agency to provide some form of plan based on the research results.

This is another crucial reason why you must be in sync with the research company. The client may ask the research company for their opinion since they are an objective third party. In this case, you should work with the research company to craft a position that you can live with.

This is particularly true when you are dealing in the creative area. Ideally, research should help the creative department do their job better. However, many times research can inhibit creative or make creative formulaic. It takes a strong hand to ensure that creative research is done properly so that all parties gain from it.

There are other times when it might be in the agency's best interests to have the research company present their interpretation of the information. This is especially true when there may be a sensitive issue regarding the client's business that is better left to a third party to discuss.

Regardless of how it is done and who does it, research is a means to an end and not the end itself. What you do with it is the most important aspect of any research project. Over time, you will be comfortable with understanding, commissioning and interpreting research that can impact your client's business.

SUMMARY

Research can be conducted internally or externally. One of the key determinations of doing external research is to eliminate bias and add credibility. There are issues with conducting both quantitative and qualitative research. In each case, you should set up specific criteria for selecting the appropriate research partner. Once you have selected a partner and conducted the research, the most important element of all research is the outcome. By understanding the process of research and working with the research partner, you should be able to provide your client with the most actionable results.

DISCUSSION QUESTIONS

1. What would be appropriate questions that would require just internal research?
2. What would be examples of questions that would necessitate external research?
3. How would you go about commissioning research?
4. What would make a good research partner?
5. How do you see the role of the research company in the strategic process?

EXERCISES

1. Locate some research in your discipline. Analyze the research. Who conducted this research? Why would this enterprise or entity be the ones to conduct this research? Who else might have conducted this research?
2. Develop some research question. Now determine whether the research should be conducted internally or externally. Who would be best in conducting this research?

ADDITIONAL READING

Berger, A. 1998. *Media research techniques.* Thousand Oaks, CA: Sage.
Hansen, A. 2009. *Mass communication research methods.* Thousand Oaks, CA: Sage.

31 | Applying Research to Advertising and Public Relations Situations

LEARNING OBJECTIVES

This chapter is intended to help you:

- Learn what types of situations require research;
- Learn the difference between marketing and advertising research;
- Understand what research techniques best fit a situation;
- Learn to assess emotional versus rational approaches to research problems;
- Learn about return on investment research.

Advertising and public relations is a part of a larger context. Whether it is a marketing program or a corporate communications program, advertising and public relations are just two of many activities that a company will use to meet their objectives.

It is important to understand this context when research situations occur. One of the key questions that you must ask is: "How does this fit within the overall plan?" For example, if you are conducting messaging research on how to best portray a brand's value, it would be good to understand any other pricing research or strategy. Similarly, if you are crafting a corporate public affairs campaign to show the environmental aspects of the company, you will want to understand how this impacts all stakeholders from Wall Street to Main Street.

The point is that you can't conduct advertising or public relations in a vacuum. Nor should you conduct research in a vacuum. There are differences between advertising and marketing research. But, there are also areas of great overlap. Before embarking on any research study, you should review your research objectives with the client to ensure that you are taking into account all aspects of the situation.

MARKETING VERSUS ADVERTISING RESEARCH

Marketing research looks at a brand from all angles. Essentially, that is the 4Ps of marketing: product, price, place (distribution), and promotion. A Chief Marketing Director or CMO usually is a very research-driven individual. Research is one of the methods that proves that his program works.

Therefore, a CMO is typically looking for a quantitative study that will be accept-

Exhibit 31.1

Comparison of Marketing vs. Advertising/Public Relations Research

Marketing Research	Both	Advertising/Public Relations Research
• Product Research	• Brand Health	• Message Testing
• Pricing Research	• Target Segmentation	• Creative Testing
• Brand Valuation	• Competitive Analysis	• Media Analysis
• Distribution Research	• Promotions Research	• Campaign Evaluation
• Marketing Mix Evaluation	• Campaign Evaluation	→ Awareness, Attitudes
	→ Return on Investment	

able to senior management. On the other hand, advertising and public relations is typically looking for the emotional aspects of a situation, which require qualitative methods that may be more intuitive than definitive. This can set up conflicts between the two groups.

It is important to recognize that marketing and advertising will be looking for different insights within the same study. For example, you can't direct an effective marketing campaign without understanding your target market. One situation that faces both marketers and advertising/public relations professionals is segmenting the target market.

The needs of the marketer may be to understand the behavior of the target market. Marketing will want to know who is buying the brand, why they are buying it versus the competition, and how often they are buying it. Marketing then constructs a usage matrix that describes heavy, medium, light, and non-users of the brand.

This information is also important to the advertising agency, particularly the media department, which may use this information to analyze and purchase media. However, the creative group will want to know more. They will want to understand not only why a consumer buys the brand but how it fits within his or her life. Is there some form of emotional attachment that the consumer has with the brand? Basically, what need does it meet?

This learning is complementary to the marketing information. However, if one group designed a target segmentation study without talking to the other, you may not be providing information that is critical to each other's use.

The same can be said regarding a competitive analysis. A marketer will want to understand how his brand compares to the competition on market share, pricing, distribution, and product benefits and promotional support. An advertiser will want to know this and what the competition is saying or communicating and where or what media vehicles they are communicating it in. Again, these are complementary activities but it is important to recognize that marketing and advertising will come at the same problem from slightly different perspectives.

ADVERTISING/PUBLIC RELATIONS RESEARCH SITUATIONS

While marketing and advertising/public relations research needs have significant overlap, there are some areas that are more discrete. The two areas that gain the most

Exhibit 31.2

Research Applications

Application	Typical Method
1. Situation/Background	Secondary research
2. Campaign Evaluation	Awareness/attitudes/usage quantitative study
3. Target Analysis/Segmentation	Behavioral- or needs-based segmentation Quantitative study
4. Advertising Message/Creative	Qualitative (focus groups, one-on-ones, or online) Quantitative (copy testing)
5. Media Analysis	Syndicated research
6. Competitive Analysis	Syndicated research

research attention in the advertising/public relations field are creative and media.

Your client comes to you and says: "My brand has a terrible reputation. What message can I say that will change the consumer's perception?" Now *that* is an advertising/public relations research problem. So, you swing into action. Once you identify the target market and confirm their perception of the brand, you now must figure out how to change it. In this case, you can test various messages with the consumer and determine which one has the highest degree of success. Message testing is one large area of advertising/public relations research.

Another client comes to you and says: "We have spent $40 million on advertising last year and less than 2 percent recall the message." Now you have a creative problem to solve. Assuming that the message is compelling to the target market, the next aspect of advertising is how to best convey that message. Testing creative executions is a business unto itself. But, the power of advertising is all about delivering a compelling message in an equally compelling manner. If the creative execution is a dud, then the advertising spending is not of great value. Creative testing in concert with message testing are the largest areas of advertising/public relations research.

A client comes to you and asks: "Is our advertising reaching our target market? Is it the most efficient and effective use of our advertising dollars?" Now you have a media problem to solve. Media, in this case, can mean paid media or unpaid media. It is the best mix of any type of consumer contact. As we have pointed out in prior chapters of this book, millions of dollars are spent on measuring and analyzing consumer media consumption. This would be the time to apply those media tools to help solve the client's question regarding the proper media mix.

RATIONAL VERSUS EMOTIONAL

Advertising/public relations are emotional businesses. Research, however, is typically a rational business. Research has its roots in science and therefore the attempt in any research study is to provide diagnostics to examine a central hypothesis. This sounds pretty sterile when you think about all the advertising that you may enjoy.

A big challenge in the advertising/public relations business is to understand the emotional connection that a message and/or creative expression of that message might have on consumers. It is always difficult to ask people how they feel and to get not only a straight answer but an in-depth one. Yet, the best advertising campaigns are the ones where you make some form of emotional connection.

For example, many consumers watch the Super Bowl to be entertained by the advertising. In this case, it is not enough to get someone to say that they liked the ad; you must get someone to talk about it. Creating this consumer connection is not easy. Measuring it or helping guide it through research is equally as daunting.

It is important as a researcher to understand that you need to provide some form of measure of emotional connection. When developing research plans and methods for assessing messages and creative expression of those messages, you may be required to conduct a variety of research to understand the consumer's reaction.

There continue to be new tools emerging to help advertisers' better gauge this emotional connection. Research methods that involve facial coding and galvanic skin response have offered a glimpse into the reaction of consumers to various stimuli. Neuroscience is another emerging technology that is now being applied to marketing and advertising. In the case of neuroscience, you are literally assessing the brain activity of the consumer in reaction to the advertising. This assessment can provide insight into the subconscious processing of advertising and public relations messages.

These and other tools to help measure the emotional connection of the consumer are important for advertising/public relations professionals to be aware of. With any advertising/public relations campaign, there will be a tug of war between the rational and emotional side of the ledger.

CAMPAIGN EVALUATION/ROI

Once you've implemented an integrated marketing communications program, the question always becomes, "Did it work?" Did it work can mean different things to different people. For example, did it work to the CEO of the company may mean, did it increase sales. Did it work to the CMO may mean, did we gain more customers or were we able to raise our prices? Did it work for the advertising agency may mean, did we gain awareness or change perception of the brand?

Clearly measuring success is crucial to any campaign. As you can see, it is important to understand what to measure as well as how to measure it. It is also important to understand how various stakeholders will judge the success of the campaign.

Typical campaign measurement is done by conducting a quantitative study that measures consumer awareness, attitudes, and intent to use the brand. This can be done with a pre-campaign benchmark study and then a post-campaign measurement to determine the difference. This study can also be conducted on a rolling basis so that you can see incremental change as the campaign is rolled out.

These campaign measures gauge the top end of the purchase funnel. Communications has historically focused on the ability to raise awareness of the brand, get it into the consideration set, and raise the intent of purchase. Although communications can play a role down the funnel, the marketer has been responsible for the actual purchase and subsequent purchases of the brand.

The knock on this type of campaign measurement is that it doesn't really tell you the real impact of the advertising/public relations program. Or in the words of the CEO:

Exhibit 31.3 **Purchase Funnel**

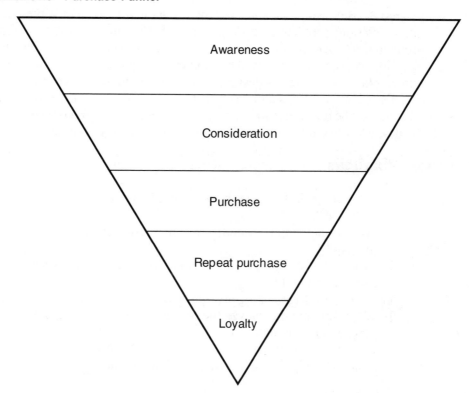

"What is the return on investment (ROI) of this program?" Not being able to quantify the ROI can leave a marketer vulnerable, as well as the advertising agency.

However, with the increasing amount of information available to a marketer, the ability to answer this age-old question is becoming much easier. The increased sophistication of retail software systems, coupled with the use of high-powered statistical models, has led many marketers to develop sales models that can explain advertising's contribution to the brand on both a short-term as well as a long-term basis.

Known as marketing mix models, these sophisticated tools allow a marketer to understand the contribution that each element has on his marketing program. So, the marketer can understand if a consumer promotion works better than a trade promotion or if advertising works better than either promotional technique. This type of analysis takes into account years' worth of information. However, it is a valuable tool for the marketer and the advertiser to answer the ultimate question: "Does advertising work?"

SUMMARY

You will face many situations that will require research as you progress in your advertising or public relations career. As you develop research plans, it is important to keep in mind that the field of advertising/public relations is a subset of marketing. Take a broader view of your research topic to ensure that it meets the marketing objectives. But also make sure that the research you conduct solves an advertising/public relations problem and not just a marketing one. Advertising/public relations problems have overlap with marketing, such as target audience segmentation, but are also discrete, such as message development. Keep in mind that much of advertising/public relations research is designed to get at the emotional connection between the brand's communications and the consumer. Making those emotional connections is what makes the difference in a campaign's effectiveness. Recognize that at the end of the day, it is critical to provide a metric for return on investment of your program.

DISCUSSION QUESTIONS

1. What are the differences between marketing and advertising/public relations research?
2. Who should direct research where marketing and advertising/public relations overlap?
3. How do you design research that provides information on a consumer's emotional viewpoint?
4. Should message testing always be done before creative testing?
5. When should you analyze the results of an advertising/public relations campaign? Semi-annually, annually, or beyond?
6. How do you segment an audience so that marketing and advertising/public relations each get the information that they need?

EXERCISES

1. Locate some marketing research that has been published. In that research, where are the direct applications to advertising? To public relations?
2. Using the public relations and advertising applications from Exercise 1 above, determine how you might expand the study to provide more and deeper information about advertising and about public relations.

ADDITIONAL READING

Morrison, M., E. Haley, and K. Sheehan. 2002. *Using qualitative research in advertising: Strategies, techniques, and applications.* Thousand Oaks, CA: Sage.
Broom, G. 2008. *Cutlip and Center's effective public relations.* Upper Saddle River, NJ: Prentice-Hall.

32 The Research Report

LEARNING OBJECTIVES

This chapter is intended to help you:

- Prepare the final research report;
- Learn the differences between academic and business research reports;
- See how the research reports may be organized;
- Combine written materials in an oral presentation.

One of the most important steps in research is among the last: the research report. If a poor report is prepared or a shoddy presentation offered, all the hard work devoted to the research can be wasted.

WRITING THE RESEARCH REPORT

In the advertising and public relations businesses, it pays to be a good writer. Much of your communication will be in writing, and even material that is presented orally will usually be scripted or at least well outlined in advance. Even simple messages by e-mail tell something about you and your abilities. So no matter what you are intending to communicate, write it well and edit and proofread carefully.

A research report is a special kind of writing, which entails detailed information, specialized terms, and sometimes mind-numbing amounts of data. It will help if you carefully explain the terms you are using and make sure that everything you write or say is easily understood by the intended audience. So if you are writing a research report for a college course and the audience is a professor, you can use standard research terminology and statistical data without much interpretation needed. On the other hand, if you are including a research study as part of a prospective campaign presentation for a client, you may need to simplify your terms and explain data carefully. If the research findings are part of a publicity release or are to be included in an advertisement that will go to the general public, you will need to summarize and simplify still further.

No matter who your audience may be, do not include all your research statistics and itemized data in the research report. Retain them for possible use later or to be able to verify that the research was actually done. You may also want to go back and reanalyze the findings, or demonstrate how the analyses were handled. Yet all the detailed data are not needed in a research report.

There are some specialized report sections that you will want to understand thoroughly. A *research abstract* is a short summary of the study, providing enough information for a reader to decide, without yet reading the entire report, whether your research will be helpful or interesting. An *executive summary* is similar but often concentrates more on the findings than on the method. Both the abstract and the executive summary come at the beginning of the report, to help the reader understand what is still to come.

A *literature review* is the secondary research that was conducted to help design this study. It is normally a thorough search and summary of all relevant previous research, along with an explanation of how each relates to the current study and what important information it provided.

Research questions, hypotheses, and *null hypotheses* were discussed in detail earlier in this book.

Conclusions are the decisions that the researcher has made about what is important or new in this research. Keep in mind that other researchers may draw different conclusions, and that empirical research does not prove anything but rather accepts or rejects hypotheses and null hypotheses. So your conclusions should be your own, clearly indicated as such.

Future research will be other studies that might evolve from the current research. Additional work that is needed because the current study did not answer the questions or solve the dilemma would also be classified as future research.

A *bibliography* is simply the list of all reference materials that are germane to this research. An annotated bibliography will include additional information, with a sentence or two telling what is found in each source. If you list only the sources that you consulted, you may want to call this section "References" instead of implying that it is a full-scale bibliography of all available materials.

An *appendix* (plural "appendices") includes information that may be useful to the reader but is not critical to understanding the method or findings. Materials such as questions asked, correspondence sent, samples of questionnaire or other data-collection forms, quotations from relevant qualitative responses, detailed charts or tables, and similar information might be included in appendices.

The inclusion of these items depends on the intentions you have for your research report, as well as the audience for which it is intended.

ACADEMIC RESEARCH REPORTS

Academic reports have strict expectations and some generally accepted formats and inclusions. A general format for an academic research report is shown in Exhibit 32.1

You will see that the order of items is relatively similar to the chronological order in which the research was conducted; the main exception is the abstract, which is usually written last, after all the other parts of the report have been competed, but usually placed early in the report.

Exhibit 32.1

Format for an Academic Research Report

Title
Abstract
Explanation of topic
Literature review
Research questions*
Hypotheses and null hypotheses*
Research method
Findings
Discussion of findings
Conclusions
Future research
Summary
Bibliography
Appendices

*The order of these items is often reversed.

If the title alone does not clearly explain the research, additional explanation should be included. Be careful: if you cannot explain your study in a brief paragraph, you may be trying to make it seem more important or more complicated than it really is—or you may not have a clear grasp of the subject yourself!

Note that, in an academic report, the findings may not be the most extensive part of the report. Many times, the literature review will be much more extensive, because it includes all other research conducted on this or similar topics. The method is needed in detail as well. So the findings and the discussion of the findings may take up less space than might be expected.

The summary does not need to reintroduce the background research or the entire study that was conducted. It should summarize the methods and the findings and it should include the most important findings.

BUSINESS RESEARCH REPORTS

Reports in adverting and public relations, as in much of business, will stress the findings and the resulting recommendations. If the reader wants more details about the original question or problem, or about the research method, that information is included later in the report. Often, however, the audience will be concerned most with the outcome and recommendations.

As Exhibit 32.2 shows, a research report in business contains most of the same elements as are included in an academic research report, but the reader of a business report will concentrate on the executive summary and the recommendations, and may be interested in the research findings. Someone who will be working with the study or who will be relying on the research findings will likely read the entire report, but the higher executives who only need to understand the general pattern and recommendations may not read much past the first two or three sections of the report.

Exhibit 32.2

Format for a Business Research Report

Title
Executive summary
Recommendations
Main research findings
Restatement of original problem or question
Detailed research findings
Research method
Future research
Appendices
Annotated bibliography

ORAL PRESENTATIONS

A written report usually has more detail than does an oral report. Oral presentations most often cover the essentials of the research and, similar to business reports, put the most emphasis on the findings and recommendations. Of course, there is usually some review of the problem or question that started the research in the first place, along with a summary of the method.

Oral presentations are usually strengthened by the use of visual elements, such as PowerPoint slides or written handouts. Although teaching how to make a good oral presentation is beyond the scope of this book, there are many sources where instruction on good oral presentations and visual supplements can be obtained.

Oral presentations are often supplemented with a written report, which contains more details, including an expansion of the method, the findings, and the appendices and bibliography. Sometimes this written report consists merely of copies of slides that were presented in the oral presentation, but many times it is more detailed and complete.

For academic research, the oral presentation may be more detailed than would be the case for an oral research presentation in business. If the academic research involves a thesis or dissertation, naturally the oral presentation will be much more detailed, but most of the material will still be contained in the written report.

SUMMARY

Research reports are a critical final step in the research process. Research reports for academic purposes contain different items and are arranged in a different order than are research reports for business. Oral presentations bring up their own formats and needs for accompanying materials.

DISCUSSION QUESTIONS

1. Why is the order for academic and business research reports different? Why does each use the format that it does?

2. What special difficulties arise with oral presentations? How do oral presentations of research complicate the situation still further?
3. What are the hallmarks of good visuals to be used in written reports? In oral presentations?

EXERCISES

1. Make a list of the differences in visual formats that might be used for written reports versus oral presentations.
2. Outline a prospective campaign presentation with a detailed section on research.

ADDITIONAL READING

Gibaldi, J. 2009. *MLA handbook for writers of research papers.* New York: Modern Language Association.

Cunningham, H., and B. Greene. 2002. *The business style handbook: An A-to-Z guide for writing on the job with tips from communications experts at the Fortune 500.* Hightstown, NJ: McGraw-Hill.

Iacone, S. 2006. *Write to the point: How to communicate in business with style and purpose.* Franklin Lakes, NJ: Career.

Thill, J., and C. Bovée. 2007. *Excellence in business communication.* Upper Saddle River, NJ: Prentice-Hall.

Bryant, M. 2004. *The portable dissertation advisor.* Thousand Oaks, CA: Corwin.

33 Research Ethics

LEARNING OBJECTIVES

This chapter is intended to help you:

- Understand the various ethical aspects of research;
- Understand the risks in recruiting respondents for research;
- Understand the ethics in the analysis and interpretation of data;
- Recognize the potential bias that can influence research;
- Understand the implications of disclosure of information.

WHY DISCUSS ETHICS IN RESEARCH?

At face value, research seems like the last topic you would need to have a discussion regarding ethics. Isn't most research just asking people questions and then reporting the results? For the most part, that is what a lot of research is all about. However, where you have people involved and issues that can be sensitive to understand, there are ethical implications.

Here are some hypothetical research situations that have ethical issues.

- A researcher is conducting an online survey regarding sexual behavior. The questionnaire states that the respondents' answers will be anonymous. However, unknown to the respondents the research company has provided respondent-level detail and their Internet IP address to the client for further follow-up.
- A researcher places a hidden camera in a store to better understand consumer behavior. After recording the interaction within the store, the research company sells some provocative footage to an online video site.
- A researcher provides a research report to the client but does not disclose all the information in the study, since some of it was contradictory.

So, there can be some serious ethical issues when conducting research. The above examples highlight the major ethical issues:

- Ensuring that the respondents engage in research in a voluntary manner.

- Ensuring that the respondents' answers and identity are kept confidential.
- Ensuring that the respondents are not deceived in any manner.
- Ensuring that the analysis and interpretation of the study is done in a professional manner that does not take a biased viewpoint.
- Ensuring that the study was conducted in an unbiased manner.
- Ensuring that there is full disclosure of methodology and results.

Let's review each of these ethical areas. In doing so, we will discuss the potential issues that can arise and how to alleviate them.

RESPONDENT RECRUITMENT

To conduct primary research, you need to recruit consumers who will be willing to participate in your study. This sounds pretty simple but when you put into play the time constraints of fielding research along with budget constraints, you have the recipe for possible ethical issues.

For example, you are conducting a telephone study for a client to understand the impact of advertising in the travel industry. You only have two weeks to field this study and have promised the client a sample of 1,000 recent travelers. Yet, a week into the survey, the research company you hired has completed only 100 interviews. They suggest that one way to get better participation would be to say that they were calling on behalf of the Department of Transportation. Do you allow them to make this change or do you tell your client that you won't meet the target number of interviews?

Voluntary participation is a key issue in recruiting respondents. This usually isn't much of a problem when you are doing mail, telephone, and/or online surveys. In each of these cases, the respondent can elect to throw it away, hang up the phone, or not click on the study. However, in the prior example, you can't deceive the respondent into participating in a survey by pretending to be someone you're not.

The same can be said of withholding from the participant the true nature of the research. For example, you recruit a number of respondents to a focus group telling them that the purpose of the focus group is to discuss views about new movies. However, when they arrive, your true purpose is to show them pornographic movies to get their reaction.

You can only imagine the reaction of a respondent who is a movie buff coming to a group to discuss buff movies.

The other aspect of respondent recruitment is in the area of coercing people to participate in a study against their will. While this is a rare occurrence in a business setting, it can occur more often in an academic setting.

For example, your professor is conducting research for a paper that is using college students as the sample. He hands out questionnaires to his advertising class and tells them that if they do not complete the survey, they will lose points towards their grade in his class.

Obviously, this is a form of coercion; the student would feel compelled to complete the questionnaire or risk getting a poor grade in the class. Of course, all major universities have policies against this type of behavior but it is something that certainly can happen.

The majority of professional research companies certainly conduct their business in an ethical manner. When recruiting participants for either a quantitative or qualitative study, they disclose who they are and the nature of the study.

Also some research studies will pay participants to be a part of the research. This is particularly true in qualitative research where a participant may have to physically go to a facility and spend a few hours discussing a topic. Certain quantitative studies can also pay respondents for their participation. This is true of panels where respondents may participate in a variety of research studies and for difficult-to-research audiences, such as senior executives. The ethic issue involved is that you must pay the respondent what you said you would.

This sounds pretty simplistic but there are occasions when it can become more complex. For example, you have recruited participants for a focus group to discuss grocery store motivations and advertising messages. However, when the focus group moderator asks the participants if they or a relative works at a grocery store; one participant raises her hand and says that she is the marketing director for a rival grocery chain. Obviously, she is asked to leave the focus group discussion. However, the question then becomes, does she get paid?

The answer is yes. Regardless of the full cooperation of a recruited participant, you must pay them if they have participated at all in the study.

RESPONDENT STUDY RISKS

Once a participant has been recruited for a study, there are other ethical considerations. This is particularly true of qualitative research. As we indicated above, quantitative research is more of a traditional question and answer type of measurement system. While there are opportunities for open-ended questions or opinions on quantitative studies, the majority of questions are geared to gaining a formal measurement.

This is just the opposite in qualitative measures. Here the researcher wants to understand the motivations, the emotional feelings and desires of the respondent. In a qualitative study, respondents are asked and encouraged to express their true feelings. As a result, any qualitative research runs the risk of damaging respondents' self-esteem, deceiving them, creating a false sense of friendship, exposing them, and invading their privacy.

A focus group can become like an encounter group where sensitive issues are discussed and very personal opinions shared. There are times when researchers will put respondents in a setting where they know they will have different viewpoints to gauge the emotional reaction. The fine line in this situation is to ensure that every respondent is treated with respect by the qualitative researcher.

For example, you are doing qualitative research for a new pharmaceutical that can mitigate depression. The focus group researcher asks respondents to describe their feelings towards depression. In this exchange, the focus group researcher makes light of one of the respondent's reasons for being depressed. After the research, the respondent is seen crying in the hallway, distraught over the researcher's actions.

In a qualitative setting, it is crucial that the researcher accept the person for what he or she is, and not criticize the person for what he or she is not. The loss of self-esteem is a real possibility when respondents are asked to dig deep and expose their emotions for others to view.

It is also the researcher's task to ensure that the respondent is not subjected to physical or mental stress. In the above example, you may be asking a respondent to remember something that was a real negative in her childhood. This could cause mental stress or anxiety. So, in the quest to get at the emotional response, it is important to understand where that response could cause undue emotional stress.

The other risk involved in any research is that of privacy. This is particularly true in qualitative research where respondents are potentially taped and/or filmed. All research should be kept confidential. It is not only ethically wrong to release information that could be damaging to a respondent but in some cases it could be illegal.

RESEARCH ANALYSIS AND INTERPRETATION

Once your research is concluded, then it is time to provide an analysis and interpretation of the results. Researchers are responsible for maintaining professional and ethical standards in analyzing and reporting their information.

Obviously, one cardinal rule of professionalism is that the data will not be tampered with. Responses and observations should not be fabricated, altered, or discarded. Also, researchers must exercise care in processing data to guard against the possibility of errors that might impact the results.

Researchers should not conceal information that might have influenced the collection of the data. For example, if you were measuring advertising awareness, you may want the research company to field the study just as the advertising has ended. However, if they failed to implement the study for two weeks, that could have a significant impact on the results with awareness levels being reported as much lower than they actually may have been.

Every research report should contain a full and complete description of the methodology and if there were any deviations from standard procedures.

Researchers are also under an ethical as well as professional obligation to draw conclusions that are consistent with the data. This is a case of "just the facts." Researchers should neither stretch or distort the interpretation of the data to fit a personal point of view nor to gain or maintain a client's favor.

Since advertising and public relations is a perception-driven business, there can be a real tendency to "spin" the information in a convenient manner. The researcher should never put a "spin" on the data. All researchers should remain as neutral as possible in reporting the information.

For example, if an advertising campaign generated a modest increase in awareness, it is not a researcher's job to suggest that if the client spent more media dollars on advertising the awareness would increase more dramatically. There are additional variables that are outside the scope of the study, such as how compelling the message is, how strong the creative execution is, and even the competitive context.

Further interpretation of the information may be done by the agency or the client for his senior management. But your role as research provider is to report the facts and not suggest other implications beyond what the information indicates.

STUDY BIAS

Another ethical issue that can arise is study bias. This is particularly true when conducting qualitative research.

For example, a focus group moderator may have had a poor experience with blond women, so every time he interviews a blond woman, he treats her with disdain. Or, the researcher has a premise that consumers are going to behave in a certain manner, so he consciously guides the discussion to fit his premise.

Since qualitative research is—by its very nature—subjective, any bias that a researcher may have could taint the results of the study. Sometimes a researcher may do this on a subconscious level. A long-held view or bias could manifest itself as he or she interacts with consumers.

This is why advertising and public relations agencies as well as clients are wise to view tapes of prior qualitative research before selecting a facilitator.

Beyond the human element in study bias are areas such as order bias. Order bias is showing a series of stimuli in a specific order and not rotating the elements to avoid bias in the manner in which they were shown. Order bias is of particular note when testing creative concepts or executions. The sequence in which ads are shown could bias the outcome. This may result in not producing the most compelling advertising campaign.

Another form of bias is methodology bias. Many times an advertiser, an agency, or researcher may automatically default to a research method that they are most comfortable with. Often times, this method may not be the best to meet the objectives of the study.

For example, an advertiser may want to determine the emotional involvement and personal memories that the brand and a specific advertising campaign evokes. The initial response to solve this problem may be to hold a focus group. However, a focus group may not allow time for respondents to fully develop their emotional feelings for the brand on a personal level, nor would they necessarily feel comfortable doing so in front of others. Other techniques such as one-on-ones or Z-mat interviews may be more appropriate. Z-mat interviews are personal interviews where the researcher does a very deep dive into the emotional feelings of the respondent.

Bias can come in many forms. It is always good to vet any research method to ensure that there is no bias to the study. In qualitative research, it is crucial to ensure that there is no bias (conscious or unconscious) by the facilitator, and specific research processes such as order of stimuli must be done in a random method.

FULL DISCLOSURE

Many researchers, advertising/public relations agencies, and clients want the research study that they have commissioned, fielded, and reported to contain a neat and tidy story. If done well, most research does tell a story. However, not all research is neat and tidy. Sometimes it has contradicting information. Other times, it may be inconclusive.

When research contains contradictory or inconclusive information, it can result in a high degree of client frustration. Imagine spending over $100,000 on a quantitative study to find out that you don't know much more now than you did prior to commissioning the study.

This pressure of telling a consistent and positive story can lead to concealment and deception of the data. Concealment is withholding certain information from the client. Deception is deliberately providing a false statement of what the data may be telling you.

In any event, it is the ethical responsibility of the researcher to fully disclose all information of the study in a professional manner even if it means that there are points of the study that may not be satisfactory to the client.

For example, suppose you embarked on a public relations effort to increase awareness of a new beverage. The research study shows that overall awareness increased significantly but that awareness among the core beverage drinking audience of 18- to 24-year-olds didn't increase at all. Is the campaign a success or a failure? If you didn't disclose that there was no increase in awareness among the 18- to 24-year-old age group, you would assume that all age groups went up proportionately. If you concealed that piece of information, a client would have a markedly different view of the results than if it was disclosed.

In this case, even if you don't conceal the information, you could convey it in a deceptive manner. For example, a researcher may say that overall awareness rose by 20 percent and varied slightly by age groups. If you read this statement, you might assume that the variance is not a great amount, probably a few percentage points one way or the other. It would certainly mask the profound lack of awareness among 18- to 24-year-olds.

It is crucial that as you read a research report, you question statements that are not concrete. You should always be looking for the facts or data that support any type of analysis. And where more subjective analyses are done, such as in qualitative research, it is important to review the study and the actual respondents' verbatim to ensure that they are consistent with the findings.

SUMMARY

There are a number of ethical issues that confront researchers and those that commission research on a daily basis. The first and foremost is that the researcher is dealing with people. And people have the right to privacy and to participate in a study only when they volunteer willingly and are not deceived in any manner. Once a study is fielded, it is the researcher's responsibility to exercise care in gathering and processing the data as well as taking all reasonable steps to assure that the results are accurate. This same level of care should be given to the recommendation of the methodology itself and its appropriateness to the problem. And there are ethical issues involved in making interpretations of the data that should be consistent with the study. All information regarding the study should be fully disclosed even if it means that it would result in a negative appearance for the researcher or the client.

Finally, with all the human interaction involved in research, there is an opportunity for unethical behavior either consciously or unconsciously to manifest itself. It is the advertising/public relations professional's role in research to ensure that any research conducted by the agency be done in an above-board, ethical manner.

DISCUSSION QUESTIONS

1. What do you feel are the largest ethical issues in conducting research? Why?
2. Have you ever been involved in a research project where you felt ethics were compromised? How?
3. How do you convey research in a persuasive manner that doesn't conceal any contradictory information?
4. What is a reasonable amount of deviance from a methodology that may not be necessary to report? Or should any deviance be reported?
5. What is your feeling about observational research where respondents may not know you are studying them?

EXERCISES

1. Read a trade publication in your field: advertising or public relations. What ethical dilemmas do you find? Why are these ethical problems difficult to solve?
2. List the major ethical problems facing your specific discipline. How would you solve each of them?
3. List your own personal ethical standards. Determine how each applies to your discipline: public relations or advertising.

ADDITIONAL READING

Smith, A. 2006. *Research ethics.* London: Taylor and Francis.

Christians, C., K. McKee, and M. Fackler. 2008. *Media ethics: Cases and moral reasoning.* Upper Saddle River, NJ: Pearson.

Spence, E.H., and B. Van Heekeren. 2005. *Advertising ethics.* Upper Saddle River, NJ: Prentice-Hall.

Parson, P. 2008. *Ethics in public relations.* London: Kogan Page.

Appendix:
Table of Random Numbers

Line	Columns									
	1	2	3	4	5	6	7	8	9	10
1	63510	11051	08401	96902	66625	08603	94800	01141	61912	31236
2	59552	37564	86322	52481	87685	93461	74510	43221	51148	40158
3	72522	06384	03142	27392	06907	53846	23115	83749	61988	12403
4	34260	39039	76124	42512	21071	76301	68523	00331	95229	06746
5	73818	57993	07573	07457	20419	70263	59034	18032	40075	27606
6	80011	70960	12977	35051	04884	54006	66521	38971	59513	74802
7	02465	50927	26599	27280	85362	77957	00935	55256	03068	05346
8	46450	77919	10369	40164	87122	64660	21960	53114	85676	08741
9	16636	24341	97598	95612	76069	43166	86546	09527	56939	04394
10	24335	75863	57458	14317	48694	55609	31044	41096	13352	85180
11	13288	87596	81982	60109	08125	51003	11510	53779	24494	88110
12	53284	16904	35536	58517	59432	15815	39195	16185	60853	75564
13	63625	96939	92490	10005	79767	54668	74989	66754	00517	97169
14	63105	59087	26830	28297	97151	94493	86406	20681	49117	59549
15	36128	93671	89353	04775	76883	56865	36681	02363	98676	46574
16	43581	43459	53521	65706	22355	49581	94138	88967	92209	86467
17	08284	57200	10347	24349	43854	25906	76566	86798	23823	73972
18	52943	78348	99252	64619	89798	90846	67361	28719	89345	61013
19	69870	27732	71649	22902	30181	33595	63997	54496	88433	76225
20	52907	09728	78365	61931	80361	58891	64140	31541	19660	86103
21	36251	79934	32016	60352	59083	65200	02429	15628	94802	72004
22	45439	21397	36506	72687	84044	04852	74618	59903	39367	65870
23	20968	31842	01850	12160	65772	27889	67881	35474	08035	79907
24	57070	12673	73971	47988	73284	33277	25477	86398	37213	61232
25	53051	04812	00492	98624	27190	07074	36331	13785	13791	87842
26	00709	50599	92685	97361	31645	08824	25921	70323	14965	35289
27	25946	88187	22309	25947	86898	70709	91704	75155	15946	94409
28	04753	40185	21823	29544	15822	01581	35949	52759	08252	81696
29	19291	51693	84336	85779	36210	49344	43601	80524	58550	39581
30	01619	30733	31603	57992	15582	10756	44950	74729	65153	52625

About the Authors

Dr. Donald W. Jugenheimer is an author, researcher, consultant, and educator. His specialties are communications, both interpersonal and mass communications, with emphasis on personal communication, advertising and media management, media economics, and advertising media.

As a consultant, Dr. Jugenheimer has worked with such firms as American Airlines, IBM, Century 21 Real Estate, Aetna Insurance, Pacific Telesis, and the U.S. Army Recruiting Command; he currently consults on a variety of research and advisory projects in advertising and marketing, including advertising media plans for class-action lawsuits. He has also conducted research for a variety of enterprises including for the U.S. Department of Health, Education and Welfare, for the International Association of Business Communicators, and for National Liberty Life Insurance.

Dr. Jugenheimer is author or coauthor of twenty books and many articles and papers. He has spoken before a variety of academic and professional organizations, including the World Advertising Congress in Tokyo. He also served as President and as Executive Director of the American Academy of Advertising and as Advertising Division Head of the Association for Education in Journalism and Mass Communication. He was Business Manager for the founding of the *Journal of Advertising*. He has testified about advertising before the U.S. House of Representatives Armed Forces Committee as well as in federal and state court proceedings.

Since earning his Ph.D. in Communications from the University of Illinois with a specialization in advertising and a minor in marketing, Dr. Jugenheimer has been a tenured member of the faculties at the University of Kansas, Louisiana State University (where he was the first person to hold the Manship Distinguished Professorship in Journalism), Fairleigh Dickinson University, Southern Illinois University, and Texas Tech University. At most of these universities, he also served as an administrator. His bachelor's degree was in advertising with a minor in economics and his master's degree was also in advertising with a minor in marketing, and all three degrees are from the University of Illinois at Urbana-Champaign. He worked at several advertising agencies in Chicago and downstate Illinois. He also served in the U.S. Air Force, first in aero-medical evacuation and later as a medical administrative officer.

Dr. Jugenheimer has lectured and conducted workshops in several countries and served on the guest faculty of the Executive Media MBA program for the Turku School of Economics and Business Administration in Finland. In addition, he has held a Kellogg National Fellowship. He is listed in *Who's Who in America, Who's Who in Advertising, Who's Who in Education,* and several other biographical references.

Dr. Jugenheimer is currently a partner and principal in the research, writing, and consulting firm In-Telligence, which concentrates on communications, marketing, and advertising.

Dr. Samuel D. Bradley is Assistant Professor of Advertising in the College of Mass Communications at Texas Tech University. He was previously Assistant Professor in the School of Communication at Ohio State University, and has taught in the Tele-communications Department at Indiana University, and the School of Journalism and Mass Communications at Kansas State University.

Dr. Bradley grew up in a family advertising agency, and earned his B.A. with honors in Journalism and Mass Communications at New Mexico State University. He spent two years working as a reporter and editor for *The Modesto Bee,* the *Las Cruces Sun-News,* and the *Albuquerque Journal* before returning to school to earn his M.S. at Kansas State in 2001.

He then earned a joint doctorate in Mass Communications and Cognitive Science at Indiana University, where his dissertation, "Exploring the Validity and Reliability of the Acoustic Startle Probe as a Measure of Attention and Motivation to Television Programming," won I.U.'s outstanding dissertation in cognitive science award in 2006.

Dr. Bradley's research involves measuring psychophysiological responses to media messages, and the formal computational modeling of underlying cognitive processes. He operates a psychophysiology lab in the College of Mass Communications at Texas Tech, where he also teaches Advertising and Mass Communications courses. Bradley has authored or coauthored more than a dozen articles in journals such as *Media Psychology, Communication Methods & Measures, Journal of Advertising,* and *Journal of Broadcasting & Electronic Media,* and presented papers at conferences of the American Academy of Advertising, the Association for Education in Journalism and Mass Communication, the Society for Psychophysiological Research, and the International Communication Association, among others.

Larry Kelley is Executive Vice President, Chief Planning Officer for FKM, the sixtieth largest advertising agency in the United States, where he is also an agency principal. Since joining FogartyKleinMonroe, now FKM, in 1990, Kelley has held senior roles in media, account planning, and interactive. Prior to joining FogartyKleinMonroe in 1990, Mr. Kelley served in senior media and research positions with BBD&O, Bozell & Jacobs, and the Bloom Agency.

Mr. Kelley has worked on a wide variety of clients and categories for both domestic and international campaigns. He has worked with such firms as American Airlines, ConAgra Foods, ConocoPhillips, Dell, Georgia-Pacific, Kroger, Minute Maid, South-western Bell, Yum Brands, and Zales.

In addition, he has written or cowritten six books on advertising as well as a popular culture book. He has been awarded with four EFFIES for advertising effectiveness and has won a series of ADDY awards. Mr. Kelley is also a Professor of Advertising at the University of Houston, where he heads the advertising sequence in the Valenti School of Communications. He also serves on numerous boards for private industry as well as the 4A's media council.

Mr. Kelley holds a B.S. in journalism from the University of Kansas and a master's degree in advertising from the University of Texas at Austin.

Dr. Jerry Hudson's primary undergraduate teaching areas are in advertising and electronic media. Among graduate courses, he has taught research methods and data analysis.

Dr. Hudson is the author or coauthor of forty-three papers, one book chapter, and thirty publications. His refereed publications appear in *Health Marketing Quarterly, Journalism Educator, Journalism Quarterly, Social Science Journal,* and *Southwestern Mass Communications Journal.* His research concentration is in dissemination-consumption of health care information and Hispanic media use-consumerism.

His experience includes commercial broadcasting for twelve years including radio and television sales, radio personality, television sports personality and weather person. During the past fifteen years, he has served as a research consultant on more than one hundred marketing/advertising projects including research and marketing plans for banks, hospitals, media companies, political candidates, shopping malls, and retail stores.

Dr. Hudson was Director of Mass Communications at Lamar University (1975–78). At Texas Tech, he served as director of the School of Mass Communications, 1987–92 and 1998–2004; coordinator of graduate studies and director of the Institute of Communications Research (1993–97); founding dean of the College of Mass Communications. Dr. Hudson has served as president of the Texas Association of Broadcast Educators and the Southwest Council of Journalism and Mass Communications. He has been recognized by three different university committees for teaching excellence. In 1995, he was awarded the President's Academic Achievement award. The American Advertising Federation's 10th District honored Dr. Hudson in 1995 as the Outstanding Advertising Educator. The Lubbock Advertising Federation awarded him the Silver Medal Award in 2002.

Index